City Essentials

An Introduction to
Investment Management

Published June 2011

ISBN 9780 7517 5400 1

British Library Cataloguing-in-Publication Data
A catalogue record for this book
is available from the British Library

Published by

BPP Learning Media Ltd
BPP House, Aldine Place
London W12 8AA

www.bpp.com/learningmedia

Cover photo by Terence O'Loughlin

Printed in the United Kingdom

Your learning materials, published by BPP Learning Media, are
printed on paper sourced from sustainable, managed forests.

© BPP Learning Media Ltd

All our rights reserved. No part of this publication may be
reproduced, stored in a retrieval system or transmitted, in any
form or by any means, electronic, mechanical, photocopying,
recording or otherwise, without the prior written permission of
BPP Learning Media. The descriptions, examples and calculations
shown in this publication are for educational purposes only. No
liability can be accepted by BPP Learning Media for their use in
any circumstances connected with actual trading activity or
otherwise. Readers should seek specific advice for specific
situations.

£25.00

Contents

		Page
1	Introduction to Investment Management	1
2	Discounted Cash Flows	27
3	Risk and Return	53
4	Fixed Income Securities	123
5	Equities	197
6	Property	211
7	Commodities and Alternative Investments	223
8	Derivative Products	229
9	Foreign Exchange	273
10	Performance Measurement and Appraisal	295
Index		321

Preface

The purpose of this book is to introduce the reader to the important principles, practices and considerations involved in the investment management process and provide an insight into the various investment vehicles available to the fund manager to achieve his investment management objectives.

Though some details such as tax and regulations may vary from country to country, the vast majority of principles and characteristics are common irrespective of geographical location or currency in which the investment management is being conducted. We have, therefore, endeavoured to keep this book as broadly relevant as possible and have only shied away from detailed country-specific regulatory and tax issues.

As we will see, the fund management process is an ongoing iterative one of continuous refinement which can never be considered to be complete unless the fund concerned is terminated and which is quite broad-ranging and generalist. Similarly, the study of investment theory and the characteristics of investment vehicles continues to evolve and so we do not hold this book out as all-encompassing. Our aim throughout has been to introduce the major issues and characteristics that take the reader a long way into each area considered. If we inspire the reader to undertake a more detailed study of any specific area then this book will have provided a firm foundation to those studies and you may be interested in considering other books from the City Essentials range covering these more specialist areas.

1 Introduction to Investment Management

Contents

1. Investment Management – An Overview 2
2. Risk/Reward Profile 8
3. Institutional Investment Management 9
4. Individual Investment Management 18
5. Making Investments 21
6. Investment Management Style 22
7. Selecting a Fund Manager 24
   Executive Summary 25

1 INVESTMENT MANAGEMENT – AN OVERVIEW

1.1 Introduction

Investment management is the management of an investment portfolio on behalf of a private client or an institution, the receipt and distribution of fund income and all other administrative work in connection with the portfolio.

In this chapter we introduce in outline:

- the key considerations and principles involved within this process
- the major institutional fund types along with their key characteristics
- the approach to fund management for an individual
- outline of the approaches we could adopt in the management of a fund

all of which we investigate in more detail in the later chapters.

1.2 So where do we start?

Investment management involves the investment of a client's assets in order to meet a number of key objectives. The objectives will vary from investor to investor and, consequently, the process of investment management must start with a detailed consideration of the client's objectives.

To satisfy the client's objectives, the fund manager also needs to appreciate the constraints that he must operate within, ie he must know such factors about the client as:

- Time horizons
- Liquidity needs
- Risk aversion/tolerances
- Tax status
- Other preferences and legal constraints, eg ethical considerations

This is needed for at least three reasons.

- It is a prerequisite to the initial portfolio structure.
- It influences the kinds of portfolio adjustment that can be made.
- It consequently influences portfolio performance.

1.3 Client objectives

1.3.1 Introduction

Broadly speaking, the requirements of clients fall into one of two categories, those who seek:

- To maximise their returns, ie positive net worth individuals looking for a portfolio to match their risk/return preferences.

- To match liabilities, eg pension funds, where the aim is to match assets and liabilities or minimise any mismatch.

1: INTRODUCTION TO INVESTMENT MANAGEMENT

1.3.2 Return maximisation

Given the choice, most investors would elect to have a high performance fund with minimal risk. However, this is not achievable and some trade-off between the two will have to take place. Understanding this **risk/reward trade-off** is crucial to grasping the overall objectives of a return maximising fund and then to establishing the policy of a fund.

Lower risk aversion or greater risk tolerance results in:

- Greater allowable portfolio risk
- Greater potential gains (and losses)

The primary concern in this type of fund is, therefore, to fully understand the client's risk tolerance, be they private or institutional clients.

1.3.3 Liability matching

The only way to guarantee the matching of any liability is through investment in government bonds where the income and capital inflows exactly match those liabilities.

If the return from bonds is insufficient to achieve this required return then we must use other assets. The result of the use of other assets is that we may achieve the higher return required. However, the risk associated with the use of these other assets means that the liabilities may not be exactly met – there may be a mismatch.

Once again, a key requirement here will be to establish the clients attitude to risk, though here we have more specific financial objectives to meet, ie a future liability to satisfy.

In assessing these liabilities we need to consider their value which may be either:

- Nominal
- Real

A **nominal liability** is one that is fixed in monetary terms irrespective of future inflation. An example of a nominal liability would be a bank loan or mortgage where the monetary sum borrowed must be paid off at the end of the term and does not alter with inflation over that time. Perhaps the best way to satisfy a nominal liability is with nominal returning assets such as normal government bonds so long as their return is sufficient.

In contrast, a **real liability** is one which changes in monetary terms as we experience inflation. For example, in order to maintain a standard of living a pension needs to pay out the same amount each year in real terms, ie a rising monetary amount to cover the impacts of inflation, and this sum needs to be paid for the remaining life from the retirement – an indeterminate term. To satisfy a real liability we probably need to consider investing in real assets, ie assets producing a higher return as we experience inflation such as inflation-linked government bonds.

Whatever the liability, assessment will involve a **present value analysis** of the anticipated future liabilities that the fund is aiming to meet. For example, to pay a pension of $20,000 pa for a period of 20 years when real returns (asset returns in excess of inflation) are 3% will require a fund value at retirement of almost $300,000 and so we would be looking to achieve this fund value at the retirement date.

1.3.4 Mixed requirements

For most institutional clients the primary requirement will be quite clear cut, for example, collective investments are generally return maximising funds whereas pension funds are liability driven as we discuss later.

For many private clients, however, the requirements may be more mixed. A wealthy private client may have certain liabilities to meet such as paying for children's/ grandchildren's school and college fees, repaying loans/mortgages or providing financial protection for relatives/dependents, but may wish that any 'spare' resources be managed to maximise returns.

1.4 Constraints on the fund

1.4.1 Introduction

Given the client's objectives, the key to understanding the investment strategy is to appreciate the various constraints that operate on the fund itself.

1.4.2 Time horizons

The time horizons for the attainment of the return, or the matching of the liabilities, will clearly influence the types of investments that will be worthwhile for the fund.

A fund whose purpose is to meet some liabilities in, say, two years' time, may find that the investment vehicle is low coupon bonds.

For a fund that has liabilities to meet in 20 years' time, such investments may be inappropriate.

The time horizon will also influence the level of risk that can be taken in order to achieve the objectives. A fund with a long-term time horizon can probably stand a higher risk, as any poor returns in one year will be cancelled by high returns in subsequent years before the fund expires. Clearly, this sort of risk cannot be taken in a very short-term fund which may only span a couple of years and, therefore, may not have counterbalancing good and bad years.

1.4.3 Liabilities

As mentioned above, certain funds have liabilities that they are obliged to meet and the investment manager's objective must take these into consideration. For example, pension funds and life assurance companies will have statistical projections of their liabilities into the future and the fund must attempt to achieve these.

A further consideration is the exposure to currency risk. A pension fund may have all its liabilities denominated in sterling. If the fund were to invest heavily in overseas assets this would expose it to an additional risk, other than the risk inherent in the assets themselves. However, if the pension fund has liabilities in, say, dollars, then buying US investments matches their currency exposure and, therefore, minimises risk as well as taking on board an acceptable investment.

1.4.4 Liquidity needs

Within any fund there must be the ability to respond to changing circumstances and, consequently, there needs to be a degree of liquidity. Government fixed interest instruments can guarantee a tranche of the investment portfolio which will give easy access to cash should the fund need it. In general, exchange traded investments (equities and bonds) tend to be highly liquid while investments that are not exchange traded, such as property, have low liquidity.

1.4.5 Risk aversion and risk tolerances

We commented above on the risk/reward trade-off and how it impacts on the ways in which the fund's requirements can be achieved and outline it in more detail in the next section.

Types of risk

The main risks that a client faces and that they need to understand are:

- **Capital risk** – the potential variability in investment values.
- **Inflation risk** – the potential variability in inflation rates that will impact significantly on return requirements for funds looking to finance real liabilities.
- **Interest rate risk** – the risk of changes in bank base rates and the knock-on effect that this may have on asset returns.
- **Shortfall risk** – the risk of the fund failing to meet any specified liabilities. This can be reduced by minimising targets, increasing sums invested or increasing investment terms.

Diversification

The principle of diversification is fundamental to the investment management process and will need to be clearly explained to the client as it will have a significant impact on the potential asset allocations.

In any investment there are two sorts of risk – the general **market risk** of investing in shares or bonds and the **specific risk** of any individual investment. For example, if an investor were to put all their money into a particular share, there would firstly be the risk that the market in all shares would fall, causing the value of the investment to fall, and secondly the risk that that particular share itself may suffer from a specific incident causing the share price to fall.

If an investor is able to buy more investments, he will be taking on board specific risks of different companies. Eventually, there will be a situation where, because of specific risks, some of the investments will fall but others will rise having a cancelling effect. Overall, through this process of **diversification**, investors are able to rid themselves of the specific risk of a stock. It is, however, **impossible to remove the market risk**.

Time scales

A client's attitude to risk will also be influenced by investment time scales.

If, for example, we are managing a pension fund, our attitude to risk will be highly dependent on time scales. If the fund is a young pension scheme with 30 or 40 years to client retirement then it can afford to take a reasonably aggressive attitude to capital risk and invest in what may be regarded as the riskier assets. By taking a high risk we may experience some poor years but we are also liable to experience some very good years. The effect is that risk averages out over time, giving rise to a good overall long-term return, thus minimising shortfall risk.

If, on the other hand, the scheme is very mature and retirement is imminent, then there is insufficient time for this averaging effect to take place. As a result, any poor performance this year may have a significantly adverse effect on the fund, ie a high capital risk in this circumstance increases the shortfall risk.

The fund managers approach will, therefore, be very much affected by investment time scales.

1.4.6 Tax status

Taxation is a consideration for all investment managers. The investment portfolio and the strategy adopted must be consistent with the fund's tax position. In some cases, the fund does not suffer taxation. For these **gross funds** the manager should, normally, avoid those stocks which involve the deduction of tax at source. For, even though it may be possible to reclaim any tax suffered, the fund will have incurred the opportunity cost of the lost interest on the tax deducted.

1.4.7 Other preferences and legal constraints

Obviously, when constructing a portfolio for any investor, the manager should consider the legal constraints that may exist and the regulatory framework adopted in the market needs to be adhered to.

The investment management industry is subject to regulation in all major financial markets. In such markets, the general thrust of these regulations is the protection of investors and local regulations have generally been developed in response to frauds and financial scandals/crimes within those countries. As a result, though the general thrust may be the same, the specific details may differ markedly between markets and we make no attempt here to cover any detailed regulatory aspects.

The investment management regulators in the major markets from whom details of local regulations may be obtained are given below.

1: INTRODUCTION TO INVESTMENT MANAGEMENT

Market	Regulator
Australia	Australian Securities and Investments Commission (ASIC)
Canada	Each province has its own regulations, the most significant of which is probably the Ontario Securities Commission (OSC)
China and Hong Kong	China Securities Regulatory Commission (CSRC)
France	Autorité des Marchés Financiers (AMF)
Germany	Bundesanstalt für Finanzdienstleistungsaufsicht (BaFin)
Ireland	Irish Financial Services Regulatory Authority (Financial Regulator)
Japan	Financial Services Agency (FSA)
Luxembourg	Commission de Surveillance du Secteur Financier (CSSF)
Switzerland	A combination of legislation and self-regulation through the Swiss Federal Banking Commission (SFBC), the Swiss Association of Asset Managers (SAAM) and the Swiss Funds Association (SFA)
UK	Financial Services Authority (FSA)
US	Division of Investment Management of the US Securities and Exchange Commission (SEC)

1.5 The role of the investment manager

While an individual investor may choose to manage his own money, the majority of investors turn towards institutional investment management to safeguard their assets. One of the reasons for this is that commissions have come down for institutional investors, while commissions for private customers remain high. Unless customers are undertaking large transactions, they may be limiting their access to the marketplace.

Equally, it is important for an investor to buy a range of assets. This restricts the level of risk he may face but, with only a limited amount of capital, it may be impossible at today's commission rates for an investor to spread his money over a portfolio wide enough to minimise risk. Consequently, it makes sense for small investors to pool their money into large funds that can be invested on their behalf by professional fund managers.

To safeguard the assets of the individual investors, funds are frequently registered in the name of a third party, rather than the managers, with the managers only having authority to undertake particular transactions, eg buying or selling securities, on behalf of the funds.

1.6 Overview of the investment management process

The process of investment management involves the investment of a third party's assets in order to meet a number of key objectives. The objectives will vary for each investor and, consequently, the process of investment management must start with a detailed consideration of the fund's objectives and constraints.

1: INTRODUCTION TO INVESTMENT MANAGEMENT

1.6.1 The approach to investment management

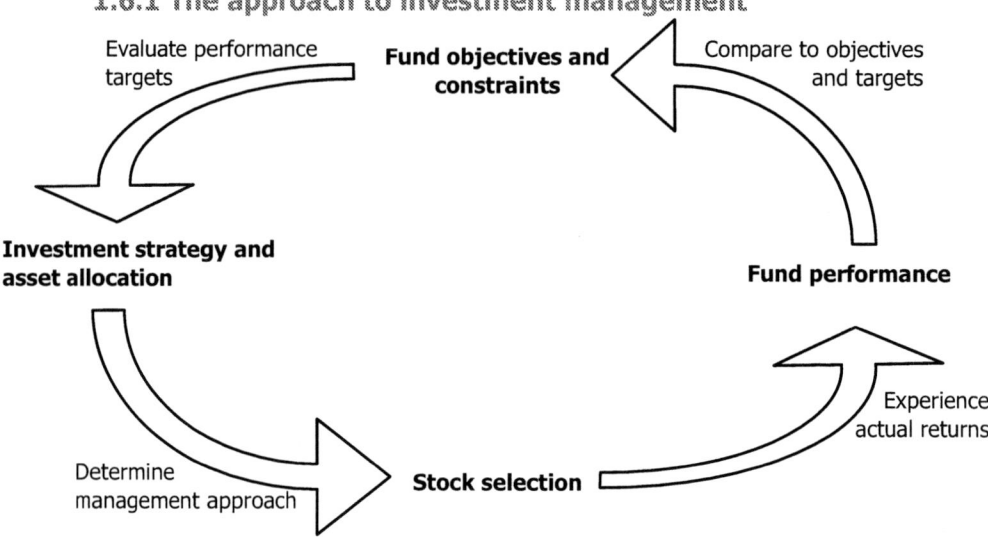

The fund management process is not a linear one which is completed once the final stage has been undertaken, rather it is a process of continuous review and refinement in the light of changing client needs and market circumstances.

The initial stage, however, is the consideration of the client's, hence the fund's, objectives and constraints. These objectives and constraints, once defined and evaluated, direct the fund manager towards certain asset classes and away from others, leading to the development of an investment strategy and an initial strategic asset allocation.

Having determined a strategy, the manager now needs to consider his management approach which directly leads to his stock selection.

Having now established a portfolio, the manager will experience the returns over time and must assess whether they are sufficient to satisfy the client's needs which then need to be fed back into the performance targets for the following period, possibly leading to revisions of the investment strategy, asset allocation, stock selection etc. In addition, any changes in client's objectives that may arise will need to be factored into this process.

That is, investment management must be viewed as a continuous iterative process of refinement.

2 RISK/REWARD PROFILE

Fundamental to an understanding of investment management is an appreciation of the relationship between risk and reward, that is:

High Risk = High Return

1: INTRODUCTION TO INVESTMENT MANAGEMENT

Investments offer a range of risk and return which can be summarised as follows.

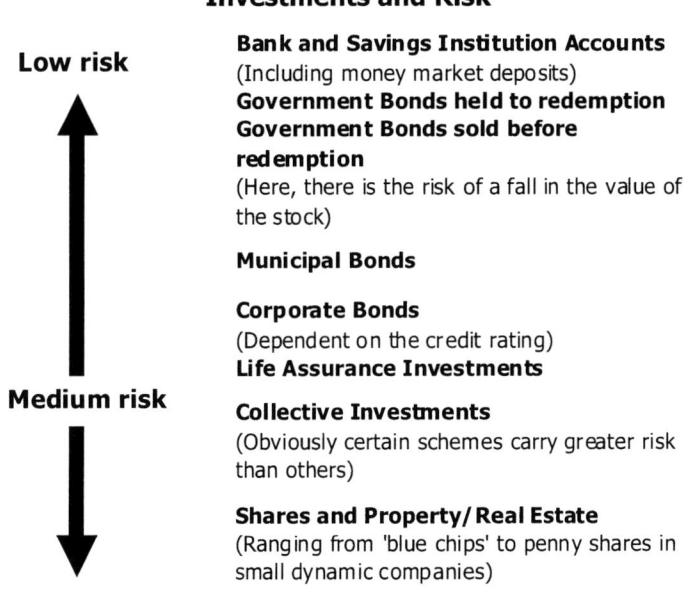

Before offering any investment advice, it is vital to ensure that the risks and returns match the customer's criteria.

3 INSTITUTIONAL INVESTMENT MANAGEMENT

3.1 Introduction

In the period since 1945, the power of the institutional investor has grown dramatically in developed markets, in line with the decline in individual investors. Taking the UK as an example, share ownership between 1963 and 2006 can be illustrated graphically as follows, and these trends have been experienced in all developed markets.

1: INTRODUCTION TO INVESTMENT MANAGEMENT

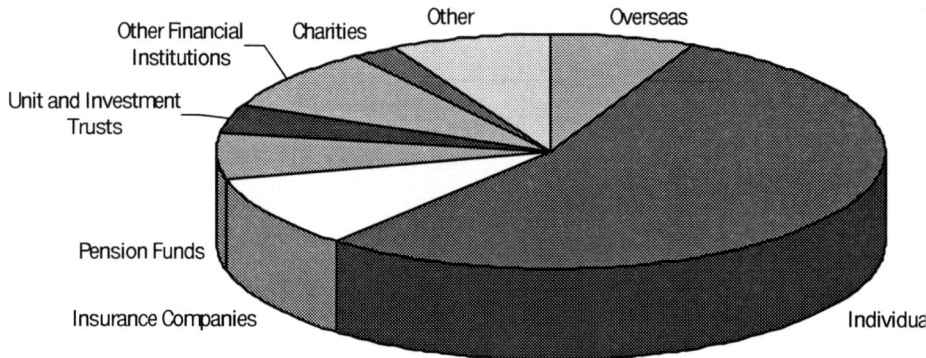

Share Ownership in 1963

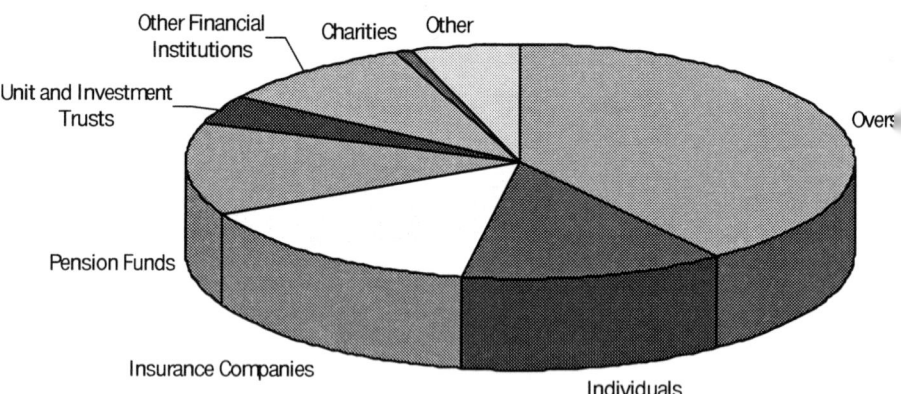

Share Ownership in 2009

While an individual investor may choose to manage his own money, the majority of investors are turning towards fund managers to manage their assets. The proportion of funds directly held by individuals has fallen rapidly over the last 40 years while the proportion managed by institutions has correspondingly risen. There are several reasons for this shift.

A major factor is that investment by individuals in the financial markets is now more likely to be indirect rather than direct. A large proportion of individual investors are likely to invest via pension funds or collective investment schemes. Ultimately, institutions represent individuals' collective involvement in the market, but why this shift to indirect investments?

One of the reasons for this shift is that commissions have reduced for institutional investors, but commissions for private customers still remain high unless customers are undertaking large transactions, this may limit their access to the marketplace.

Equally, it is important for an investor to buy a range of assets. This restricts the level of risk he may face but, with only a limited amount of capital, it may be impossible at today's commission rate for an investor to spread his money over a wide enough portfolio to minimise risk. Consequently, it makes sense for small investors to pool their money into large funds, which can be invested on their behalf by professional fund managers. The growth of investment advisors servicing the individual investor has probably also contributed here. Investment advisors have tended to focus mainly on packaged products rather than individual equities. An increased awareness of the benefits of diversification and the need for 15 – 20 holdings has led advisors to only recommend individual equities to those with considerable funds to invest.

A further advantage of using a managed fund is that it provides the private customer with easier access to overseas markets and, therefore, exposure to new industries and economic conditions.

One final reason can be found in marketing – a company is not allowed to advertise to promote its existing shares directly to the public. By contrast, the public has been besieged with adverts from providers of insurance, pension and collective investment products. The effect of this is hard to ascertain but is likely to have encouraged individuals into packaged products and away from individual shares.

3.1.1 Implications

With the majority of funds under the control of professional fund managers, this is likely to lead to greater market efficiency. Thus, it is harder for the active fund manager to add significant value. The difficulty that active fund managers are experiencing in beating benchmarks has led to an increase in tracker funds.

Individual funds have grown in size. Such large institutional funds experience difficulties as the liquidity in the market for many equities may be insufficient for them to efficiently achieve their investment objectives. This has led institutions to focus most heavily on the constituents of the major indices.

With such large quantities of funds in the hands of institutional fund managers, the competition for new issues will be considerable, particularly for any large new issues that managers are anxious to include within their portfolios. Individual managers may find applications scaled down or fail to secure stock.

The greater proportion of institutional shareholders gives fund managers far more influence in company affairs. It would not be uncommon for a company meeting to be effectively controlled by a small number of fund managers. This has allowed fund managers to be far more involved in corporate affairs, for instance removing a board if they do not feel shareholder value is being created. It is institutional shareholders who will generally determine the success or failure of a takeover bid. Thus, fund managers may be required to take a more active role in the governance of companies in which they have a significant stake.

3.2 Types of fund

A variety of funds exist. Each has its own particular risk/reward profile stemming from:

- Its initial objectives, return maximising/liability matching.
- The value and time horizons of the liabilities it has to meet (if any).
- The assets it can invest in.
- The liquidity required within the fund.

- The risk that can be tolerated in the fund.
- Its tax status.
- Legislation governing its powers.

As already noted, we do not attempt to cover here the legislative or regulatory aspects and constraints that the investment manager faces as these are completely country-specific. Likewise, though in practical terms it is very important, we do not attempt here to cover the taxation of the fund or the investor as this is equally country-specific. The one observation we do make with regard to taxation, however, is that in most countries income (dividends from shares, income from bonds, rental income from real-estate) and gains (appreciation of asset values) are taxed differently with income being taxed at higher rates than gains. As a result, many investors prefer to benefit more from gains than income, especially higher-rate taxpayers.

3.2.1 Pension funds

A pension fund is an example of a liability matching fund or a return maximising fund depending on how it is structured. It represents a pool of money to be invested now, to achieve either:

- A specific return based on the employee's salary and number of years' service with the company – a **defined benefit/final salary scheme**; or
- A general increase in value of the contributions paid on behalf of the employee – a **defined contribution/money purchase scheme**.

Occupational pension schemes, where the scheme is set up by the employer for the benefit of the employees, tend to be defined benefit schemes, though defined contribution schemes have become increasingly popular since the 1980s.

Personal pension schemes, set up by an individual who is, perhaps, self-employed or is not a member of an occupational scheme, are defined contribution pensions.

Generally speaking, pension funds have fairly **long-term horizons** and, therefore, are prepared to take on board a higher degree of risk, since any shortfall in the fund can be made up in future investment performance. This **investment policy** depends on the **maturity** of the fund. If the fund beneficiaries are close to retirement, then it would be more appropriate to select relatively short-term safe investments. However, in general the above comment is applicable.

Pension funds also have to keep control over the real rate of return that they earn since their liabilities, the potential pension payments calculated by the fund actuaries, will be expanding in line with inflation. As a consequence, pension funds tend to invest in slightly more speculative assets often referred to as **real assets**, such as **equities** and **property**, since these offer a degree of protection against the impact of inflation.

In addition, they tend to keep only a small proportion of the fund in fixed interest instruments. In particular, they will tend to be substantial holders of inflation-linked issues, partly because these guarantee real returns over a period of time, but also because the bonds themselves tend to have fairly high durations and are therefore sensitive to movement in real interest rates.

Equally, the pension fund will need to keep some assets in a liquid form and government bond markets represent a highly liquid marketplace in which to invest money gaining a moderate but **risk-free** return.

1: INTRODUCTION TO INVESTMENT MANAGEMENT

3.2.2 Life assurance funds

Life assurance is a form of insurance against an eventuality that is **assured** (hence the name) to arise, ie that people will die. Generally speaking, internationally the word 'insurance' is taken to refer to an event that may or may not happen, whereas 'assurance' refers to an event that is inevitable. However, in some markets, such as the US, the term 'insurance' is generally applied to both situations.

As such, life assurance represents another form of liability matching fund. Life assurance policies take one or two forms.

- **Protection policies or Temporary policies** – Policies paying a benefit in the event of the death of the insured. There are some standard international versions of such policies including:
    - **Term assurance policies** – where an individual's life is insured for a specific period or term (usually ten years or more) in a similar way to normal car or household insurance.
- **Investment policies or Permanent polices** – Policies designed to provide an investment return over a specified period, such as:
    - **Whole of life policies** – where a capital sum will be paid upon the death of the policyholder, whenever that may be.
    - **Endowment policies** – which combine life insurance and savings. These policies are generally associated with mortgages where the savings element is designed to pay off the capital borrowed at the end of the term of the policy, and the life insurance will repay the mortgage should the policyholder die before the end of that term.

In common with pension funds, life assurance companies tend to have reasonably **long-term** liabilities and, as such, are able to take on board a higher degree of risk. Once again, this tends to involve a high proportion of their assets being invested into equities and property with only a smaller proportion being invested into the fixed interest markets.

As a long-term fund, life assurance companies are able to take a reasonably high degree of risk and again may be tempted towards the higher duration stocks in the bond markets.

Within the industry there are a variety of policies available ranging from with profits policies, which share in the profits of the fund but attract higher premiums, to without profits or non-profit policies, where the premiums are lower but the profits go to the insurance company.

3.2.3 General insurance companies

General insurance companies clearly aim to be able to match their liabilities. They have a much shorter liability profile than life funds. In essence, insurance is like taking a bet. The insured person pays the company the premium.

The insurance company makes money if they are able to take in this premium and earn investment income on it that exceeds the amounts of any claims arising on the policy.

1: INTRODUCTION TO INVESTMENT MANAGEMENT

Since claims are likely to arise in the immediate future, for example in the next year, then they are unable to take substantial risks, forcing them to invest a greater proportion of their fund into **short-term** 'risk-free' government securities. While the returns may not be as high, the fund simply cannot take any risk.

Both life assurance funds and general insurance funds tend to be closely monitored to ensure that the solvency of the company is in no way called into question. Overall, this tends to make both of them more risk adverse than pension funds but there is a marked difference between life assurance companies and general insurance companies in the risk/reward profile they adopt.

3.2.4 Collective investment vehicles

Collective investment schemes are return maximising funds. They are operations where a large number of small investors pool their money together to achieve a large fund which is placed under professional investment management. These funds can be in either of the following forms.

- Closed-end
- Open-end

Closed-end funds

Closed-end funds are **public limited companies** whose shares are listed on the Stock Exchange. The general term 'closed-end fund' is recognised internationally though the funds themselves go by different names in different countries. In Australia they are known as 'Listed Investment Companies' in much of Europe (Belgium, France, Italy, Luxembourg, Spain, Switzerland) they are called 'Société d'Investissement à Capital Fixe (SICAF)' in the UK they are called 'Investment Trusts' and in the US they are called 'Closed-end Companies'.

Closed-end funds initially raise money by issuing shares. If an individual wishes to liquidate his investment, or make a new investment, he needs to either sell the shares to or buy some shares from someone else.

Unlike pension funds and life assurance funds, closed-end funds do not have liabilities to be met, hence the money is invested by the fund manager on behalf of the investors to generate a combination of capital growth and income in accordance with the fund's objectives. Other than to pay income distributions, money will not be repaid from the fund unless it is terminated.

As a result, closed-end funds are not faced by inflows and outflows of funds as pension funds and life assurance funds are. For closed-end funds, the size of the fund itself is independent of the buying or selling of shares. It is a function of the initial capital subscribed and the gains generated on that capital.

Furthermore closed-end funds are able to gear up the portfolio by borrowing money. This has the potential to increase the risk of the fund, as well as increasing the potential for returns.

The objective of the investment manager is to maximise the value of the shares of the closed-end funds which, if the fund has a **split capital structure**, may be:

- **Dividend shares** – which entitle their holders to dividend distributions. Their value is, therefore, a function of the level of dividend payments and the **timescales over which these will be received**.
- **Capital shares** – which are entitled to the redemption value of the fund when it is terminated. Their value is, therefore, a function of the capital value of the fund, ie the value of the underlying investments that the fund holds.

Open-end funds

Open-end funds tend to be structured either as corporations/companies or as trusts and will correspondingly issue shares or units which confirm the entitlement of the investor to a proportion of the fund.

Again, the general term 'open-end fund' is recognised internationally though the funds themselves go by different names in different countries. In Australia they are known as 'Unit Trusts', in much of Europe (Belgium, France, Italy, Luxembourg, Spain, Switzerland) they may be either 'Société d'Investissement à Capital Variable (SICAV)' or 'Fonds Commun de Placement (FCP)', in the UK they may be either 'Unit Trusts' or 'Open-Ended Investment Companies (OEICs)' and in the US they may be called 'Mutual Funds'.

Unlike closed-end funds, open-end funds may suffer significant inflows and outflows of cash as a result of the way in which the funds operate. Open-end funds raise money by issuing shares or **units** that are **created** by the fund manager when cash is subscribed. This cash forms the initial pool of funds invested by the manager for the unit-holders. As a result, open-end funds need to maintain a reasonable degree of liquidity.

The manager must then act as a market-maker for the units, quoting **bid** and **offer** prices based on the bid and offer values of the underlying investments and the level of his initial charge. If an individual wishes to buy/sell units, then the fund manager must accommodate him. The manager will attempt to match buys and sells, though this may not always be possible. If the buys exceed the sells, the fund manager will have to create new shares or units and invest, as part of the fund property, the excess money received. If, however, the sells exceed the buys, the fund manager will have to liquidate some shares or units, ie sell some of the underlying investments of the fund and cancel the units.

Consequently, the number of shares or units in issue and the capital value of the fund may vary considerably.

The overall objectives of each fund are determined in advance in the documents setting-up the corporation or trust. These state the objectives in terms of risk/reward profile and may indicate the appropriate markets in which to invest. For example, it may be felt worthwhile for a fund manager to establish a fund investing in highly speculative emerging markets in order to maximise returns for its investors.

On the other hand, other groups of investors may wish to have their money placed into reasonably secure short-term liquid issues, eg short-dated government bonds, generating a reasonable income flow. Each scheme will have its own particular emphasis and a selection of stocks, and a strategy will be determined by this emphasis.

3.2.5 Exchange traded funds (ETFs)

Exchange Traded Funds (ETFs) are structured as open-ended collective investment vehicles that allow exposure to an index through the purchase of a share at relatively low cost to the investor. Unlike other open-end funds, however, they trade and settle like shares.

3.2.6 Venture capital funds (VCFs)

These are a type of investment company or partnership that invest in new and growing small businesses and allow investors to get indirect exposure to the private equity market by buying a share in the venture capital fund.

3.2.7 Charities

What defines a charity or charitable organisation differs from country to country, however they are generally entities that the government of that country considers to be acting for the benefit of society rather than seeking to make profit (sometimes referred to as non-profit organisations). As a result of their non-profit status and their benevolent nature they tend to be exempt from taxes.

The assets of a charity will produce an investment return that will be applied as required in the terms of the charity. Investment managers may run investment funds specifically for charities known as Common Investment Funds or Common Deposit Funds.

These pooled investment funds provide a simple and low-cost investment approach for smaller charities.

3.2.8 Hedge funds

Hedge funds originally intended to offer investments against the market using derivatives and short selling. Hedge funds have moved away from this and now different hedge funds will have different strategies. Some are geared while some consider the macroeconomy and gamble on interest rates and currencies. The one thing that all hedge funds have in common is their desire to search for **absolute returns**.

The hedge fund manager is not concerned about performance compared to benchmarks and therefore has the freedom to try to generate high returns and hence high personal rewards. This will create the need for a risky portfolio, and therefore the name hedge fund is slightly misleading. A better name would probably be isolation fund, since the hedge fund manager looks for specific bets to try to generate high returns.

Fees

Hedge fund managers will receive a fixed base management fee, which is a percentage (often between 1% and 2%) of the value of assets under management and an incentive fee which is related to profits. As this cannot be negative if losses are made, there will often be a clause stating that if losses are made, these losses have to be repaid in any subsequent profits before an incentive fee can be paid.

Example

A hedge fund has a base fee of 1%. The incentive fee is 25% for any returns made over and above the risk-free rate. Gross returns during the year were 38% and the risk-free rate is 6%. What is the net return?

Solution

Fee = 1% + 25% × (38% − 6%) = 9%

Net return = 38% − 9% = 29%

Types of hedge funds

Hedge funds represent a variety of different investment strategies, some of which are highlighted below.

- **Long/short funds** take positions in stock and are often geared. They are not normally market neutral, but instead have a long or short bias.
- **Market-neutral funds** take long positions in stocks that are considered undervalued and short positions in stocks that are considered overvalued. The fund is neutral, in that the value of short positions is equal to the value of long positions and the sensitivity of long and short positions is the same. Other strategies of a market neutral portfolio are to look for arbitrage opportunities in warrants or derivatives. They should therefore be relatively intuitive to changes in the underlying market.
- **Global macrofunds** bet on macroeconomic variables such as currencies or interest rates. They are often highly geared and use derivatives. Subgroups of macrofunds are **futures funds**, which use futures to bet on certain asset classes such as currency, fixed income and commodities and **emerging-market funds**. These can sometimes be referred to as speculative or tactical funds.
- **Event-driven funds** bet on events specific to a company or security. One example of this would be to invest in distressed securities or shares involved in a merger or acquisition.

Fund of funds

A fund of funds is, as the name suggests, a fund that invests in a selection of hedge funds. It enables small investors to access hedge funds. The benefits of a fund of funds are as follows.

- The fund of funds will invest in a variety of hedge funds, allowing the investor to diversify.
- A fund of funds provides easy access to investors who may be otherwise unable to use hedge funds. There may also be the opportunity to invest in funds that have otherwise closed to new investors.

- The manager of the fund of funds will have more expertise than the investor. He will have better access to information and will be more experienced in the due diligence required prior to investing in a hedge fund.

There are, of course, disadvantages, primarily the fee that the fund manager will charge.

3.2.9 Banks

The western world has a highly developed banking market ranging from the high-street banks to the large international banks. The range of services is considerable, from the straightforward deposit-taking and lending to the more sophisticated corporate finance and money market activities run of the merchant banks and capital markets divisions. In general, however, bank liabilities are **short term**, since the bulk of their assets are derived from deposit-taking, most of which is repayable on demand.

In recent years, the commercial pressure on the conventional banking activities through the process of diversification has forced the banks to expand their activities into the areas of financial services and, in particular, the provision of investment advice to the individual customer.

3.2.10 Saving and loan institutions

Saving and loan institutions have their foundation as mutual community-based institutions for savings and mortgages. They go by different names in different countries, being called building societies or trustee savings banks in the UK and many commonwealth countries and saving and loan associations or thrifts in the US.

In the past, saving and loan institutions have provided an extremely limited range of services mainly linked to long-term lending on property, though more recently they have expanded the range of services they provide such as:

- Transact business in the **forex** market.
- Operate estate agencies.
- Establish and manage personal investment funds.
- Provide **investment services**
- Make **unsecured loans**, making the institutions much more like retail banks.

4 INDIVIDUAL INVESTMENT MANAGEMENT

4.1 Assessing the client's objectives

As we noted earlier, for most institutional clients the primary requirement will be quite clear cut, for example collective investments are generally return maximising funds whereas pension funds are liability driven.

For many private clients, however, the requirements may be more mixed. A wealthy private client may have certain liabilities to meet such as paying for children's/grandchildren's school and college fees, repaying loans/mortgages or providing financial protection for relatives/dependents, but may wish that any 'spare' resources be managed to maximise returns.

1: INTRODUCTION TO INVESTMENT MANAGEMENT

There are, therefore, a number of stages that need to be undertaken when considering client objectives.

4.1.1 Quantifying and prioritising client's objectives

The first stage is to determine all of the objectives that the client is looking to meet and to prioritise and quantify those objectives, especially quantifying any liability targets since they will invariably be the top priorities.

From a priority viewpoint, this will clearly be specific to, and determined by, the client.

From a quantification viewpoint, as already mentioned the fund liabilities may include such factors as school/college fees, loans, dependent pensions etc, and a primary consideration here will be whether those liabilities are nominal or real.

4.1.2 Affordability of client's objectives

Based on the quantification, the fund manager will be able to determine any lump sum or annual contributions that need to be paid into the fund in order to establish the required pool and at this stage the issue of affordability needs to be considered.

If the current assets and/or disposable income of the client are more than sufficient to meet the liability needs then the surplus funds are available for (return maximising) savings. If, on the other hand, there is a deficit or shortfall then the client's targets and, potentially, priorities will need to be reconsidered.

4.1.3 The fact find process

Key to the assessment of the affordability, therefore, is the client's current personal and financial circumstances which may be determined through a fact find.

The fact find will seek to establish both personal and financial information. **Personal information** detailed in the fact find would, for a retail client, include family names and addresses, dates of birth, marital status, employment status, tax status. **Financial information** would include current income and expenditure levels, levels of savings and investments, the scale of any financial liabilities (usually mortgages, loans and credit cards), the existence of any life assurance policies and pensions etc.

The client will have much of this information easily to hand, however certain information may need to be obtained from third parties. For example, the current performance and value of any pension schemes or life policies such as endowments will probably need to be obtained from the relevant pension fund manager or life assurance fund manager. The overall financial plan will need to take account of any payments that are committed to such funds, any receipts that may be expected from them and whether it is worth considering changing providers.

Other areas that may be considered at this stage are current mortgage terms and the terms of other loans as it may again be appropriate to refinance at better rates.

The objective information regarding the client's personal and financial situation may be referred to as **hard facts**. One final aim of the fact find will be to seek to understand the more subjective information that may be relevant, such as client aspirations, risk tolerances and any other subjective factors such as their attitude towards issues such as

1: INTRODUCTION TO INVESTMENT MANAGEMENT

socially responsible investment. This subjective information may be referred to as **soft facts**.

Understanding such soft facts requires face-to-face meeting with the client to discuss and consider the issues alongside them. Establishing a client's risk tolerance, for example, is far from straightforward as standard risk measures are far from familiar to most retail clients. Such approaches are covered below.

4.1.4 Client's risk tolerance

There are two approaches that a fund manager will utilise in order to get an understanding of the client's risk tolerance, specifically the fact find soft facts discussion and undertaking a review of any current investments. Since a full appreciation of risk is essential to how the fund is managed, the fund manager will investigate both.

The process will probably start with a review of the client's current investments and risks, which will clearly illustrate the client's historical attitude to risk. As we noted above, however, risk tolerance changes over time, so this historical information, while a very useful insight, is not of itself sufficient for a full understanding of the client's risk tolerance.

To augment this, the fund manager will also undertake the fact find soft facts review. The standard fact find approach is to ask the client to select a mix of, say, equities and bonds, to give an idea of the normal mix (and hence risk) that the client wishes to face. We noted above that as part of the fact find process the fund manager will illustrate various possible asset allocations and discuss in detail the potential returns and risks of each. Such targeted discussions should enable the manager to get an understanding of the client's general risk tolerance. The fund manager will also be looking to establish limits for each asset class, maximum and minimum holdings of the different assets available, representing investment risk limits.

4.2 Offshore investment

Another advantage of using a managed fund is that it provides the private customer with easier access to overseas markets, and therefore exposure to new industries and economic conditions.

4.3 Types of customer and services provided

4.3.1 Discretionary customers

Discretionary customers are those who have given the firm discretion in deciding how to manage their investments. The firm makes investment decisions and implements these on behalf of the customer in line with investment objectives and criteria agreed with the customer in advance.

This can be contrasted with non-discretionary customers where the firm may advise the customer but where all investment decisions are made by the customer himself.

4.3.2 Advisory customers

An advisory customer is one to whom the firm gives advice and investment management services. However, any investment decisions are always ultimately made by the customer.

4.3.3 Execution-only customers

Execution-only customers are those who are not given any advice by the firm when they make investment decisions. The only responsibility of the firm to such customers is one of 'best execution'; to implement the customer's investment decisions at the best price available.

4.3.4 Nominee service

A firm may offer clients this service, whereby stock is registered into the name of a nominee. This simplifies the administration for the client.

5 MAKING INVESTMENTS

5.1 Introduction

There are three investment activities involved in the investment management process, specifically:

- Strategic asset allocation
- Tactical asset allocation or market timing
- Stock selection

Each of these activities is outlined briefly below.

5.2 Strategic asset allocation

Strategic asset allocation is the allocation of the funds available between the various instruments or financial markets.

All fund managers require a knowledge of strategic asset allocation according to more fundamental principles. This is perhaps the most subjective area of fund management, and one where there will never be a single correct answer. Given the same fund and client, it is unlikely that any two fund managers would produce exactly the same asset allocation and make exactly the same investment decisions. However, it would be reasonable to assume that any allocations would have a broadly similar effect. The justification for this last statement is that the fund manager has a duty to base the asset allocation on the client's wishes with particular regard to the criteria discussed above when identifying the client's objectives, specifically the following.

- Matching liabilities
- Meeting any ethical considerations
- Remaining within risk tolerances
- Maximising fund performance

1: INTRODUCTION TO INVESTMENT MANAGEMENT

There are three basic rules the fund manager should bear in mind when trying to satisfy the client's investment objectives.

- The fund manager should take every step to diversify risk, a process requiring an understanding of the different risk factors affecting all the investments in which he may be investing as well as the impact of foreign exchange.

- The fund manager should be aware that the best way to match the client's liabilities if they are fixed in money terms is by investing in bonds, since this will generate cash flows from interest and redemption proceeds which will allow the liabilities to be met as they arise.

- Asset allocation is effectively a compromise between matching investments to client liabilities and investing assets in more attractive markets in order to maximise fund performance.

5.3 Tactical asset allocation or market timing

Market timing involves adjusting the sensitivity of the portfolio to anticipated changes. A fund manager engages in market timing when he does not agree with the consensus about the market, ie he is more bullish or more bearish than the market, and rebalances his portfolio asset allocation in the short term to take advantage of this view.

5.4 Stock selection

Stock selection is the selection of the specific stocks within each asset class. The precise approach adopted depends on the investment management style adopted, ie active or passive.

6 INVESTMENT MANAGEMENT STYLE

6.1 Active versus passive

There are two overall styles that the investment manager can adopt. On the one hand, an active investment manager is one who intervenes with the portfolio on a regular basis, attempting to use individual expertise in order to enhance the overall return of the fund. Passive investment management, on the other hand, establishes a strategy which, once secured, should guarantee the appropriate level of return for the fund. These are, perhaps, two extreme versions of investment management. There are alternatives that represent hybrids between the two extremes.

6.2 Active

As mentioned above, active investment management means the fund manager constantly takes decisions and appraises the value of investments within the portfolio. While, to many, this may seem the only thing a fund manager could do, it has to be appreciated that in practice there are costs involved with all transactions, and hence limits on the number of active interventions taking place are likely to be to the advantage of the fundholder.

1: INTRODUCTION TO INVESTMENT MANAGEMENT

Moreover, from a more theoretical point of view, there are a number of theories that suggest that markets are efficient and therefore the prices currently quoted in the market contain within them all available information. If this is so, then the only reason that a price will move is because of information which is not already known to the market and, as such, fund managers buying and selling (switching between stocks) will only make money if they are 'lucky' and switch to the right stock at the right time.

Active fund managers do not believe that the securities markets are continuously efficient. Instead, they believe that securities can be misvalued and that at times **winners** can be found. They also attempt to correctly **time** their purchase or sale on the basis of specific stock information, market information, economic factors, etc.

Active fund managers may obtain research from external sources such as investment banks. In this instance analysts are referred to as 'sell-side' analysts. Alternatively, they may establish an in-house research department, made up of 'buy-side' analysts. The benefit of generating unbiased internal research needs to be weighed against the costs of setting-up the department.

6.3 Passive

6.3.1 Introduction

Passive management involves the establishing of a strategy with the intention of achieving the overall objectives of the fund. Once established, this strategy should not require active intervention, but should be self-maintaining. The simplest strategy is to 'buy and hold'. However, perhaps the most common form of passive management is indexation.

6.3.2 Indexation

With indexation, the fund manager selects an appropriate index quoted in the marketplace. Having established the index, the fund manager builds a portfolio which mimics the index, the belief being that this portfolio will then perform in line with the index numbers. Such funds are known as **index** or **tracker** funds.

Overall, the likelihood is that the fund will underperform the index for a number of reasons. First, there is the initial cost of creating the portfolio. Second, and perhaps more importantly, all index funds tend to be based on a sampling approach and consequently exhibit a degree of **tracking error**.

It should be noted that indexation itself is not a totally passive form of investment management since the constitution of each index will, over time, change and the portfolio will also be required to change. Tracker funds will, however, incur lower transaction costs as a result of the lower levels of turnover, an advantage over actively managed funds.

6.4 Hybrids

Increasingly, fund managers are being requested to outperform indexes, rather than merely track them, and this inevitably requires a less passive, more interventionist approach, potentially with an **indexed core fund** and a **peripheral** or **satellite fund** (which is more actively managed and potentially involves the use of derivatives in order to establish larger trading positions than the fund itself can obtain).

Alternatively, the fund manager may combine both active and passive fund management methods by **tilting** the fund. Tilting involves holding all (or a representative sample) of the constituents of an index (like a passive tracker fund), but with larger proportions in areas that the manager favours. This asset allocation decision constitutes the active management component.

7 SELECTING A FUND MANAGER

The factors considered by sponsors in selecting a fund manager include the following.

Past performance

Past performance should be considered in relation to the risk profile of the assets under management. It should also be considered over a long period to assess the variability in performance rather than simply contemplating short-term absolute performance. Absolute performance should also be considered against an appropriate benchmark for the industry peer group or the markets invested in. It could also be argued that for funds, such as pension funds, it is the generation of a real return, rather than nominal return, that is of consequence.

Consistency of management

Sponsors need to take care that they do not select a fund manager on the basis of a performance history that relates to a particular fund manager or methodology that is no longer a feature of that firm. Certain skill-based investment approaches will be very dependent on the individual fund manager.

Internal controls and regulation

In the wake of regulatory problems that have been well publicised, sponsors are likely to be increasingly concerned as to the effectiveness of regulatory controls within any fund manager. Particular areas of concern might include investment restrictions, custody and segregation.

Management style

An assessment of the approach is critical to the needs of the fund itself. The fund sponsor must select a style that is compatible with the fund's objectives. This would necessitate a consideration of active or passive management and their respective risks and returns.

Fees

The level of management fees will obviously be an issue. The adverse publicity surrounding the performance failures of active managers has led to increasing focus on performance fees. Active management will increasingly need to prove its worth by achieving good performance to justify its charging structure.

1: INTRODUCTION TO INVESTMENT MANAGEMENT

Executive Summary

We have looked to lay down some foundations in this chapter and identify the issues of primary importance to the fund manager. We have introduced a number of ideas which we will be expanding on as we move forward, but it is appropriate to highlight them now to give some context to the following chapters.

We started by describing investment management as the management of an investment portfolio on behalf of a client or institution with the aim of matching future liabilities or maximising returns, we introduced an outline of the investment management process as follows:

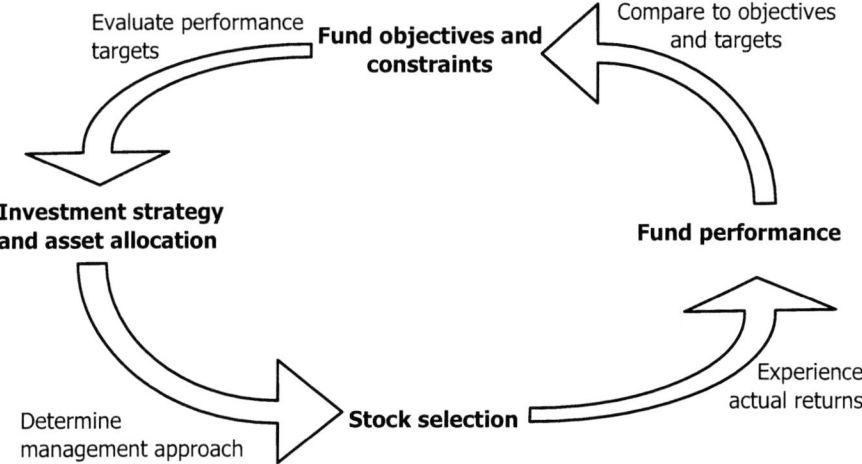

and introduced the concept of diversification and the risk-return profiles of various assets available.

Key issues raised in this chapter have been

- Investment management is the management of an investment portfolio on behalf of a private client or an institution.

- The objective of the fund/investors will either be to match future liabilities or to maximise returns within given risk parameters.

- While the investment manager will take primary responsibility for managing the money, the role of protecting the assets is often passed over to a third party.

- There are two main types of pension scheme: defined benefits schemes which pay a proportion of final year's salary at retirement; and defined contribution schemes which pay a pension based on the amount of contributions and investment performance up to retirement.

1: INTRODUCTION TO INVESTMENT MANAGEMENT

- Life assurance and general insurance companies also invest the premiums they receive to generate returns.

- Collective investment schemes include closed-end and open-end funds, venture capital funds and exchange traded funds (ETF). All offer investors benefits of diversification, professional fund management and the opportunity to invest in worldwide assets.

- Hedge funds are a form of unregulated fund able to take on any one of many different strategies and approaches.

- Discretionary, advisory and execution-only are all different service levels offered to clients.

- The investment management process involves asset allocation, market timing and stock selection.

- Investment managers may follow an active process of trying to outperform the market, a passive approach of merely aiming to track the market or some hybrid combination.

The important issues we have introduced in this chapter are therefore:

- The evaluation of any future liabilities and assets that the fund may have. This is considered in Chapter 2 where we introduce the fundamentally important evaluation tool of discounted cash flows.

- The principles of risk, return and diversification. These principles are expanded on in Chapter 3 – Risk and Return, though further specific details are included in the later investment-specific chapters.

- The characteristics (pricing, returns and risks) of the major assets we may consider investing in are covered in Chapters 4 to 9. Please note that we only consider the main asset classes in this book.

- The uses of such assets to try to achieve the fund objectives are examined in Chapter 10.

- The assessment of actual performance against any target in order to determine our success or otherwise as a fund manager, is considered Chapter 10.

2 Discounted Cash Flows

Contents

1. Introduction 28
2. The Time Value of Money and Interest Rates 29
3. Terminal/Future Values 33
4. Present Values and Net Present Values 37
5. Internal Rate of Return 46
6. Securities Evaluation and DCF 49
7. Assumptions Underlying the IRR and NPV Approaches 50
   Executive Summary 52

2: DISCOUNTED CASH FLOWS

1 INTRODUCTION

Central to all our theories regarding the valuation of securities is DCF (Discounted Cash Flows) and the time value of money. It is therefore essential that we thoroughly understand this topic and the relevance of the measures that we derive.

The various valuation ideas are based on the dividend valuation model which states that:

"The market value of a security is the present value of the future expected receipts, discounted at the investors' required rate of return."

We will see this idea time and time again, hence the importance placed on the basics.

The important consideration in this section is consistency. That is consistency in terms of the currency used, the required rates applied and the period covered. For example, if we wish to evaluate future annual US dollar cash flows we would measure time in years and apply annual US rates to the annual US dollar values. Alternatively, if we wished to evaluate semi-annual Euro cash flows we would measure time in half years and apply semi-annual Euro required rates to the semi-annual Euro cash flows. The principles introduced here are independent of currency or timescales but simply require consistency.

However, before we can go on to use this idea, we need to consider how an investor may establish their required rate of return.

Suppose a bank lends you $100 to be repaid with interest in one year's time with inflation running at 3%.

For the bank to be just as well off in real terms, it will need to receive $103 in one year to cover inflation, ie the minimum interest it can charge would equate to the rate of inflation.

However, banks are in business to make profits (being better off), not to be just as well off, so the bank will charge more than this.

The rate the bank will charge is given by the Fisher equation.

$$(1 + r) = (1 + i)(1 + R)$$

Where:

r = nominal rate (total annual rate)
i = inflation rate
R = real rate of return

The real rate being the excess return required by the bank to compensate for:

- Its loss of flexibility (you have its cash).
- The risk it is taking (you may default).

2 THE TIME VALUE OF MONEY AND INTEREST RATES

2.1 Introduction

A starting point is the realisation and appreciation of the time value of money, which we will all be aware of as a result of the payment (or possibly the receipt) of bank interest.

Bank interest can take one of two forms:

- Simple interest; or
- Compound interest.

Each of which are illustrated below with the aid of the following example.

2.2 Simple interest

If a bank account were to offer a **simple interest** rate, then the interest received each year would be based on the **original capital invested only**. Hence, in relation to the above example, we would have the following solution.

Example

$100 is deposited in an account paying interest at 10% per annum (simple interest). How much interest will be earned during, and what will be the value of the deposit at the end of:

- The first year?
- The nth year (say 5th)?

Solution

First year

The interest earned in this year would be based on the capital originally invested ($100) and the simple rate of interest (10%). The interest could be calculated using the formula:

$$i_1 = D_0 \times r$$

where:

i_1 = interest earned by the end of the first year (time = 1)
r = interest rate stated as a decimal, here 10% or 0.10
D_0 = original capital invested at the start of the first year (time = 0)

Giving:

$$i_1 = \$100 \times 0.10 = \$10$$

At that date, the deposit will be worth $110.

n^{th} year

With simple interest, the interest generated each subsequent year will be exactly the same, since it is only based on the original capital invested. Hence, we can apply the same formula to calculate this year's interest as:

$i_n = D_0 \times r$

giving for the fifth year:

$i_5 = \$100 \times 0.10 = \$10$

We can see that the value of our deposit is growing by $10 each year.

In conclusion, with simple interest, we earn the same amount of interest each year. At the end of n years, the total interest we will have earned will be:

n × Annual interest

or:

$i_{tot} = n \times (D_0 \times r)$

which, when added to our starting capital of D_0, gives the value of our deposit as:

$D_n = D_0 + n \times (D_0 \times r)$

Applying this to the above example gives:

$D_5 = D_0 + n \times (D_0 \times r) = \$100 + 5 \times (\$100 \times 0.10) = \$150$

which is perhaps the result we expected. Five years' interest at 10% per annum should add a total of 50% to the value of the deposit with flat interest.

2.3 Compound interest

2.3.1 Annual compounding

Interest rates are described as **compound interest** if, in each year, interest is earned on the **total value of the deposit at the start of the year**, ie original capital plus any interest previously earned. With compound interest, we receive interest on our previous interest.

Example

$100 is deposited in an account paying interest at 10% per annum (compound interest). How much interest will be earned during, and what will be the value of the deposit at the end of:

The first year?

The nth year (say 5th)?

Solution

First year

The interest earned in this year would be based on the value of the deposit at the start of the year, ie the capital originally invested ($100) and the compound rate of interest (10%). The interest could again be calculated using the formula:

$$i_1 = D_0 \times r$$

where:

i_1 = interest earned by the end of the first year (Time = 1)
r = interest rate stated as a decimal, here 10% or 0.10
D_0 = original capital invested at the outset (time = 0)

Giving:

$$i_1 = \$100 \times 0.10 = \$10$$

At that date, the deposit will be worth $110, which we could have calculated directly using the formula:

$$D_1 = D_0(1 + r) = \$100 \times (1 + 0.10) = \$100 \times 1.10 = \$110$$

where D_1 = the value of the deposit at Time 1. We can see that, so far, this is identical to the simple interest example above. However, this is only true for the first year.

n^{th} year

With compound interest, the interest generated each subsequent year will be based on the value of the deposit at the start of each year. We could state this in a formula as:

$$i_n = D_{n-1} \times r$$

In order to calculate the interest for the fifth year, we would need to know the value of the deposit at the start of the fifth year/end of the fourth year. From our Year 1 illustration above, we noted that the value of the deposit at the end of the first year/start of the second was given by:

$$D_1 = D_0(1 + r)$$

This amount would then grow by the end of the second year/start of the third year to:

$$D_2 = D_1(1 + r) = D_0(1 + r)^2$$

In a similar way, we could calculate the value of the deposit at the end of each subsequent year as:

$$D_3 = D_2(1 + r) = D_0(1 + r)^3 - \text{end of third/start of fourth}$$
$$D_4 = D_3(1 + r) = D_0(1 + r)^4 - \text{end of fourth/start of fifth}$$
$$D_5 = D_4(1 + r) = D_0(1 + r)^5 - \text{end of fifth/start of sixth}$$

which could be described generally as:

$$D_n = D_0(1 + r)^n - \text{end of } n^{th}/\text{start of } (n + 1)^{th}$$

Hence, at the end of the fourth year/start of the fifth the value of the deposit would be:

$$D_4 = D_0(1 + r)^n = \$100(1 + 0.10)^4 = \$100 \times 1.1^4 = \$146.41$$

and, hence, the interest generated in the fifth year would be:

$$i_5 = D_4 \times r = \$146.41 \times 0.10 = \$14.641$$

taking the value of the total deposit up to $161.051 ($146.41 + $14.641) by the end of the fifth year, which we can confirm with the formula:

$$D_5 = D_0(1 + r)^5 = \$100 (1 + 0.10)^5 = \$100 \times 1.1^5 = \$161.051$$

This is a larger sum than under simple interest, since we are getting interest on our previously earned interest.

2.3.2 Non-annual compounding

Generally, bank accounts quote an annual interest rate that is liable to be compounded, though the compounding may be more regular than once per annum. There is no standard in relation to the frequency of compounding. Many bank accounts compound monthly, while others are compounded quarterly, six-monthly or annually.

Generally, two rates are quoted.

- A flat rate
- An Annual Percentage Rate (APR)

What are these quotes and what difference does this make to our deposit?

Flat rate

Example

$100 is deposited in an account quoting an annual flat rate of 10% compounding quarterly. Calculate the interest earned and value of the deposit by the end of the first year.

Solution

A flat rate of r per annum which compounds m times a year would generate interest of $\frac{r}{m}$ each period, ie with a flat rate of 10% compounding quarterly (four times per annum), the interest generated each period would be $\frac{10\%}{4} = 2.5\%$.

We can now suppose that we are generating an interest rate of 2.5% per period, hence at the end of four periods (one year), the value of our deposit will have grown to:

$$\$100 (1 + 0.025)^4 = \$100 \times 1.025^4 = \$110.38$$

which is slightly more than when interest is compounded annually.

Example

$100 is deposited in an account quoting an annual flat rate of 10%, compounding monthly. What is the value of the deposit at the end of one year?

Solution

The rate per month would be $\dfrac{10\%}{12} = 0.83333\%$.

Hence, at the end of 12 months (one year), the value of our deposit will have grown to:

$$\$100\,(1 + 0.0083333)^{12} = \$100 \times 1.0083333^{12} = \$110.47$$

which is slightly more than when interest is compounded both annually and quarterly.

What we can conclude is:

- The more frequent the compounding, the better.
- The higher the interest rate, the greater the benefit of frequent compounding.

Annual percentage rate

We can see from the above that if the interest compounds monthly we have generated interest of $10.47 over the first year based on our initial $100 deposit – an effective rate of 10.47%. This effective rate is the APR. It tells you exactly how much you will earn over a year (or pay if you are borrowing) based on the flat rate and the frequency of compounding.

3 TERMINAL/FUTURE VALUES

3.1 Introduction

A **terminal value** or **future value** is the value of a deposit at the end of a period of time having received interest over that period, ie D_n is the terminal value in the above examples.

A **present value** is the equivalent value of the same deposit before the effects of interest, ie D_0 is the present value in the above examples.

Calculating terminal or present values for investment opportunities provides a means of appraising them. Indeed, as we noted at the outset, the calculation of a present value provides a method for evaluating a security, ie determines its market value.

All calculations with regard to these ideas utilise the concept of **compound interest**.

3.2 Terminal/future values

3.2.1 Introduction

Terminal/future value calculations consider:

- Each cash flow generated by an investment.
- The timing of the cash flow.

They calculate how much cash could be generated to the end of the investment period if the earlier returns were banked each year to generate additional compound interest.

2: DISCOUNTED CASH FLOWS

If the returns plus the interest that they can accumulate exceeds the total that could be generated had we simply banked the cash at the outset rather than buying the investment, then we accept the investment. The decision criteria could be stated as:

"An investment should be accepted if it produces a surplus in cash terms after accounting for interest."

Example

Two alternative investments to banking $100 are Investments A and B, both of which will terminate in three years. Investment A will return $41.00 per annum for the next three years, giving a total return of $123 and a total profit of $23. Investment B will return $134.00 at the end of the third year, a profit of $34.

Which investment opportunity is superior and which, if either, should be accepted if the interest rate is 10%?

Solution

Since we can receive 10% per annum on any cash generated, then the effects of selecting A or B would be as follows.

Investment A

Time	Balance b/f $	Interest for year $	Receipt at year end $	Balance c/f $
1	–	–	41.00	41.00
2	41.00	4.10	41.00	86.10
3	86.10	8.61	41.00	135.71

Undertaking Investment A will result in cash in the bank of $135.71 at the end of the three years – this is its terminal value.

Investment B

Investment B will result in a receipt of $134.00 at the same time, hence this is its terminal value.

Bank account

Time	Balance b/f $	Interest for year $	Receipt at year end $	Balance c/f $
1	100.00	10.00	–	110.00
2	110.00	11.00	–	121.00
3	121.00	12.10	–	133.10

Banking the $100 today will result in cash in the bank of $133.10 at the end of the three years.

2: DISCOUNTED CASH FLOWS

Conclusion

Both investments produce a better end position than the simple investment in the bank. Investment A will result in $2.61 more cash ($135.71 – $133.10) and Investment B $0.90 more ($134.00 – $133.10). Comparing the two, Investment A now appears preferable to Investment B.

It would certainly seem that it is in the investor's interest to pay more attention to the cash flows expected from an investment and to the timing of these cash flows than to consider solely the level of profit.

Alternative solution

An alternative way of dealing with the example would be by compounding the interest on each flow individually, using our earlier compound interest ideas.

Investment A

Time	Cash flow $	Compound factor	Terminal value $
1	41.00	1.10^2	49.61
2	41.00	1.10^1	45.10
3	41.00	1	41.00
Terminal value at t_3			135.71

Investment B

Time	Cash flow $	Compound factor	Terminal value $
1	0.00	1.10^2	0.00
2	0.00	1.10^1	0.00
3	134.00	1	134.00
Terminal value at t_3			134.00

Here, we have compounded each flow by adding on interest at 10% per annum for the number of years remaining until the end of the investment lives. To achieve this, we have in each case multiplied the cash flow by the compound factor, which in general terms may be written as:

Compound factor with n years to run = $(1 + r)^n$

where r is the rate of interest expressed as a decimal (here r = 0.10) and n is the number of years' compounding required.

Clearly, the calculations have produced the same result, but the method used here is somewhat neater. We have compounded the flows to produce what is termed the terminal value of each flow.

2: DISCOUNTED CASH FLOWS

Again, this can be compared to the $133.10 terminal value from the bank account to show that the investments are both worthwhile.

3.2.2 Net Terminal Value (NTV)

The net surplus or deficit from the investment ($2.61 for Investment A, $0.90 for Investment B as calculated above) is known as the Net Terminal Value (NTV), and since it is positive, indicating a surplus, the investments are worthwhile and should be accepted. Had it been negative, indicating a deficit, we would have rejected the investments.

Rather than calculating separately the terminal values of the investment and the bank account, we can combine them in one net terminal value calculation, as follows.

Investment A

Time	Cash flow $	Compound factor	Terminal value $
0	(100.00)	1.10^3	(133.10)
1	41.00	1.10^2	49.61
2	41.00	1.10^1	45.10
3	41.00	1	41.00
Net terminal value at t_3			2.61

Here, we are considering the $100 invested initially as a cash outflow on which we will lose interest. In turn, we get the investment inflows that generate interest, but it is the net difference we are interested in.

Investment B

Time	Cash flow $	Compound factor	Terminal value $
0	(100.00)	1.10^3	(133.10)
1	0.00	1.10^2	0.00
2	0.00	1.10^1	0.00
3	134.00	1	134.00
Net terminal value at t_3			0.90

3.3 Conclusion

Net terminal values will be useful for evaluating individual investments or investments with the same end date. If, however, we are trying to evaluate investments with different end dates, then we cannot compare the terminal value of one directly to the terminal value of the other.

For example, how could we compare the terminal value of Investment A of $135.71 at the end of three years, to the terminal value of a third investment of $150 at the end of six years?

In order to do this comparison, we must compound the interest out to a common end date. Here, six years would be sensible. However, this method will get very cumbersome, especially if we have some investments that will continue forever and never terminate, such as an investment in irredeemable bonds.

4 PRESENT VALUES AND NET PRESENT VALUES

4.1 Introduction

One way of accounting for the interest is by compounding the flows and calculating the terminal values, as we have just seen. However, as we stated earlier, if we are to compare investments, we will have to calculate to a common date, say, the end of the longest investment time. An alternative approach is to use present values where we take the common date as the present.

4.2 Present values

4.2.1 Introduction

Present value calculations consider for any investment:

- Each relevant cash flow; and
- The timing of the cash flow.

and calculate how much cash we would need to have invested now to generate these same amounts of cash at these same future dates.

If we can get the same amounts of cash at the same future dates by investing less upfront now, then we should accept the investment.

Example

Two alternative investments to banking $100 are Investments A and B, both of which will terminate in three years.

Investment A will return $41.00 per annum for the next three years; Investment B will return $134.00 at the end of the third year.

Which investment opportunity is superior and which, if either, should be accepted if the interest rate is 10%?

Solution

Investment A

Investment A generates the following cash flows.

Time	Cash flow $
1	41.00
2	41.00
3	41.00

2: DISCOUNTED CASH FLOWS

Looking at each of these in turn, how much cash would we need to invest now at our 10% rate of return to have $41.00 in each year?

Year 1

If we invest x now, then in one year it will grow to x × 1.10 = 1.10x. Since we know that this is $41.00, then we can calculate x as:

$$1.10x = \$41.00$$

Or:

$$x = \frac{1}{1.10} \times \$41.00$$

$$x = \$37.27$$

Year 2

Similarly, x invested now will grow to x × 1.10² = 1.21x after two years, hence:

$$1.21x = \$41.00$$

Or:

$$x = \frac{1}{1.21} \times \$41.00$$

$$x = \$33.89$$

Year 3

And x invested now will grow to x × 1.10³ = 1.331x after three years, hence:

$$1.331x = \$41.00$$

Or:

$$x = \frac{1}{1.331} \times \$41.00$$

$$x = \$30.80$$

Conclusion

Putting these all together, we have:

Time	Cash flow $	Discount factor	Present value $
1	41.00	$\frac{1}{1.10^1}$	37.27
2	41.00	$\frac{1}{1.10^2}$	33.89
3	41.00	$\frac{1}{1.10^3}$	30.80
Present value at t_0			101.96

2: DISCOUNTED CASH FLOWS

In total, the present value of these receipts is $101.96. This means that, given the 10% rate of return, we would be indifferent between $41.00 each year for three years and $101.96 now.

Rather than compounding up the cash values for interest generated to the end of the investment, we are **discounting down**, ie reducing future cash values to their equivalent value today.

This discounting is effectively the reverse of our compounding process and in a similar way, we could apply a general formula for any year.

$$\text{Discount factor at time n} = \frac{1}{(1+r)^n}$$

where r is the **discount rate**, ie rate of interest expressed as a decimal (here r = 0.10) and n is the number of years' discounting required.

Solution

Investment B

Calculating the present value for Investment B gives:

Time	Cash flow $	Discount factor	Present value $
3	134.00	$\frac{1}{1.10^3}$	100.68
Present value at t_0			100.68

This means that we would be indifferent, given the 10% rate of return, between $134.00 in three years and $100.68 now.

4.2.2 Bank

What is the present value of our option to bank the cash for a comparison? Under this option, we left the cash in the bank until Year 3 when it had grown to $133.10. This is then the cash flow to discount giving:

Time	Cash flow $	Discount factor	Present value $
3	133.10	$\frac{1}{1.10^3}$	100.00
Present value at t_0			100.00

2: DISCOUNTED CASH FLOWS

This one really proves the idea, as it shows that we would be indifferent between $133.10 in three years and $100.00 now, which stands to reason as to get $133.10 in three years, we will need to invest $100.00 in the bank now.

4.2.3 Net present value

The present value of Investment A is $1.96 higher than could be expected from the bank. Investment B has a present value which is $0.68 higher than that from the bank. These represent the **net present values** of these investments.

In a similar way to net terminal values, we could calculate a net present value in one go, rather than calculating separately the present value of the investment and the banking option, as follows.

Solution

Investment A

Time	Cash flow $	Discount factor	Present value $
0	(100.00)	1	(100.00)
1	41.00	$\frac{1}{1.10^1}$	37.27
2	41.00	$\frac{1}{1.10^2}$	33.89
3	41.00	$\frac{1}{1.10^3}$	30.80
Net present value at t_0			1.96

You will note in this that the cash flow at Time 0 (now) is not discounted. $100 now is worth $100 now. Discounting takes account of the time value of money.

Investment B

Similarly, for Investment B, we get:

Time	Cash flow $	Discount factor	Present value $
0	(100.00)	1	(100.00)
3	134.00	$\frac{1}{1.10^3}$	100.68
Present value at t_0			0.68

Conclusion

For an accept or reject decision, the criterion is as before – a positive net present value (NPV) indicates a cash surplus after accounting for interest and therefore we should accept. A negative NPV indicates a cash deficit and we should therefore reject.

If we were to choose between various investments, we would now simply select the investment with the highest NPV.

4.3 Discount factors

4.3.1 Single cash flow discount factor

We established above that the general term for a discount factor to be applied to cash flows at Time$_n$ is:

$$\text{Discount factor at Time n} = \frac{1}{(1+r)^n}$$

The above formula is suitable if we are only dealing with a few cash flows, or have a spreadsheet model to cope with a large number, but what if this is not the case? There are some other situations for which we can establish discount factor formulae to make manual calculations more straightforward, specifically in the situation of:

- Level annuities; and
- Level perpetuities.

4.3.2 Annuity discount factor

An annuity describes the situation where we have equal annual cash flows for a set period, such as in Investment A above. Here, we have $41.00 received at the end of each of the next three years and, so far, we have appraised each flow separately.

However, since for all the receipts we are multiplying the relevant discount factor by $41.00 each time, we can simplify the calculation by multiplying $41.00 by the sum of the discount factors, ie:

$$\$41.00 \times \left(\frac{1}{1.10^1} + \frac{1}{1.10^2} + \frac{1}{1.10^3} \right)$$

$= \$41.00 \times 2.48685$

$= \$101.96$ as before

The discount factor of 2.48685 is termed the **three-year annuity discount factor** at 10%.

This annuity discount factor for cash flows arising from Time 1 to Time 0 can be calculated using the following formula:

$$\text{Annuity discount factor for Time 1 to Time n} = \frac{1}{r}\left(1 - \frac{1}{(1+r)^n}\right)$$

2: DISCOUNTED CASH FLOWS

where r is the rate of interest per annum expressed as a decimal which must be constant throughout the period.

Using this formula

Wherever we pay or receive a level stream of payments over a period of time, eg a regular coupon from a bond assuming constant interest rates, we can use this formula to calculate their present value.

Example

Using this formula to calculate the three-year annuity discount factor at 10% gives:

Annuity discount factor for Time 1 to Time n = $\dfrac{1}{0.10}\left(1 - \dfrac{1}{1.10^3}\right)$

$= \dfrac{1}{0.10}\left(1 - \dfrac{1}{1.10^3}\right)$

$= \dfrac{1}{0.10}(1 - 0.751315)$

$= \dfrac{1}{0.10}(0.248685)$

$= 2.48685$

Solution

Using this approach, we could calculate the net present value of Investment A above (which we earlier calculated as $1.96) as follows.

Time	Cash flow $	Discount factor	Present value $
0	(100.00)	1	(100.00)
1 – 3	41.00	$\dfrac{1}{0.10}\left(1 - \dfrac{1}{1.10^3}\right)$	101.96
Net present value at t_0			1.96

This approach can lead to significant time savings as the annuity period gets longer.

4.3.3 Perpetuity discount factor

A perpetuity refers to an equal annual flow which will continue **indefinitely**.

NB: Any series of flows that continue beyond 50 years could be approximated to a perpetuity without much impact or loss of accuracy.

Clearly, it will be impossible for us to evaluate each individual cash flow going on forever. For this situation, we must have a short cut.

Example

We are going to receive $10,000 per annum in perpetuity and the interest rate (which we will now start to refer to as a required rate of return or cost of capital) is 10% per annum. How would we value this series of flows?

To get a present value, we need to know how much cash invested now at 10% per annum would provide $10,000 pa in perpetuity. We would be indifferent between these two things which, by definition, means that it is the present value.

Solution

If we are to receive exactly the same amount in perpetuity, then we must never add to or take out of our capital invested. We are looking for an income of exactly $10,000 per annum.

Since our interest rate is 10% per annum, we can achieve this level of income by investing $100,000, the relationship being $100,000 × 10% = $10,000.

Now, we know that $10,000 × Perpetuity discount factor = $100,000 (the present value), hence the perpetuity discount factor in this case is $\frac{1}{0.10}$.

NB: What we have found is the discount factor for a stream of cash flows starting in one year, ie at Time 1.

The general discount factor formula for a level perpetuity stream of cash flows starting at Time 1 is:

$$\text{Perpetuity discount factor for Time 1 to } \infty = \frac{1}{r}$$

where r is the rate of interest per annum expressed as a decimal.

4.4 Annuities and perpetuities not starting at Time 1

4.4.1 Introduction

As we noted in the calculation of the annuity or perpetuity discount factor, the first cash flow always arises at the end of the first time period (at Time 1). However, there will be situations when this will not be the case.

Example

An investment pays $41 at the end of Years 3, 4 and 5. Calculate the present value of the receipts assuming a 10% required rate of return.

2: DISCOUNTED CASH FLOWS

Solution

Time	Cash flow $	Discount factor	Present value $
3	41.00	$\dfrac{1}{1.10^3}$	30.8039
4	41.00	$\dfrac{1}{1.10^4}$	28.0036
5	41.00	$\dfrac{1}{1.10^5}$	25.4578
Present value at t_0			84.2653

4.4.2 Alternative approaches

There are two alternative approaches that we could have adopted to calculate this, which could prove very useful in longer annuity or perpetuity situations.

Deducting unwanted years

We could view this cash stream as a normal five-year annuity (Time 1 to Time 5), but assume we must repay the Time 1 and Time 2 cash flows (hence not receive them).

Example

An investment pays $41 at the end of Years 3, 4 and 5. Calculate the present value of the receipts assuming a 10% required rate of return.

Solution

Time	Cash flow $	Annuity discount factor (ADF)	Present value $
1 – 5	41.00	$\dfrac{1}{0.10}\left(1 - \dfrac{1}{1.10^5}\right)$	155.4224
1 – 2	(41.00)	$\dfrac{1}{0.10}\left(1 - \dfrac{1}{1.10^2}\right)$	(71.1571)
Present value at t_0			84.2653

Discounting back

The alternative approach is to recognise that this is a three-year annuity, which starts to pay at Time 3 rather than Time 1, ie two years later than a standard annuity which starts at Time 1. If all of the cash flows are two years later than in a normal annuity or perpetuity, they must be discounted back a further two years. Hence:

$$\text{ADF}(3-5) = \text{ADF}(1-3) \times \frac{1}{(1+r)^2}$$

Example

An investment pays $41 at the end of Years 3, 4 and 5. Calculate the present value of the receipts assuming a 10% required rate of return.

Solution

Time	Cash flow $	Discount factor	Present value $
3 – 5	(41.00)	$\frac{1}{0.10}\left(1 - \frac{1}{1.10^3}\right) \times \frac{1}{1.10^2}$	84.2653

Conclusion

There are three alternative approaches.

- Evaluate each separate cash flow.
- Calculate by deducting the unwanted years.
- Calculate by discounting back.

All approaches will give the same answer, and you may choose whichever approach you prefer.

4.5 Relationship between present and terminal values

One final point to note is that there is a direct relationship between present and terminal values, either gross or net. If we take the present or net present value of any investment and compound it up for the appropriate number of years, we will get the corresponding terminal or net terminal value as we can see from our sample investments.

Solution

Earlier, we calculated the terminal value, net terminal value, present value and net present value of two investments (A and B), A paying $41.00 each year for three years and B paying $134 at the end of the third year. Comparing the net present values and net terminal values we calculated earlier based on a required rate of return of 10%, we get:

2: DISCOUNTED CASH FLOWS

	Net present value $	Compound factor	Net terminal value $
Investment A	1.96	1.10^3	2.61
Investment B	0.68	1.10^3	0.90

We can use this idea to determine the terminal value or net terminal value of anything for which we can calculate a present value or net present value (other than a perpetuity). That is, we can calculate the present value of the cash flows, then compound them up to give the corresponding terminal value.

5 INTERNAL RATE OF RETURN

5.1 Definition

The **Internal Rate of Return (IRR)** is defined as follows.

> IRR = The rate of interest that discounts the investment flows to a net present value of zero.

5.2 Use of the IRR

The IRR may be used as a method for assessing the total return from an investment or a portfolio, and you will find this approach necessary in calculating the gross redemption yield for a bond or the money-weighted return for portfolio performance.

Example

An investment is bought for $100 and sold one year later for $110. Calculate the return realised.

Solution

Here we are making a $10 gain on a $100 investment, corresponding to a 10% return.

Clearly, with this very simple investment it was very easy to assess the return without recourse to DCF. However, if we were to discount this investment's cash flows at different rates we would find the following.

2: DISCOUNTED CASH FLOWS

Time	Cash flow $	Discount factor (5%)	Present value $	Discount factor (10%)	Present value $	Discount factor (15%)	Present value $
0	(100.00)	1	(100.00)	1	(100.00)	1	(100.00)
1	110.00	$\frac{1}{1.05^1}$	104.76	$\frac{1}{1.10^1}$	100.00	$\frac{1}{1.15^1}$	95.65
Net present values			4.76		0.00		(4.35)

What we can see here is that there is an inverse relationship between NPVs and required rates of return; as rates rise, NPVs fall, and appreciating this relationship is the key to understanding the examination approach to these questions.

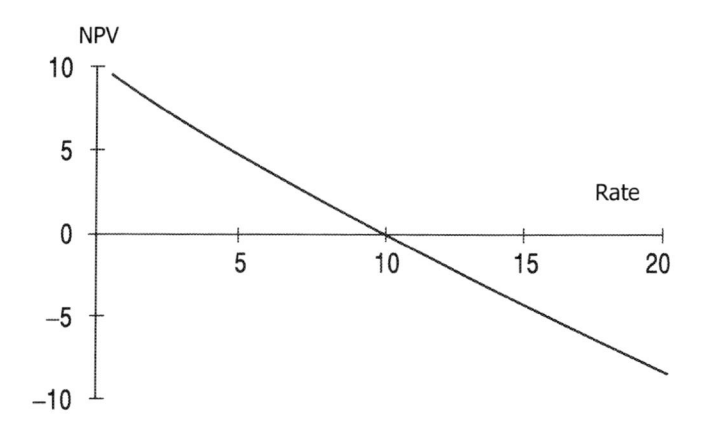

What we can also see in this example is that the IRR is 10% (the rate corresponding to a zero NPV), telling us that this investment is returning 10%. Clearly, we already knew the return from this very simple security was 10%, however the strength of this IRR approach is that it can be applied to investments that provide a much more complicated series of cash returns.

5.3 Assessment

An approximation to the IRR can be determined through a process called **interpolation**, though a trial and error approach is really the only way of finding the exact IRR. Through knowledge of the inverse relationship, however, the number of trials and errors can be minimised in a multiple choice exam where four alternative rates are offered.

5.3.1 Steps

Calculate the NPV of the various cash flows using the second highest rate, which will give rise to three possibilities.

- If the NPV is zero, then the correct rate has been selected first time.

- If the NPV is positive, then the selected rate is too low and the IRR is a higher rate. Since the second highest rate was originally selected, the correct answer must be the highest rate offered.

- If the NPV is negative, then the selected rate was too high and the IRR is one of the two lower rates offered in the question. One of these two lower rates will need to be tried to determine which it is.

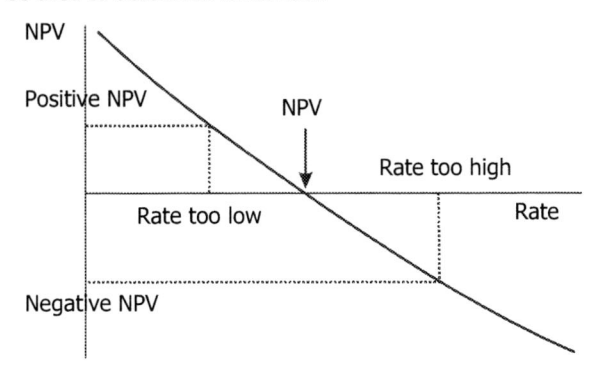

Example

An investment is bought for $88.33. It returns $6 each year for the next five years and is then sold for $100. Calculate the return realised on this investment.

- A   8.7%
- B   9.0%
- C   9.3%
- D   9.5%

Solution

Trying the second highest rate of 9.3%

Time	Cash flow $	Discount factor	Present value $
0	(88.33)	1	(88.33)
1 – 5	6.00	$\dfrac{1}{0.093}\left(1 - \dfrac{1}{1.093^5}\right)$	23.16
5	100.00	$\dfrac{1}{1.093^5}$	64.11
Net present value at t_0			(1.06)

Since this is negative, the rate we have selected is too high, so the correct answer must be either 8.7% or 9.0%.

2: DISCOUNTED CASH FLOWS

Try 9.0%

Time	Cash flow $	Discount factor	Present value $
0	(88.33)	1	(88.33)
1 – 5	6.00	$\dfrac{1}{0.090}\left(1 - \dfrac{1}{1.090^5}\right)$	23.34
5	100.00	$\dfrac{1}{1.090^5}$	64.99
Net present value at t_0			0.00

The NPV is zero, hence the rate of return (the IRR) is 9.0%.

6 SECURITIES EVALUATION AND DCF

6.1 Introduction

The Dividend Valuation Model (DVM) is the basis for all our calculations relating to the market value of any investment.

In order to raise finance, a company must attract investors, ie the investors must believe that they will receive a return sufficient to match their requirements. If they do not believe this, they will not invest.

As a result, the market value of a security at any point in time is determined by two factors.

- The returns (dividends/interest/capital growth) that the investors expect.
- The rate of return that the investors require.

The dividend valuation model states that the:

> Market value = Present value of the future expected receipts discounted at the investor's required rate of return.

That is, we assume investors rationally evaluate the returns in order to determine what they are willing to pay. Though we may be cynical about particular investors, in the UK we can be fairly sure that the majority of dealing is rationally assessed.

Alternatively, the investor's required rate of return can be calculated as the IRR of the current market value and subsequent repayments (dividends, interest, capital, etc).

NB: These comments relate equally to **all** investments.

6.2 Illustration

We will see the application of this idea to various types of securities in the following sections, but the Example below is included for illustration.

Example

A bond pays an annual coupon of $9 and is to be redeemed at $100 in three years. The required return on the bond (prevailing interest rate) is 8%. What will be the market value?

Solution

The market value can be established by calculating the present value of the associated cash flows at the required rate of 8%. The cash flows from the bond will be a $9.00 coupon at the end of each year, and $100 capital redemption at the end of the third year, ie $109 is received in total at that time.

The market value can, therefore, be calculated as:

Time	Cash flow $	Discount factor	Present value $
1	9.00	$\dfrac{1}{1.08^1}$	8.33
2	9.00	$\dfrac{1}{1.08^2}$	7.72
3	109.00	$\dfrac{1}{1.08^3}$	86.53
Market value			$102.58

7 ASSUMPTIONS UNDERLYING THE IRR AND NPV APPROACHES

7.1 Introduction

At this stage, it is worthwhile to consider the assumptions we have implicitly been making in all of the NPV and IRR calculations made to date.

7.1.1 The basic assumptions

- The cash flows expected to accrue from any investment can be considered in isolation, and are independent of decisions relating to any other investment.
- The cash flows are known with certainty.
- No firm or individual has sufficient funds to affect the price of funds.
- Investors have a time preference for money and make rational decisions accordingly.

7.1.2 The assumptions as to reinvestment rates

The fundamental difference between NPV and IRR is the assumption made about reinvestment rates. Under NPV, we are implicitly assuming that any surplus funds generated can be reinvested to earn a return equal to the required rate of return.

However, the IRR calculation assumes that surplus funds will be reinvested to earn a return equal to the IRR, that the time value placed on money is this rate.

Conceptually, NPV is superior because, regardless of the actual investment that is generating the cash flows, we always assume the flows can be reinvested at the same rate. There is no real justification for saying that returns from one investment can be reinvested to earn a return in excess of the returns earned from any other investment, as assumed with the IRR.

7.1.3 Multiple IRRs

If there are multiple sign changes in the series of cash flows, eg (Outflow – Inflow – Outflow – Inflow), there may be multiple IRRs for a single project. This means the IRR decision rule may be impossible to implement. Examples of this type of project would be nuclear power plants where there is usually a large cash outflow at the end of the project to clean up the site.

2: DISCOUNTED CASH FLOWS

EXECUTIVE SUMMARY

- DCF provides a mechanism for evaluating both fund liabilities and the various assets we may hold.
- To calculate a present or terminal value there are three relevant factors.
    - **Cash flow** – value to be multiplied by the relevant compound or discount factor.
    - **Timing** – determines which factor to use, basic, annuity, perpetuity.
    - **Rate** – determines the rate r for that factor.
- Fisher equation:
  $(1 + r) = (1 + i)(1 + R)$
- Simple interest is where interest is received on an original capital sum only. **Compounding** occurs when interest is earned on reinvested interest.
- A **terminal value** or **future value** considers the cash flows of an investment and the timing of the cash flows to calculate the value of a deposit/investment at the end of a period.
- A **present value** calculation considers the cash flows of an investment and the timing of the cash flows and discounts these to calculate a value at the present time. Present value calculations are fundamental to valuation of many financial investments.
- Present value calculations may take the form of single cash flows, annuities and perpetuities.
- Discount factors:
    - Basic

    $$\frac{1}{(1+r)^n}$$

    - Annuity

    $$\frac{1}{r}\left(1 - \frac{1}{(1+r)^n}\right)$$

    - Perpetuity

    $$\frac{1}{r}$$

    - IRR

    Calculated by guessing two rates then interpolating using:

    $$IRR = R_1 + \left(\frac{N_1}{N_1 - N_2} \times (R_2 - R_1)\right)$$

- Net present value calculations may be used as a form of investment appraisal.
- The IRR is the rate of interest that discounts the investment flows to a net present value of zero.

3 Risk and Return

Contents

1 Introduction 54
2 Risk 54
3 Portfolio Theory – The Effect of Diversification 73
4 The Capital Asset Pricing Model 95
5 Arbitrage Pricing Theory 116
   Executive Summary 121

1 Introduction

In a certain world, the return from an investment would always be exactly as expected and there would be no risk. The investor would merely have to compare the returns available on different investments and choose those which offered the highest returns.

Unfortunately, the existence of uncertainty means that the returns from investments are not always as expected – there is some risk involved.

In our analysis so far, we have largely avoided the problem of risk. We have assumed that we know with certainty the future expected cash flows and required rates of return. Clearly, this is unrealistic.

Almost all investment opportunities involve a risk. All securities quoted on the Stock Exchange are subject to risk. Different types of security will have different kinds of risk associated with them, for example UK government securities do not suffer the risk of default, but are vulnerable to changes in interest rates. However, the effect of all these different kinds of risk is the same – the actual returns achieved may differ from those expected by the investor. The riskier the investment, the more likely it is that the hoped-for return will not be reached or the greater the shortfall from the expected return.

One of the fundamental assumptions of investment appraisal is that investors are rational and risk averse, ie they will demand a higher return if they are to face a higher risk, or:

> The return that investors demand will be commensurate with the risk that they face.

But how can we use this idea to rationally appraise any investment alternatives?

If we are to undertake a systematic appraisal of an investment opportunity, we must be able to incorporate all relevant factors. In order to incorporate these factors into our analysis, we must be able to answer the following questions.

- What causes risk?
- How can we measure/quantify risk?
- How can risk be avoided?
- How can we relate risk and return?

2 Risk

2.1 Causes of risk

There are several different factors that give rise to risk, ie lead to variability in return on an investment. Some investments, such as gilts, will have few risks associated with them, whereas company shares will be subject to many possible reasons for fluctuations in return. Factors contributing to risk in investment returns include the following.

- Uncertainty of income
- Interest rates
- Inflation
- Exchange rates
- Tax rates
- Economic state

- Default risk
- Liquidity risk, ie the risk of not being able to sell the investment

That is, we are uncertain about the future economic state of the world, hence we are uncertain about our investment returns.

2.2 Measurement of return and risk

2.2.1 Introduction

Having identified the different types of risk that exist and realised that they are the result of the possibility of different states of the world occurring in the future, how can we quantify the risk and likely return of any investment?

There are two possible approaches here depending on the information that is available to us, ie:

- Use economic forecasts and probabilities to describe the likelihood of each possible state of the world occurring and estimate the returns and values arising given that state of the world.

- Use historically observed returns and associated frequencies on the assumption that this past data will be representative of the future.

2.2.2 Based on economic forecasts and probabilities

Return measure

Arithmetic mean

The most commonly used measure of return is the arithmetic mean, the calculation of which reflects the values and probabilities of the various possible returns. The arithmetic mean may be described mathematically as either:

$$\bar{r} = \sum pr$$

where we have probabilities p of each return r occurring; or

$$\bar{r} = \frac{\sum fr}{n}$$

where f is the frequency of occurrence of each return r and we have n items in total.

Example

The shareholders in an ungeared company have a required rate of return of 10% pa It can invest $100 in a one-year project from which the terminal values are expected to fall within the following range of possibilities (with associated probabilities derived from inspecting past frequencies – **objective probabilities**).

3: RISK AND RETURN

Probability	Return $
0.25	100
0.45	110
0.30	120

Should the investment be undertaken?

Solution

We should first calculate the percentage returns realised in each state of the world and hence, the expected rate of return as:

Probability	×	Return (%)	=	Expected (%)
0.25	×	0	=	0.0
0.45	×	10	=	4.5
0.30	×	20	=	6.0
Expected return (r)			=	10.5

On the basis that the expected return is 10.5% and the required rate of return of the shareholders is 10%, we may be tempted to believe that we should accept the project. The problem is that while returns considerably in excess of 10% could occur, so could returns considerably below 10%, which may not be acceptable.

This variability is the risk that we face and in deciding on any investment, we have to cope with the fact that there is a range of possible outcomes.

In determining their required return of 10% for the company, the shareholders will have taken account of the risk that they expect to face from its current operations, ie the variability of the current returns. However, that is unlikely to be identical to the risk from this project, hence the 10% required return may not be appropriate. If the project is riskier, the investors would require a higher return as we noted above.

Thus, we need to quantify the level of risk involved.

Geometric mean

The arithmetic mean is the most appropriate measure when, as above, we are assessing the expected return in any one year. However, it is less appropriate when we are assessing the average annual return from an accumulated total over several years. For example, if we had experienced a 12% return over a three-year period, would it be appropriate to say that the mean return is 4% pa (the arithmetic mean 12% ÷ 3)? This is clearly not appropriate as it ignores the compounding of those earlier returns. A more appropriate measure here would be the geometric mean which would reflect the compounding. The geometric mean, like DCF, deals with compounding situations and the formula and ideas are very closely related to DCF.

3: RISK AND RETURN

Sticking with the example to establish the geometric mean.

- If $1 had been invested across the three years it would now be worth $1.12.
- If $1 had been invested at the average (geometric mean) rate for those same three years, using terminal value ideas it would be worth:

$1 × (1 + r)^3, where r is the average (geometric mean) rate.

We must, therefore, have:

$(1 + r)^3$ = 1.12

$1 + r$ = $\sqrt[3]{1.12}$ = 1.0385

r = 0.0385 or 3.85%

More generally we can say:

$(1 + r)^n = 1 + R$

where:

r = geometric mean for year
R = return for longer period
n = number of years in this longer period

In turn, to get to R we may need to compound together the effects of a number of earlier years. For example, if the returns over the last four years had been 4%, 6%, 4% and 3% respectively, then the cumulative return over the four-year period would be:

$(1 + R) = (1 + r_1)(1 + r_2)(1 + r_3)(1 + r_4)$

or:

$(1 + R) = 1.04 \times 1.06 \times 1.04 \times 1.03 = 1.1809$

so:

R = 0.1809 or 18.09% for the four years.

and if we wanted the geometric mean we would have:

$(1 + r)^4 = 1 + R = 1.1809$

$(1 + r) = \sqrt[4]{1.1809} = 1.0424$

r = 0.0424 or 4.24%

Putting these ideas together and trying to generalise them we have:

$(1 + r) = \sqrt[n]{(1+R)}$

and:

$(1 + R) = (1 + r_1)(1 + r_2)...(1 + r_n)$

so the geometric mean is:

$(1 + r) = \sqrt[n]{(1+r_1)(1+r_2)...(1+r_n)}$

ie the nth root of the compound returns over those n years.

Comments

We need to be very careful in the application of the arithmetic mean and the geometric mean.

The arithmetic mean is appropriate if we are looking to determine the average return for a single period based on either what we have seen in the past or expect to see in the future. For example if in the last three years we have experienced returns of 3%, 4%, 5%, then the average is 4%.

If we wish to work out (or are given) the accumulated return over several periods, however, we should use the compounding geometric approach.

- The arithmetic mean is most appropriate for assessing possible returns in any one year/periods or when looking to forecast future periodic returns from historical periodic returns.

- The geometric mean is most appropriate for assessing compounded returns over several consecutive years/periods.

- The geometric mean will always be less than (or in rare cases, equal to) the arithmetic mean, since it takes account of compounding.

Risk measure

To measure the degree of variability of an investment i, we can use either:

- The standard deviation (usually designated by σ_i); or
- The variance (usually designated by σ_i^2),

where each possible return r_i occurs with probability p and the expected (arithmetic mean) return is denoted by $\bar{r}_i$.

These two risk measures are related. The variance is the expected value of the squares of the deviations about the expected return $\bar{r}_i$. The standard deviation is the square root of the variance. As a result, each summarises as a single figure the variability of the return (either up or down) about the expected value.

The standard deviation has the benefit that it is expressed in the same units as the returns (% in the example above), whereas the variance is in the original units squared [%^{2} or per 10,000 rather than per 100%]. The standard deviation can be thought of as the average deviation from the expected value. The standard deviation for this could be mathematically described as:

$$\sigma = \sqrt{\sum p(r - \bar{r})^2}$$

Other single measures could be calculated, for instance by only looking at variances below the expected value, but none is as widely used as either the variance or standard deviation.

Though this formula looks a little daunting, the measure can be quite easily be calculated using a standard tabular approach as illustrated below.

Example

For the above example, determine the expected return and risk.

Solution

Probability (p)	Return (r_i) (%)	Expected value (%)	$r_i - \bar{r}_i$	$(r_i - \bar{r}_i)^2$	$p(r_i - \bar{r}_i)^2$
0.25	0	0.0	−10.5	110.25	27.5625
0.45	10	4.5	−0.5	0.25	0.1125
0.30	20	6.0	9.5	90.25	27.0750
Expected return ($\bar{r}_i$) =		10.5	variance (σ_i^2) =		54.7500

Variance of returns (σ_i^2) about $\bar{r}_i$ = 54.75

Standard deviation of returns $\sigma_i = \sqrt{54.75}$ = 7.399%

Interpretation of the result

Being able to calculate the expected return and associated risk is one thing, interpreting and using those results is another. How can we compare the project's expected returns and risk with the investors' required rate of return?

From the above example, we have:

- Expected net return $\bar{r}_i$ = 10.5%.
- Associated risk σ_i = 7.399%.
- Company's required rate of return is 10%.

It is clear that the expected return does exceed that currently required by the company's shareholders, but how can we take account of the level of risk? What happens if the project increases their risk? Is the extra return sufficient compensation? How can we relate risk and return?

In order to answer these questions, we need to look at the idea of risk-return **indifference curves**, which we consider below.

2.2.3 Based on historically observed data

Return measure

When calculating the average periodic return based on historically observed data, the approach (as above) is to calculate the mean return historically observed over the period selected.

NB: Here, we are using past data in the hope that it will be representative of the future. If there have been no fundamental economic changes or changes in the security we are investigating (eg the nature of business a company conducts if

3: RISK AND RETURN

we are appraising its shares), then this approach may not be unreasonable. If either of these factors has changed, the results of this analysis will be of historical interest only and of little use for the future.

What we need to consider, therefore, is recent past data in relation to the returns of the security concerned over a period where the factors influencing the economy and the security have been stable, and the following analysis assumes that this is the case.

Example

The following quarterly returns have been observed for two securities over the last two years.

Year	Quarter	Security A (%)	Security B (%)
1	1	16	14
	2	18	15
	3	12	12
	4	15	14
2	1	14	13
	2	15	15
	3	17	17
	4	13	12

Calculate the average return for each quarter.

Solution

Year	Quarter	Security A (%)	Security B (%)
1	1	16	14
	2	18	15
	3	12	12
	4	15	14
2	1	14	13
	2	15	15
	3	17	17
	4	13	12
		120	112

From which, we can calculate the means returns as:

- **Security A** – return, $\bar{r}$ = $\frac{120}{8}$ = 15%

- **Security B** – return, $\bar{r}$ = $\frac{112}{8}$ = 14%

Risk measure

Once again, the risk measure that we will apply is the standard deviation, this time based on the observed frequencies. There are two possibilities here.

Population standard deviation

The population standard deviation can be calculated as:

$$\sigma = \sqrt{\frac{\sum f(r - \bar{r})^2}{n}}$$

where f is the frequency of occurrence of each observed value.

This calculation is appropriate where the values and frequencies observed represent the full range of all possibilities, ie we have observed the entire population. It is useful, for example, in calculating the probabilities of particular hands in card games (where the population of a pack of cards is well known), but not in our situation here, since we are only examining a part of the past data and have no idea about what may be experienced in the future.

Sample standard deviation

The sample standard deviation can be calculated as:

$$\sigma = \sqrt{\frac{\sum f(r - \bar{r})^2}{n - 1}}$$

This calculation is appropriate where the values and frequencies observed represent just a sample of the full range of possibilities, ie we have observed just a subset of the entire population. It is therefore the appropriate basis for the calculations here.

Example

Calculate the risk of the two earlier securities A and B.

3: RISK AND RETURN

Solution

Security A ($\bar{r}_a = 15\%$)

Year	Quarter	r_a	$r_a - \bar{r}_a$	$(r_a - \bar{r}_a)^2$
1	1	16	+1	1
	2	18	+3	9
	3	12	−3	9
	4	15	0	0
2	1	14	−1	1
	2	15	0	0
	3	17	+2	4
	4	13	−2	4
		120		28

$$\sigma_a = \sqrt{\frac{28}{8-1}} = \sqrt{4} = 2\%$$

Security B ($\bar{r}_b = 14\%$)

Year	Quarter	r_b	$r_b - \bar{r}_b$	$(r_b - \bar{r}_b)^2$
1	1	14	0	0
	2	15	+1	1
	3	12	−2	4
	4	14	0	0
2	1	13	−1	1
	2	15	+1	1
	3	17	+3	9
	4	12	−2	4
				20

$$\sigma_a = \sqrt{\frac{20}{8-1}} = \sqrt{2.857} = 1.690\%$$

Interpretation of the results

When we compare the returns and risks of the two securities, we have:

	Security A %	Security B %
Return	15.00	14.00
Risk	2.00	1.69

Clearly, Security A offers a higher return, but at a higher risk. How can we determine which is the superior alternative? The answer, once again, is to look at the idea of risk-return **indifference curves** examined below.

2.2.4 Limitations of the standard deviation measure

The standard deviation is the primary risk measure used in almost all of the finance theories that we will be considering, however the use of this measure is not without limitations. The limitations of standard deviation inherently become limitations of the models it is used in, specifically:

- Portfolio theory (combining returns and risks)
- CAPM and APT (comparing systematic risks)
- The basic Black-Scholes model
- Value at Risk

All of which rely on the idea of returns following the pattern of a normal distribution, a symmetrical statistical distribution defined by a mean (the return) and a standard deviation (the risk). If security returns are not normally distributed, then the results that we may derive from these theories will not be completely valid.

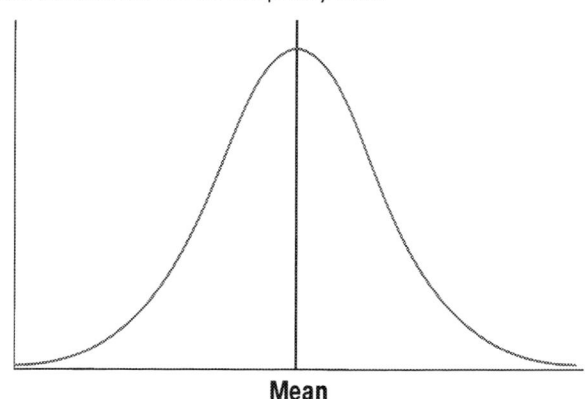

Mean

One of the assumptions of a normal distribution is that the probability of a gain will be equal to that of an equivalent loss, the distribution being symmetrical. If the distribution is not symmetrical (is skewed) then upside and downside risk will be misstated. As a result, the probability of experiencing gains or losses of a certain scale will be misstated.

Another assumption is that the possible returns follow a bell-shaped distribution where more central values are most likely to be observed and the more extreme the movement the less likely it is to occur – the distribution is said to be mesokurtic or mesokurtotic.

Observations show that this may not be the case in extreme times and that the true distribution of security returns may be leptokurtotic (have fat tails). The practical implication of this is that extreme price movements may be significantly more likely to arise than would be suggested by a normal distribution. Another possibility would be that the return distribution is much flatter than the normal distribution bell-shape – the distribution could be platykurtic or platykurtotic.

A further assumption underlying a normal distribution is that it has a single standard deviation across the entire range of possible values and through time – it is homoskedastic. It may be that the security's risk varies, that the distribution is heteroskedastic and that any conclusions that are drawn on the assumption of homoskedasticity will be invalid.

One final assumption underlying a normal distribution is that the standard deviation takes just one value, ie risk is constant (the distribution is homoskedastic).

2.2.5 Semi-deviation and semi-variance

One further criticism of the standard deviation is that it does not differentiate between what people may consider to be positive variations and what they may consider negative. The standard deviation and variance assess the average deviation from the mean, considering variations both above and below the mean. Arguably, applying the standard deviation as the chosen risk metric inherently assumes that investors have symmetrical views about risk – equally concerned by upswings as by downswings.

Arguably, however, for most investors an above average return would be welcomed and they are only concerned by the prospects of a below average return which is where the semi-deviation and semi-variance come in. These are calculated in the same way as a standard deviation and variance, except that only the observations that fall below the mean return and the extent to which they fall below this mean return are included, ie this ratio uses the standard deviation of the below-average returns and is sometimes referred to as downside standard deviation. For a skewed distribution, the semi-deviation offers some additional information that the standard deviation does not.

Example

Using the earlier economic forecast example in which a security offered the following returns:

Probability	Return
0.25	0%
0.45	10%
0.30	20%

We assessed this security as offering an expected return of 10.5% at a standard deviation of 7.399%. We now wish to calculate its semi-deviation.

Solution

The approach is as above but only considering the returns falling below 10.5%, giving:

Probability (p)	Return (ri) (%)	$r_i - \bar{r}_i^-$	$(r_i - \bar{r}_i^-)^2$	$p(r_i - \bar{r}_i^-)^2$
0.25	0	−10.5	110.25	27.5625
0.45	10	−0.5	0.25	0.1125
			Semi-variance =	27.6750

Semi-deviation = $\sqrt{27.6750}$ = 5.26%

Note: this 5.26% semi-deviation should not be compared in any way to the 7.399% standard deviation. When comparing risks it is essential to compare like-for-like, ie compare one standard deviation to another, or compare one semi-deviation to another. Consistency is all important here.

2.2.6 Covariance

Before moving on, however, there is one further statistic that will prove useful to us, and that is the covariance. The covariance gives a measure of how the returns of two securities vary in relation to one another. We may need to apply the calculation when using either of the above methods.

Economic forecasts and probabilities

On this basis, the formulation for two securities a and b would be:

$$\text{Cov}_{ab} = \sum p(r_a - \bar{r}_a)(r_b - \bar{r}_b)$$

Historically observed data and frequencies

Using historical data, the formulation for two securities a and b would be as follows.

Population calculation

$$\text{Cov}_{ab} = \frac{\sum f(r_a - \bar{r}_a)(r_b - \bar{r}_b)}{n}$$

Sample calculation

$$\text{Cov}_{ab} = \frac{\sum f(r_a - \bar{r}_a)(r_b - \bar{r}_b)}{n - 1}$$

The difference between these two formulations is the denominator (n or n − 1), and the relevance/applicability is as expressed above. Once more, the second formulation is slightly more convenient manually.

3: RISK AND RETURN

Example

Based on the two-year data example above, calculate the covariance of the returns of A and B.

Solution

The sample formulation is the appropriate measure here, hence:

Year	Quarter	$(r_a - \bar{r}_a)$	$(r_b - \bar{r}_b)$	$(r_a - \bar{r}_a)(r_b - \bar{r}_b)$
1	1	+1	0	0
	2	+3	+1	3
	3	−3	−2	6
	4	0	0	0
2	1	−1	−1	1
	2	0	+1	0
	3	+2	+3	6
	4	−2	−2	4
				20

Giving:

$$\text{Cov}_{ab} = \frac{20}{8-1} = 2.8571$$

Interpretation

An appreciation of this measure can be gained by looking at one of the formulations, eg the probability formulation.

$$\text{Cov}_{ab} = \sum p (r_a - \bar{r}_a)(r_b - \bar{r}_b)$$

If a and b tend to move together, then they will both be:

- Above average at the same time, making $(r_a - \bar{r}_a)$ and $(r_b - \bar{r}_b)$ both positive, hence their product will be positive and indicative of the scale of the deviations.

- Below average at the same time, making $(r_a - \bar{r}_a)$ and $(r_b - \bar{r}_b)$ both negative, hence their product will again be positive and indicative of the scale of the deviations.

A positive covariance value therefore indicates:

- That the returns tend to move together.
- The scale of the deviations involved.

On the other hand, if a and b tend to move in opposition, then:

- When a is above its average, b will be below, making $(r_a - \bar{r}_a)$ positive and $(r_b - \bar{r}_b)$ negative, hence their product will be negative and indicative of the scale of the deviations.

- When a is below its average, b will be above, making $(r_a - \bar{r}_a)$ negative and $(r_b - \bar{r}_b)$ positive, hence their product will be negative and indicative of the scale of the deviations.

A negative covariance value therefore indicates:

- That the returns tend to move in opposition.
- The scale of the deviations involved.

The usefulness of this measure will be seen later on in this section.

Correlation

The covariance demonstrates both:

- How securities move in relation to each other (positive or negative).
- The scale of the co-movements.

Sometimes it may be preferable to have an indication of the degree of any co-movements alone, ie in the absence of any scale measure. This can be done using the correlation coefficient.

The correlation coefficient achieves this by dividing the covariance by the scale of the observed volatilities, thus removing this scale factor and simply leaving a measure of the degree of any co-movements:

$$Cor_{ab} = \frac{Cov_{ab}}{\sigma_a \sigma_b}$$

Which can alternatively be written as:

$$Cov_{ab} = \sigma_a \sigma_b Cor_{ab}$$

A correlation coefficient will have any value between +1 and −1. The meaning of the correlation coefficient can best be understood by considering the extremes.

Perfect positive correlation – (correlation coefficient = +1)

If the returns from two securities are perfectly positively correlated, then they move up and down together in proportion.

Perfect negative correlation – (correlation coefficient = −1)

If the returns from two securities are perfectly negatively correlated, then they move up and down in exact opposition and in proportion.

Uncorrelated – (correlation coefficient = 0)

If the returns from two securities are uncorrelated, then they move independently of each other, ie if one goes up, the other may go up or down or not move at all.

Conclusion

The sign of the correlation coefficient tells us the relative direction of movement. A positive correlation implies that returns move up and down together, negative correlation means that they move in opposition. The value of the figure, ignoring the sign, gives an indication of the strength of the relationship. The closer to a value of 1, the stronger the relationship.

2.3 Decision-making with risk

2.3.1 Introduction

Consider an investor comparing a number of possible investment opportunities. For each investment, the expected return and risk (standard deviation) can be measured, then we can select the one that offers the best combination of risk and return for that investor – the best **risk-return profile**. This, however, may be easier said than done.

Example

Consider an investor who has the following choices of mutually exclusive investments, which offer the following returns from an investment of $100.

Security	Return ($\bar{r}$) $	%	Risk (σ) $	%
A	110	10	6	6
B	111	11	5	5
C	119	19	11	11
D	120	20	10	10

Assuming that our investor is rational and risk averse, which project will he choose?

Solution

We can represent the options we have on the following diagram.

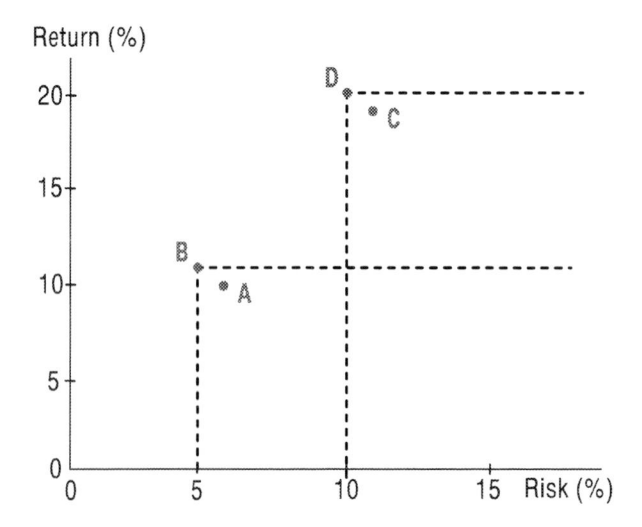

3: RISK AND RETURN

Comparing investments in turn

- **A and B**

    Comparing A and B, it is clear that B is preferable. It has a higher return for a lower level of risk. In fact, B dominates all investments in the rectangle shown (with B in the top left-hand corner).

- **C and D**

    Similarly, D will dominate C and any others in its rectangle.

- **B and D**

    But which of B and D is preferable? While D offers the higher return, it does so at a higher risk than B. Which combination of return and risk is preferable to the investor?

    We cannot answer this question without further information about this particular investor's reaction to risk.

2.3.2 Indifference curves

An indifference curve shows combinations of return and risk that are perceived as equivalent by an individual. The investor is indifferent between any investment opportunities lying on the same indifference curve. As such, they may be useful in choosing between different investments offering both differing risks and returns. They may not be necessary to make a decision in certain circumstances, but they are in others.

For example, if our rational and risk averse investor was able to obtain either a risk-free return of $100 or an investment with a risk (σ_i) of $5, we would expect him to require a somewhat higher expected return from the risky investment if it were to be as attractive as the one with zero risk. He may, for instance, require an expected return of $107 to be indifferent.

Continuing this idea, considering more investments with higher level of risk, we would expect our investor to require still higher returns to make them as attractive as the initial risk-free $100 investment and we would perhaps end up with the following results.

Return $	Risk $
100	0
107	5
121	10
142	15
170	20
205	25

3: RISK AND RETURN

Our particular investor is indifferent between each of these investments and would, in each case, regard the extra return as exactly compensating for the additional risk.

Having ascertained our investor's attitude to risk, we could plot this on a graph, as follows.

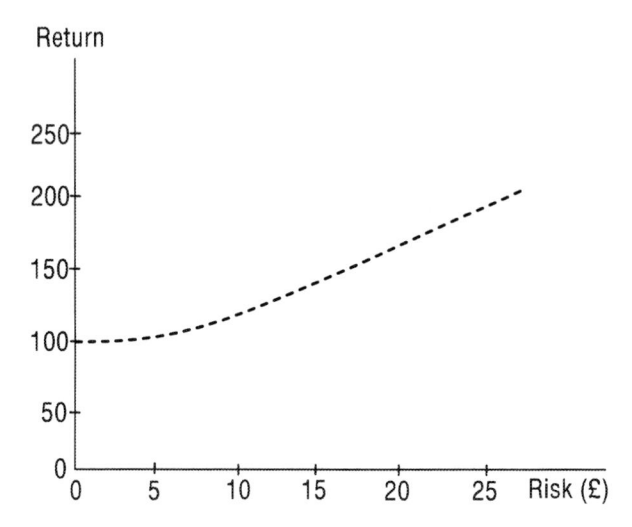

This curve is known as an **indifference curve**, in that our investor would be indifferent between all investments on the curve and a risk-free return of $100.

Note that this curve is upward sloping due to the economic idea of diminishing marginal utility. In basic terms, the law of diminishing marginal utility suggests that the more of a given positive factor you acquire, the less you are prepared to pay for additional units. For example, while one slice of pizza may be very nice and a second one also very pleasant, would you still want more after nine or ten slices? Would a tenth slice provide as much satisfaction as the first? If the satisfaction or benefit derived from extra units is lower, the cost you are prepared to face for those extra units is also lower.

Applying this idea to risk and return, return is the benefit we get and risk is the cost faced. As the benefit (return) rises, the cost we are prepared to pay for each additional unit (the additional risk we are prepared to take on for an extra 1% return) falls leading to the increasing gradient.

Clearly, there are plenty of other investment opportunities that do not fall on this line. We have only considered those that would be thought of as equal to a risk-free $100. To get a complete picture of the investor's attitude to risk and return, we would need to establish the curves equivalent to all the various possible risk-free levels, giving us something like this.

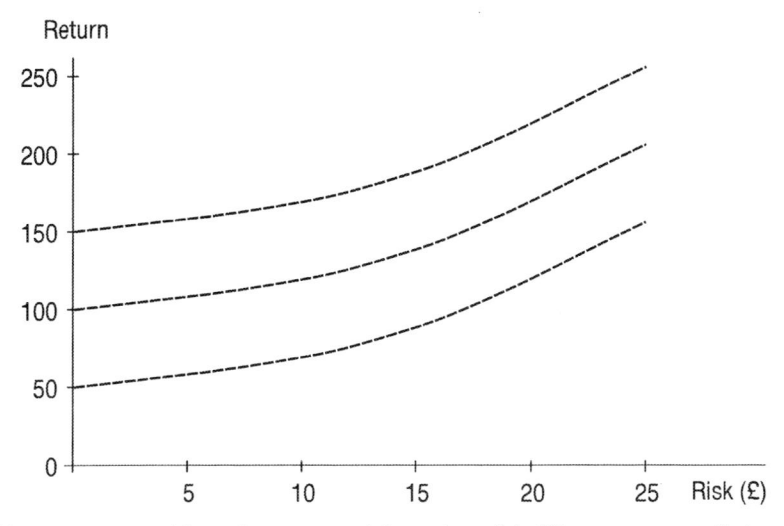

3: RISK AND RETURN

[Graph showing Return vs Risk (£) with three upward-sloping indifference curves, Return axis 0 to 250, Risk axis 0 to 25]

In this way, we would produce a complete series of indifference curves that would, between them, show our investor's overall attitude to risk.

2.3.3 Characteristics of indifference curves

The general characteristics of indifference curves are as follows.

- They are upward-sloping curves indicating greater aversion to risk (a greater risk results in a greater required return).

- The more steeply they curve upwards, the more risk averse the investor (indifference curves are individual).

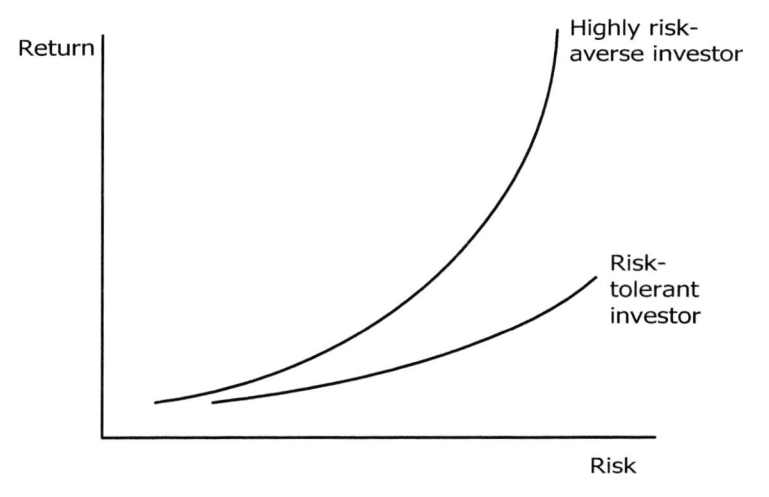

[Graph showing Return vs Risk with two curves: a steeply rising curve labelled "Highly risk-averse investor" and a more gradual curve labelled "Risk-tolerant investor"]

- All investments on one particular curve are viewed by the particular investor as equivalent to a risk-free investment, giving the return shown on the vertical axis where the curve meets it.

3: RISK AND RETURN

- Comparing the risk-free equivalent for investments on each curve shows that the higher the curve, the more attractive it is to the investor.

NB: These indifference curves only represent the attitude of one particular investor and each investor will have a differing attitude and hence, a different family of indifference curves. The more risk averse an investor is, the steeper his indifference curves.

2.3.4 Decision-making

Example

Having established the indifference curves for our investor, can they be used to help us decide between our two investments B and D in the example above **for him**?

Solution

We had shortlisted two alternatives with the following returns and risks.

Investment	Return $	Risk $
B	111	5
D	120	10

Plotting these on our graph of indifference curves gives:

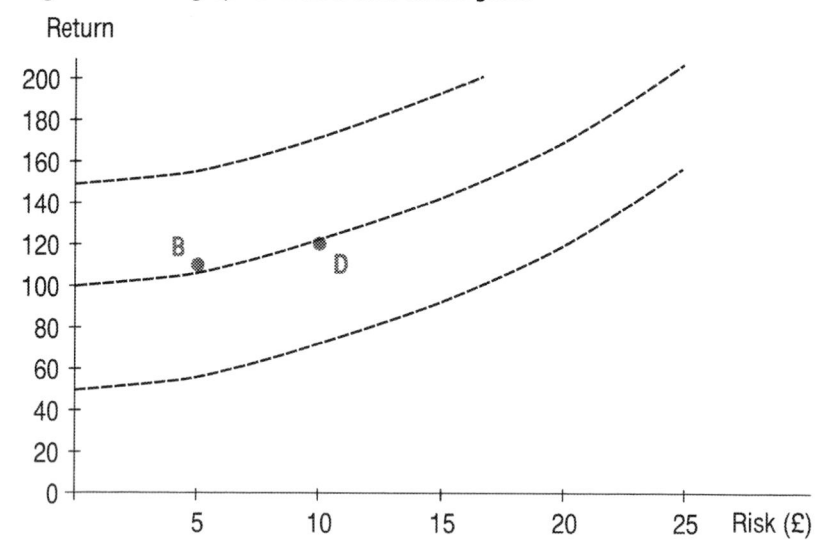

[Graph showing Return (y-axis, 0-200) vs Risk £ (x-axis, 0-25) with three upward-curving dashed indifference curves. Point B plotted near (5, 111) just above the middle curve; Point D plotted near (10, 120) just below the middle curve.]

We can see from this that Investment B lies just above the indifference curve equivalent to a $100 return with zero risk, whereas Investment D lies just below it. We may, therefore, conclude that **our investor** would prefer Investment B. For him, the additional return offered by Investment D does not make up for the additional risk.

NB: This decision would be reversed by a less risk averse investor with flatter indifference curves – indifference curves are individual.

2.3.5 Conclusion

In more general terms, we have seen that the higher the indifference curve on which a particular investment lies, the more attractive the investment is to our investor.

3 PORTFOLIO THEORY – THE EFFECT OF DIVERSIFICATION

3.1 Diversification

There is an old adage that says "do not put all your eggs in one basket". This means that by spreading the risk of holding something, we can minimise our potential losses without necessarily reducing the value of our holding.

Though a simple and reasonably obvious idea in the context of the farmyard, it is equally applicable in the context of investment management. By spreading the total investment fund over several securities that offer the desired level of return, we get the same return that any one of them can offer but face a much lower risk since, though one may become worthless, it is unlikely that they will all do so simultaneously. Hence, there is a chance of losing all our money if it is all invested in just one share, but this possibility is vastly reduced when we hold a number of shares. Obviously, the more shares we hold, the more the risk is reduced.

Therefore, diversification reduces risk without necessarily reducing returns.

Here we have considered only default risk, the risk of losing all our money. The same principle applies, however, to other forms of risk such as fluctuations in earnings.

If we invest all our cash in one share, then our income will vary as the company profits, hence returns from that share, vary. However, it is unlikely that returns from all shares will move in exactly the same way. Therefore, if we invest in a range of shares, it is likely that as the returns from some are falling, the returns from others are stable or rising. The result will be that we will realise a steadier overall return when we hold a spread of securities, with the losses on one being cancelled by profits on another.

3.2 Portfolio theory principle

The basic premise of portfolio theory is that risks and returns in isolation are irrelevant. What we must consider is the combined effect, which may result in the elimination or diversification away of some risk. We demonstrate this with a rather simple example, however, it does illustrate the point.

3: RISK AND RETURN

Example

An investor is considering either of two additional investments, A or B. The returns from his existing investments and from A and B are dependent on the prevailing economic climate. They are expected to be:

Economic condition	Probability	Current investments %	A %	B %
I	0.30	0	5	20
II	0.40	10	10	10
III	0.30	20	15	0

He is considering halving his investment in the current portfolio and investing the cash freed up in one of the alternatives. Which investment should be accepted (if any)?

Solution

From this data, we can calculate the following.

Current portfolio of investments

Probability (p)	Return (r_i) (%)	Expected value (pr_i) (%)	$r_i - \bar{r}_i$	$(r_i - \bar{r}_i)^2$	$p(r_i - \bar{r}_i)^2$
0.30	0	0.0	(10.0)	100.0	30.0
0.40	10	4.0	0.0	0.0	0.0
0.30	20	6.0	10.0	100.0	30.0
Expected return ($\bar{r}_i$) =		10.0	Variance (σ_i^2) =		60.0

Hence:

- Expected return $\bar{r}_i$ = 10.0% pa
- Risk $\left(\sqrt{Variance_i}\right) = \sqrt{60} = 7.746\%$

Investment A

Probability (p)	Return (r_a) (%)	Expected value (pr_a) (%)	$r_a - \bar{r}_a$	$(r_a - \bar{r}_a)^2$	$p(r_a - \bar{r}_a)^2$
0.30	5	1.5	(5.0)	25.0	7.5
0.40	10	4.0	0.0	0.0	0.0
0.30	15	4.5	5.0	25.0	7.5
Expected return ($\bar{r}_a$) =		10.0	Variance$_a$ (σ_a^2) =		15.0

Hence:

- Expected return $\bar{r}_a$ = 10.0% pa
- Risk $\left(\sqrt{\text{Variance}_a}\right) = \sqrt{15} = 3.873\%$

Investment B

Probability (p)	Return (r_b) (%)	Expected value (pr_b) (%)	$r_b - \bar{r}_b$	$(r_b - \bar{r}_b)^2$	$p(r_b - \bar{r}_b)^2$
0.30	20	6.0	10.0	100.0	30.0
0.40	10	4.0	0.0	0.0	0.0
0.30	0	0.0	(10.0)	100.0	30.0
Expected return $(\bar{r}_b)$ =		10.0	Variance$_b$ (σ_b^2) =		60.0

- Expected return $\bar{r}_b$ = 10.0% pa
- Risk $\left(\sqrt{\text{Variance}_b}\right) = \sqrt{60} = 7.746\%$

Summarising

	Current investments %	A %	B %
Expected return $\bar{r}$	10.000	10.000	10.000
Risk σ	7.746	3.873	7.746

At first sight the answer may appear obvious, since Investment A offers the same return as both the current portfolio and Investment B, but at a much lower risk. However, the important point to the investor is how this investment fits with his other investments. After all, he will be combining the chosen investment with his current portfolio, and it is the effects of each investment on his overall portfolio risk-return profile that we must consider.

As you will see, it is not only the individual returns and risks we must consider, but how they vary in relation to each other. To appreciate this, we must first calculate the expected returns and risks of combinations of investments.

This can be tackled in two ways:

- By tabulating each possible combined return and calculating the expected return and risk of these combined returns as before.
- By using formulae that give the expected return and risk of a combination, given information about the individual investments and how they correlate.

3.3 Tabulation

3.3.1 When used

We would use a tabulation approach when we have information regarding various possible returns and associated probabilities, as above.

Example

Using the above example data, calculate the potential alternative 50:50 portfolio risk-return profiles.

Solution

Current investment + A

If we calculate the various returns that would result if Investment A was added to the portfolio, we get:

Economic condition	p	Current return (r_i) (%)	A (r_a) (%)	50:50 return (r_{i+a}) (%)	Expected value (pr_{i+a}) (%)^2
I	0.30	0	5	2.5	0.75
II	0.40	10	10	10.0	4.00
III	0.30	20	15	17.5	5.25
					10.00

And if we go on to calculate the risk, we find:

Probability (p)	Return (r_{i+a}) (%)	Expected value (%)	$r_{i+a} - \bar{r}_{i+a}$	$(r_{i+a} - \bar{r}_{i+a})^2$	$p(r_{i+a} - \bar{r}_{i+a})$
0.30	2.5	0.75	(7.5)	56.25	16.875
0.40	10.0	4.00	0.0	0.00	0.000
0.30	17.5	5.25	7.5	56.25	16.875
	Expected return $(\bar{r}_{i+a})$ =	10.00	Variance (σ_{i+a2}) =		33.750

What we can see from this is that by combining the current portfolio with an equal amount of Investment A, we can reduce our risk to 5.81% $(\sqrt{33.75})$ while still maintaining a 10% return. Hence, accepting Investment A would be beneficial.

Current investment + B

If we now calculate the various returns that would result if Investment B was added (50:50) to the portfolio, we get:

3: RISK AND RETURN

Economic condition	p	Current return (r_i)(%)	B (r_b)(%)	50:50 (r_{i+b})(%)	Expected value (pr_{i+b})(%)
I	0.30	0	20	10	3
II	0.40	10	10	10	4
III	0.30	20	0	10	$\dfrac{3}{10}$

And if we go on to calculate the risk, we find:

Probability (p)	Return (r_{i+a}) (%)	Expected value (%)	$r_{i+b} - \bar{r}_{i+1}$	$(r_{i+b} - \bar{r}_{i+b})^2$	$p(r_{i+b} - \bar{r}_{i+b})$
0.30	10.0	3	0	0	0
0.40	10.0	4	0	0	0
0.30	10.0	$\dfrac{3}{10}$	0	0	$\dfrac{0}{0}$

Expected return $(\bar{r}_{i+b}) =$ Variance $(\sigma_{i+b\,2}) =$

What we can see from this is that by combining the current portfolio with an equal amount of Investment B, we can eliminate risk! Our return is 10% regardless of the state of the economy, it does not vary, hence it is risk-free as is demonstrated by the calculation of the standard deviation.

Our investor now has three options, which we can summarise as follows.

Portfolio	Return %	Risk %
Existing portfolio	10	7.746
Existing + A	10	5.81
Existing + B	10	0

It is clear that the best course of action is to invest in B, since in this way, he can reduce the degree of risk suffered considerably. This is despite the fact that Investment B has more risk than Investment A, in isolation.

3.3.2 Conclusion

When considering risk, it is not the risk of the investment in isolation, but the effect of the investment on the overall level of risk that is important. This illustrates the portfolio effect, ie that diversifying investments may potentially reduce the level of risk suffered without necessarily reducing the level of return.

3.3.3 Importance of correlation

What this shows is that the effectiveness of this cancellation will depend on the degree of correlation between the movements of the returns. As noted above, correlation is a measure of how two variable factors move in relation to each other and will have any value between +1 and –1.

Perfect positive correlation – (correlation coefficient = +1)

If the returns from two securities are perfectly positively correlated, then they move up and down together in proportion. The consequence of this is that if they were combined in a portfolio, we would not get the cancelling effect that we were looking for.

Perfect negative correlation – (correlation coefficient = –1)

If the returns from two securities are perfectly negatively correlated, then they move up and down in exact opposition and in proportion. As a result, if we were to combine two such securities in a portfolio, we could achieve an exact offset of profits from one against losses from the other.

Uncorrelated – (correlation coefficient = 0)

If the returns from two securities are uncorrelated, then they move independently of each other, ie if one goes up, the other may go up or down or not move at all. As a result, if we were to combine two such securities in a portfolio, we would expect to see a cancellation of profits and losses on some occasions but not on others. However, this is still a better position than investing in just one share, where there is no cancellation of gains and losses at all.

Limitations of correlation coefficient

Correlation coefficients may not always be a reliable measure when outliers are present. These are small numbers of observations at the extremes of a sample of data. The analyst must decide whether it is better to include or exclude outliers on a case-by-case basis.

Furthermore, a correlation between two variables may reflect a chance relationship in a particular set of data, or may arise because the two variables are themselves correlated to a third variable. For example, bee stings may be positively correlated to ice cream consumption, but the underlying relationships are between sunshine and bee stings, and sunshine and ice cream consumption.

Finally, correlation coefficients are susceptible to change in times of market turbulence. A portfolio may be thought of as risk averse with a basket of uncorrelated equities, only to find the correlation between the securities becomes increasingly positive in times of market turmoil, removing many of the diversification benefits which previously existed.

Conclusion

The sign of the correlation coefficient tells us the relative direction of movement. A positive correlation implies that returns move up and down together, negative correlation means that they move in opposition. The value of the figure, ignoring the sign, gives an indication of the strength of the relationship. The closer to a value of 1, the stronger the relationship.

The effectiveness of the diversification will depend on the degree of correlation between the returns on the securities. In practice, we are unlikely to encounter perfect positive or perfect negative correlation (though we may get close with certain derivative instruments). Most shares show a small degree of correlation in practice and hence we see some benefit from diversification.

3.4 Formulae

3.4.1 Introduction

The alternative to tabulating all of the possible combined returns and associated probabilities is to apply the portfolio theory formulae below. This will be the most convenient approach if we are aware of the correlation coefficient of the returns. If this is not available and needs to be calculated through tabulation, then the above approach would be more efficient.

3.4.2 Basic formulae

Two formulae permit us to combine returns and risks more conveniently when we have the correlation coefficient. If a portfolio is made up of two investments as follows:

	A	B
Expected return	r_a	r_b
Risk	σ_a	σ_b
Proportion of funds invested	p_a	p_b
Correlation coefficient	Cor_{ab}	

Then, the portfolio will have a combined return and risk of

3.4.3 Return of portfolio

$$r_{a+b} = p_a r_a + p_b r_b$$

3.4.4 Risk of portfolio

$$\sigma_{a+b}^2 = p_a^2 \sigma_a^2 + p_b^2 \sigma_b^2 + 2 p_a p_b \sigma_a \sigma_b Cor_{ab}$$

or, since $Cov_{ab} = \sigma_a \sigma_b Cor_{ab}$

$$\sigma_{a+b}^2 = p_a^2 \sigma_a^2 + p_b^2 \sigma_b^2 + 2 p_a p_b Cov_{ab}$$

3: RISK AND RETURN

Before using these formulae, let us examine what they say about combining investments.

- Returns simply combine on a weighted average basis.
- The key to the effect of a combination on risk is the correlation coefficient, as we have already seen.

Example

Using the above example data, calculate the potential 50:50 portfolio risk-return profiles using a formula approach.

Solution

Current investments + A

Based on the figures we calculated above for $(r_i - \bar{r}_i)$ and $(r_a - \bar{r}_a)$, we can calculate the covariance, correlation coefficient, return and risk as follows.

Covariance

Probability (p)	$(r_i - \bar{r}_i)$	$(r_i - \bar{r}_i)$	$p(r_i - \bar{r}_i)(r_i - \bar{r}_i)$
0.30	(10.0)	(5.0)	15.0
0.40	0.0	0.0	0.0
0.30	10.0	5.0	15.0
		Covariance =	30.0

Correlation coefficient

$$Cor_{ia} = \frac{30.0}{7.746 \times 3.873} = +1$$

That is, these investment opportunities are perfectly positively correlated.

Return

$r_{i+a} = p_i r_i + p_a r_a$

$r_{i+a} = 0.5 \times 10\% + 0.5 \times 10\% = 10\%$

Risk

$\sigma_{i+a}^2 = p_i^2 \sigma_i^2 + p_a^2 \sigma_a^2 + 2 p_i p_a \sigma_i \sigma_a Cor_{ia}$

$\sigma_{i+a}^2 = 0.5^2 \times 7.746\%^2 + 0.5^2 \times 3.873\%^2 + 2 \times 0.5 \times 0.5 \times 7.746\% \times 3.873\% \times (+1)$

$= 33.75$

$\sigma_{i+a} = \sqrt{33.75} = 5.81\%$

Current investments B

Based on the figures we calculated above for $(r_i - \bar{r}_i)$ and $(r_b - \bar{r}_b)$, we can calculate the covariance, correlation coefficient, return and risk as follows.

Covariance

Probability (p)	$(r_i - \bar{r}_i)$	$(r_i - \bar{r}_i)$	$p(r_i - \bar{r}_i)(r_i - \bar{r}_i)$
0.30	(10.0)	10.0	(30.0)
0.40	0.0	0.0	0.0
0.30	10.0	(10.0)	(30.0)
		Covariance =	(60.0)

Correlation coefficient

$$Cor_{ib} = \frac{-60.0}{7.746 \times 7.746} = -1$$

That is, these investment opportunities are perfectly negatively correlated.

Return

$r_{i+b} = p_i r_i + p_b r_b$

$r_{i+b} = 0.5 \times 10\% + 0.5 \times 10\% = 10\%$

Risk

$\sigma_{i+b}^2 = p_i^2 \sigma_i^2 + p_b^2 \sigma_b^2 + 2p_i p_b \sigma_i \sigma_b Cor_{ib}$

$\sigma_{i+b}^2 = 0.5^2 \times 7.746\%^2 + 0.5^2 \times 7.746\%^2 + 2 \times 0.5 \times 0.5 \times 7.746\% \times 7.746\% \times (-1)$

$= 0.0$

$\sigma_{i+b} = \sqrt{0} = 0.0\%$

Conclusion

Our investor again has three options, which we can summarise as before.

Portfolio	Return %	Risk %
Existing portfolio	10	7.746
Existing + A	10	5.81
Existing + B	10	0

3.4.5 Special cases

It is worth our while at this point to consider three special cases, specifically when:

- $Cor_{ab} = +1$
- $Cor_{ab} = -1$
- $Cor_{ab} = 0$

3: RISK AND RETURN

When correlation coefficient is +1

When the correlation coefficient is +1, the risk combination formula:

$$\sigma_{a+b}^2 = p_a^2\sigma_a^2 + p_b^2\sigma_b^2 + 2p_ap_b\sigma_a\sigma_b Cor_{ab}$$

becomes

$$\sigma_{a+b}^2 = p_a^2\sigma_a^2 + p_b^2\sigma_b^2 + 2p_ap_b\sigma_a\sigma_b$$

which algebraically can be reduced to

$$\sigma_{a+b}^2 = (p_a\sigma_a + p_b\sigma_b)^2$$

Hence:

$$\sigma_{a+b} = p_a\sigma_a + p_b\sigma_b$$

Thus, for two perfectly positively correlated securities, the combined risk is a weighted average of the individual components risks (as, you will recall, is the combined return).

When correlation coefficient is −1

When the correlation coefficient is −1, the risk combination formula:

$$\sigma_{a+b}^2 = p_a^2\sigma_a^2 + p_b^2\sigma_b^2 + 2p_ap_b\sigma_a\sigma_b Cor_{ab}$$

becomes:

$$\sigma_{a+b}^2 = p_a^2\sigma_a^2 + p_b^2\sigma_b^2 - 2p_ap_b\sigma_a\sigma_b$$

which algebraically can be reduced to:

$$\sigma_{a+b}^2 = (p_a\sigma_a - p_b\sigma_b)^2$$

As a result, the combined risk can be reduced to zero if:

$$p_a\sigma_a = p_b\sigma_b$$

$$\frac{p_a}{p_b} = \frac{\sigma_b}{\sigma_a}$$

This implies that we can eliminate risk within a portfolio if:

- The securities are perfectly negatively correlated.
- The portfolio is weighted correctly (inverse of the relative risk/volatility).

When correlation coefficient is 0

When the correlation coefficient is zero, the risk combination formula:

$$\sigma_{a+b}^2 = p_a^2\sigma_a^2 + p_b^2\sigma_b^2 + 2p_ap_b\sigma_a\sigma_b Cor_{ab}$$

Becomes:

$$\sigma_{a+b}^2 = p_a^2\sigma_a^2 + p_b^2\sigma_b^2$$

3: RISK AND RETURN

Which cannot be reduced further algebraically. Hence, to combine the risks of completely independent (uncorrelated) returns/securities, we must combine the variances appropriately weighted.

3.5 Portfolio selection – The minimum variance frontier and the efficient frontier

3.5.1 Introduction

We have seen that the correlation coefficient governs the extent of diversification that can be achieved within a portfolio of two investments, but can we use this information to determine a range of superior investments (on efficient frontier), or even an optimal portfolio? To consider this, we need to establish the risk-return profiles of combinations of securities, given different correlation coefficients.

The diagram below illustrates the expected return and risk for possible combinations of two risky investments A and B (ie different proportions of funds invested in each) assuming three different degrees of correlation.

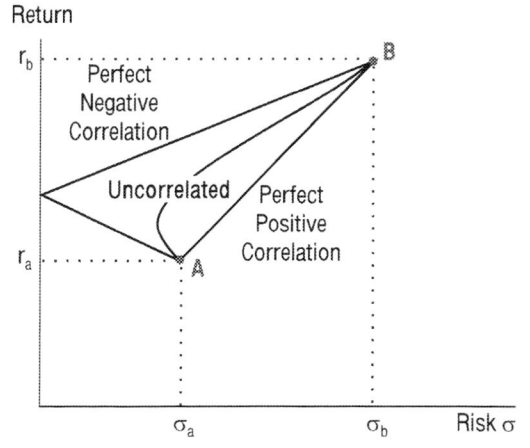

If we have all of our funds invested in B, we will receive all of its returns (r_b) and face all of its risk (σ_b). As we start to invest in A, we will start to move along the appropriate line towards A. How far along that line we are depends on what proportion of our funds are invested in A. Ultimately, when we are 100% invested in A, we will be at A, ie receive just A's return r_a and face just A's risk σ_a.

Perfect positive correlation

With perfect positive correlation the resultant risk and return are simply the weighted average of the two investments risks and returns – there is no benefit from diversification. We saw this to be the case when we combined Investment A with our current portfolio above.

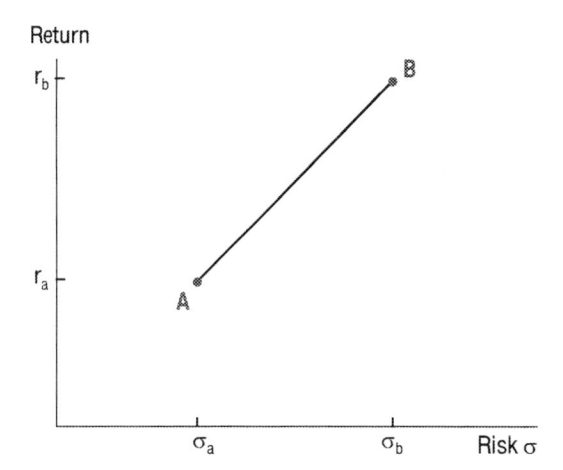

Here the entire line from A to B is both the:

- Minimum variance frontier – the minimum risk achievable for any available returns.
- Efficient frontier – the maximum return achievable for any available risks.

Perfect negative correlation

When the investments are perfectly negatively correlated it is possible to find appropriate proportions such that risk is completely diversified away. We saw this to be the case when we combined Investment B with our current portfolio above.

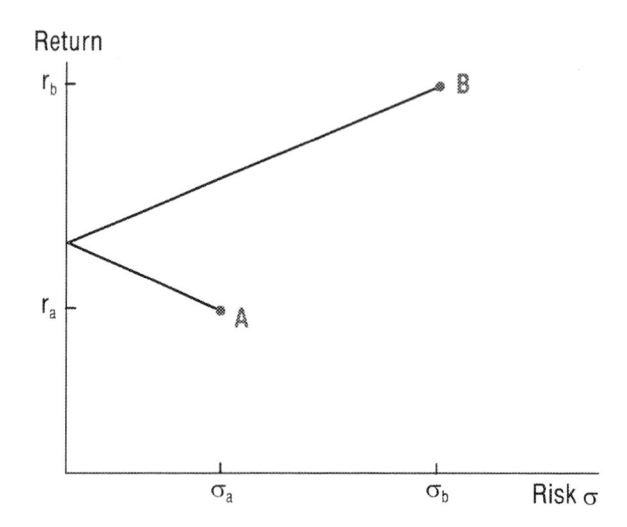

In this situation, the:

- Minimum variance frontier is the entire line from A to B (minimum risk for any available return).

- Efficient frontier is just the part from the zero risk point to B (maximum return for any available risk).

Imperfect correlation

The middle curved line shows the risk-return profile if A and B are imperfectly correlated (cor_{ab} between −1 and +1, the most likely situation). The particular choice of portfolio (ie the split of funds between the two investments) will depend, as always, upon the indifference curves.

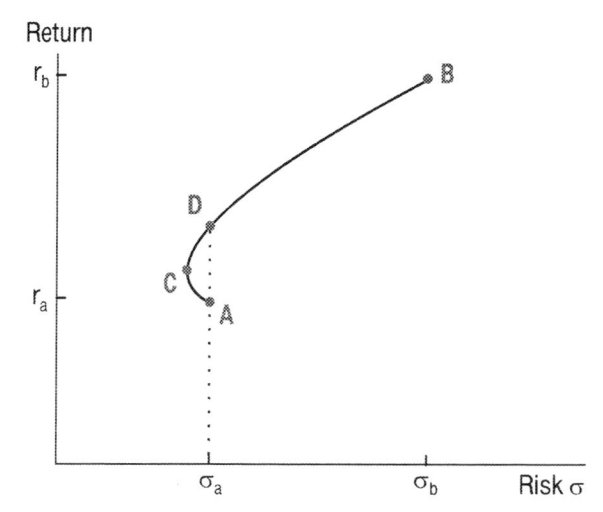

Considering the 'normal' imperfect correlation situation, some portfolios can be eliminated without knowing the indifference curves. All those on the part of the curve from A to C offer lower returns for the same risks as those on the part of the curve from C to D. We would, therefore, only consider investments on that part of the curve BC, since it offers the highest possible returns for any given level of risk.

In this situation, the:

- Minimum variance frontier is the entire line from A to B (minimum risk for any available return);
- Efficient frontier is the line from C to B (maximum return for any available risk).

And the importance here is that rational risk-averse investors would choose to invest along the efficient frontier, maximising their return at any acceptable level of risk.

3.5.2 Using indifference curves

If we now consider the possible indifference curves of our investors, we can see from the diagram below that:

- The highly risk averse investor would prefer to hold more of Investment A.
- The less risk averse investor would prefer to invest more in Investment B.

A fairly obvious conclusion, but now quantifiable. We can calculate specific proportions of investments for each individual investor that will best suit his requirements based on his indifference curves.

3: RISK AND RETURN

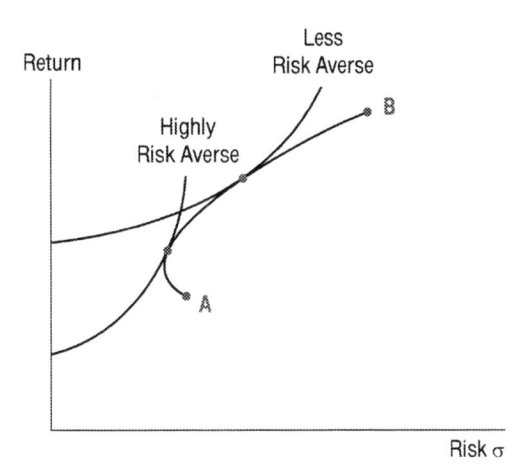

3.5.3 More than two investments

With more than two investments, the number of different portfolios multiplies, introducing various combinations of investments as well as differing proportions invested in each.

The calculations of combined risks and returns of multiple-investment portfolios becomes more time-consuming, but the underlying principle of diversification remains.

Suppose we are considering constructing a portfolio from, say, five risky securities. There will be five possible portfolios of only one security, ten of two, ten of three, five of four and one of all five – 31 possible portfolios in total, each offering an infinite variation of possible proportions invested in each security. The number of possible investment alternatives is enormous, even with just five securities. The diagram below shows the risk and return for each security.

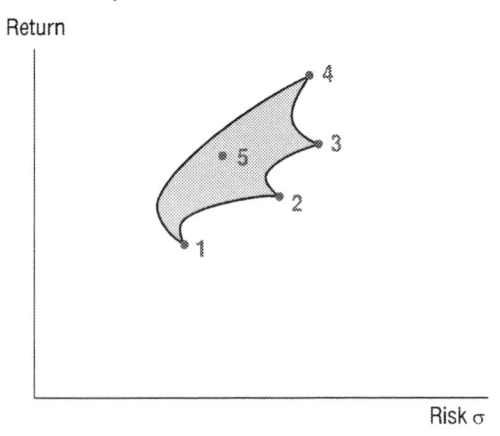

The diagram above shows the risk and return for each security (1 to 5). The shaded area shows the risk-return of the various possible portfolios that could be constructed from these five securities, the opportunity set. Some of the portfolios will involve all five securities, while others will use less. Once again the smooth convex shape of the left/upper surface should be noted.

3: RISK AND RETURN

In this situation, the:

- Minimum variance frontier is the smooth convex curve connecting 1 and 4 on the above diagram (the minimum risk for any available return).

- Efficient frontier represents just the part of this minimum variance frontier that extends from the point of minimum risk up to point 4.

If a diagram were plotted of risk and return for portfolios constructed from all the possible available risky securities (rather than just the five above), then we would obtain something more like the opportunity set below.

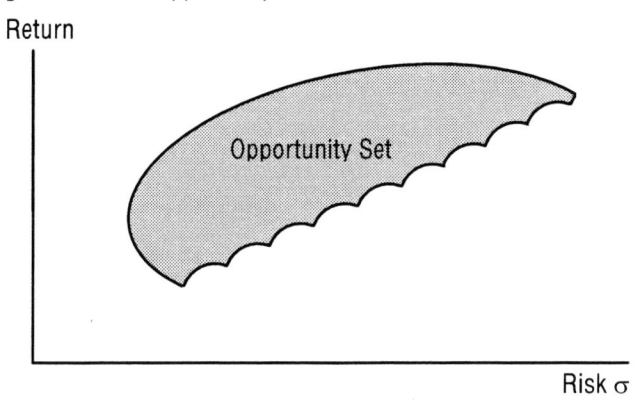

[Diagram: Return (y-axis) vs Risk σ (x-axis) showing a shaded "Opportunity Set" region]

You will note that the maximum return from this opportunity set declines at the highest levels of risk. At these higher levels we have fewer available portfolios (as a result of diversification) until, ultimately, there is only one portfolio at the maximum level of risk which is not necessarily the highest returning one. Though in theory risk and return go hand-in-hand, there is no guarantee that a higher risk investment will definitely produce a higher return

Implication for the investor

Which of the possible portfolios would investors actually select?

Even without indifference curves, we can rule out all portfolios except those falling on the upper edge of the area between points X (the minimum risk portfolio) and Y (the maximum return portfolio) below. This line is the efficient frontier in this situation because it dominates all other possible portfolios.

3: RISK AND RETURN

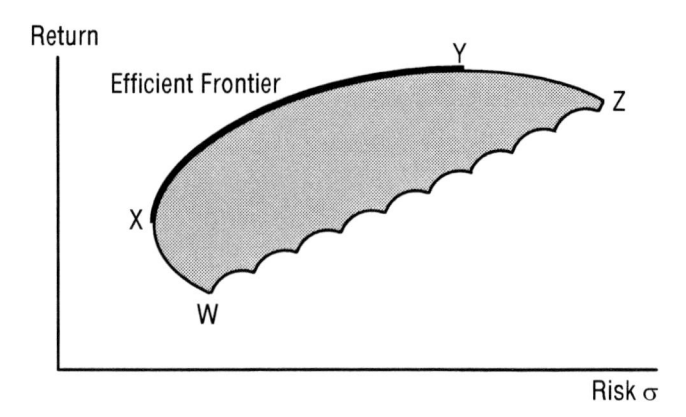

Returning to a point made earlier, in this situation the:

- Minimum variance frontier is the smooth convex curve connecting W, X and Y on the above diagram (the minimum risk for any available return).
- The efficient frontier represents just the part of this minimum variance frontier that dominates other possibilities, providing the best risk-return possibilities, ie from X to Y.

You should note that this diagram shows the opportunity set and efficient frontier when we consider unlimited investment levels in long-only portfolios. What impact does short selling have on this analysis. Intuitively, expanding the range of possible portfolios should expand the opportunity set and efficient frontier, but how?

If short-investing is permitted then an investor would be able to sell portfolio W and buy portfolio Y thereby generating a return from, at least in theory, ignoring dealing costs and spreads, a zero net investment – an infinite return, however this is also at an infinite risk. Similarly, an investor holding X would be able to short-sell W and invest the proceeds in X, potentially expanding the opportunity set. Unlimited short-selling therefore extends the opportunity set at the extremes, however empirical studies have shown that it makes little difference to the majority of the efficient frontier.

The diagram below shows the original long-only efficient frontier and the extension that appears to arise from short-selling. We can see that now the new minimum risk point is a little lower, so X has shifted down, and that Y is no longer the maximum return point.

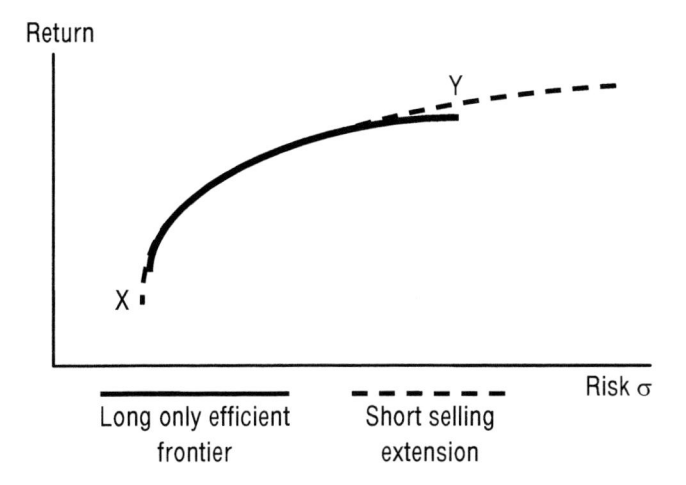

3: RISK AND RETURN

[Diagram: Return vs Risk σ, showing long only efficient frontier (solid curve from X to Y) and short selling extension (dashed line beyond Y)]

In conclusion, the efficient frontier is extended at the extremes by short-selling but remains a smooth convex curve.

The question that still needs answering, however, is where would individual investors choose to invest. With indifference curves, we could be specific but would find (as always) that different investors would prefer different points along the efficient frontier.

We can see from the diagram below that the highly risk-averse investor will choose portfolio A, whereas the less risk-averse individual may select portfolio C, and someone with a mid risk-return preference may choose B – all on the efficient frontier.

[Diagram: Return vs Risk σ, showing efficient frontier from X to Y with indifference curves tangent at points A, B, and C]

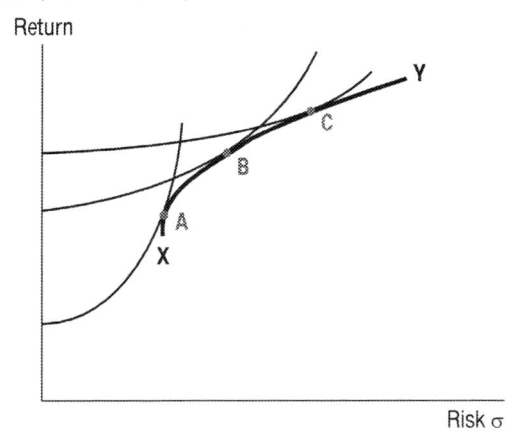

3.5.4 Size of efficient portfolios

The investor, given a set of **n** securities, can now choose the combination of those securities that is optimal for him. It may include only two securities or it may include all **n**, depending on the correlations of the securities. The question the investor will now no doubt ask is: how many securities should he consider in the first place?

He knows he should diversify to gain the benefits of risk reduction, but to what extent? The small investor will be particularly concerned to know the answer to this question, since he will have higher transaction costs the more securities he buys.

How quickly does the risk of a portfolio decrease and tend towards the average market risk as we increase **n**? Experiments have been carried out on different sizes of randomly selected portfolios of UK shares. Portfolios from one to 50 securities were chosen and the **average** risk of each size of portfolio calculated. This average risk was then expressed as a percentage of the average risk of holding only one share. Diagrammatically, the results were:

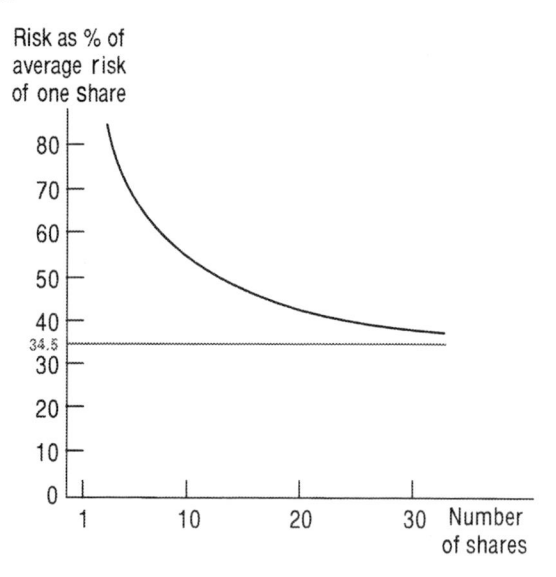

We can see from this that average risk decreases quickly as we increase the number of securities held. Each time another security is added risk is reduced by a smaller amount, but no matter how many securities are held, risk cannot be reduced on average to below 34.5% (in this particular study) of the risk of holding only one share.

This indicates that there is a certain amount of risk common to all shares quoted on the UK stock market that cannot be diversified away. This is intuitively obvious, since if an investor held all quoted UK shares, he would not be holding a riskless investment.

These results have two major implications for investors.

- Small investors can achieve substantial diversification benefits with as few as 30 shares in their portfolio. By even only holding ten randomly selected shares in equal amounts, an investor may expect to diversify away roughly 90% of the average shares' diversifiable risk.

- Institutional investors do not need to hold vast numbers of securities to be diversified. The extra reduction in risk gained by holding 150 rather than 50 securities is very small and may well be more than outweighed by the additional transaction and monitoring costs involved in holding the extra 100 shares.

So far, in discussing how many securities the investor should hold, we have considered naive diversification (randomly chosen securities held in equal amounts) and average levels of risk for different sizes of portfolios. This misses the more dramatic reductions in risk, which can be achieved by carefully selecting securities and then calculating efficient frontiers. It may be that two negatively correlated shares could be found, in which case a minimum risk portfolio would include only those two shares. If another share were added, it would add risk. Therefore, on a naive diversification policy, at least 30 shares should probably be held to reduce risk to near the average market risk level, whereas a careful examination of covariances could lead to a smaller efficient portfolio.

3.6 Risk-free investments – The Capital Market Line

3.6.1 Introduction

So far, there seems to be no single portfolio preferred by all investors. However, that is only the case if risky securities alone are included.

Not all securities are risky. In the UK, gilt-edged stocks, for instance, give a certain return if held to maturity (the interest and the capital repayment are known for certain at the time of initial issue and are guaranteed by HM Government).

If a portfolio is formed comprising a risk-free investment (say a gilt, returning r_f) and a risky investment (m, returning r_m) then, as we have seen before, the exact risk and return given by the combination will depend on the relative split of funds between the two components. In each case, the average return and standard deviation depend on the relative split of funds.

The relationship between return and standard deviation for different mixes is linear, since the risk-free investment, by definition, makes no contribution to the combined risk. This can be proved with the aid of the equations that we established earlier for combining risk and returns as follows.

Return

$$r_{m+f} = p_m r_m + p_f r_f$$

now:

$$p_f = 1 - p_m$$

giving:

$$r_{m+f} = p_m r_m + (1 - p_m) r_f$$

$$r_{m+f} = p_m r_m + r_f - p_m r_f$$

$$r_{m+f} = r_f + p_m (r_m - r_f)$$

Risk

$$\sigma_{m+f}^2 = p_m^2 \sigma_m^2 + p_f^2 \sigma_f^2 + 2 p_m p_f \sigma_m \sigma_f \text{Cor}_{mf}$$

Now $\sigma_f = 0$, since it is risk-free, hence:

3: RISK AND RETURN

$$\sigma_{m+f}^2 = p_m^2 \sigma_m^2 + 0 + 0 = p_m^2 \sigma_m^2$$

$$\sigma_{m+f} = \sqrt{p_m^2 \sigma_m^2} = p_m \sigma_m$$

Gearing

If we can borrow at the same risk-free rate of interest, then the possibilities increase. Whereas before with, say, $1,000, we could invest it all in m or in r_f (or split it between the two), it would now be possible to borrow, say, $500 at r_f, and put the whole $1,500 into m, which would give the point labelled j below.

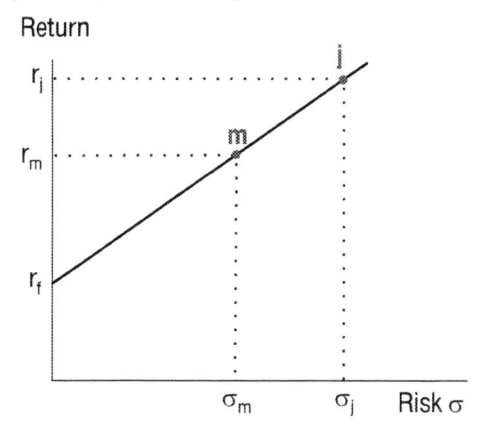

3.6.2 The Capital Market Line

Referring back, we saw how (in the absence of the risk-free stock) each investor selects the best portfolio from the efficient frontier based on his own personal indifference curves.

If we now include the possibility of borrowing or lending at the risk-free rate, then any point falling on a straight line through r_f and any point on or beneath the efficient frontier is now a potential portfolio.

Looking at just two alternatives, N and M, on the efficient frontier, which would an investor choose? The answer is the one that maximises his risk-return profile.

3: RISK AND RETURN

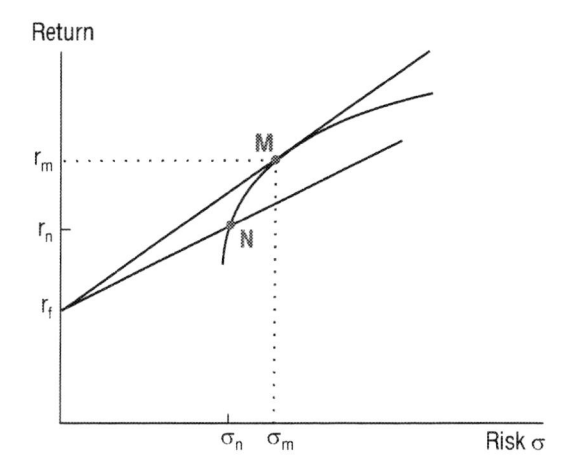

Previously, we have always needed to refer to the investor's indifference curves, but no longer. Regardless of the investor's attitude to risk, portfolios constructed from a combination of r_f and M provide a higher return for the same level of risk as those constructed from a combination of r_f and N and therefore must represent the optimal set of opportunities. The line through M gives the greatest return at any level of risk, hence all diversified investors would choose to invest somewhere along this line, known as the Capital Market Line (CML).

The exact proportions in which any one investor would choose to invest could, once again, be determined by reference to his indifference curves. However, all would choose some combination of r_f and M.

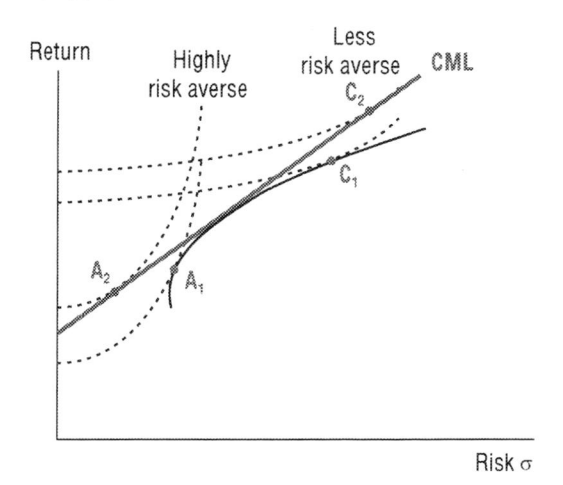

For example, our risk-averse investor who previously invested on the efficient frontier at A_1 will now choose to invest on the CML at A_2, which puts him on a higher indifference curve. Similarly, the less risk-averse investor, who previously invested at C_1 on the efficient frontier, would now choose to invest at C_2.

3.6.3 The market portfolio

We can conclude from the above that all investors will choose to invest in one combination of portfolio M and risk-free stock, each investor's utility profile dictating the precise combination chosen.

There remains one very important question to answer – what is this portfolio M?

Suppose that there was an investment (say x?) not contained in portfolio M. Since everyone wants to hold portfolio M, no one would wish to buy x, so its price would be zero. But x presumably gives some level of return, so at a price of zero it must be undervalued compared to other securities actually included within M.

If markets are efficient, then investors would sell these other securities and buy the relatively undervalued x until the price of x had risen to the point where it was correctly valued.

This leads us to the conclusion that M must contain a proportion of all investments on the market – it must be a 'scaled-down' version of the market for securities – the 'market portfolio', a tracker fund perhaps.

The Capital Asset Pricing Model theory assumes that diversified investors do hold the market portfolio plus risk-free stock. This may seem to be an extremely limiting assumption, since it would clearly be impractical to hold every single security on the market. As we have already noted, however, research has shown that a well-constructed portfolio of even as few as 30 shares is a good approximation to the market portfolio.

4 The Capital Asset Pricing Model

4.1 Nature of risk

4.1.1 Systematic and unsystematic risk

Our conclusion above was that diversification reduces risk and that the more shares we hold, the greater the risk reduction. However, we could not completely eliminate risk. As we saw, studies have indicated that a certain proportion of risk can be eliminated through diversification, though not all. Some residual risk cannot be diversified away.

Thus, it would appear that we can analyse the total risk of an investment into two subcategories as follows.

3: RISK AND RETURN

```
                    ┌─────────────────────┐
                    │   Total risk of     │
                    │    Investment       │
                    │        σᵢ           │
                    └──────────┬──────────┘
                               │
                ┌──────────────┴──────────────┐
                │                             │
```

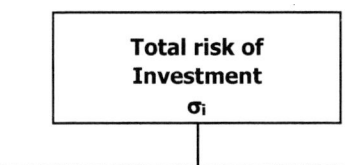

Systematic risk/market risk	Unsystematic risk/idiosyncratic risk/ specific risk
σ_s	σ_u
Potential variability in the returns offered by a security caused by general market influences, eg	Potential variability in the returns offered by a security as a result of factors specific to the company, eg
▪ Interest rate changes ▪ Inflation rate changes ▪ Tax rate changes ▪ State of the economy	▪ Quality of management ▪ Susceptibility to demands of suppliers and customers ▪ Profitability margins and levels
Cannot be eliminated through diversification	**Can be eliminated through diversification**

As we note, the unsystematic risk can be eliminated through diversification. This arises as a result of the trade between companies. If one company makes a mistake and undertakes a bad deal (loses money), then its trading partner will be making a corresponding amount of money. Hence, by investing in both companies, we can eliminate this variability from our portfolio. We get the combined return regardless of which company generates it.

The systematic or market risk is something that impacts on the economy in general, which all companies are part of, hence this is the type of risk that cannot be eliminated.

4.1.2 Consequences

An **undiversified investor** (ie one who has most/all of his money invested in the shares of one company) will **face the full risk** of that investment, σ_i. He will, therefore, look for a return commensurate with this full level.

A **diversified investor** will have eliminated, through diversification, the unsystematic risk inherent in the individual securities in his portfolio and **face just the systematic risk**, σ_s. Hence, he will seek a return commensurate with the level of systematic risk only.

4.1.3 Decomposition of risk

In order to undertake calculations, we may need to decompose this total risk into its two sub-components, which can be achieved using the relationship:

$$\sigma_i^2 = \sigma_s^2 + \sigma_u^2$$

NB: Risks are combined by adding variances (the square of the standard deviation) as we did with portfolio theory above.

4.2 The model

4.2.1 Introduction

We are now in a position to derive the basic Capital Asset Pricing Model (CAPM). Let us consider a highly diversified investor who has spread his funds across the full stock market, with some also invested in a risk-free security. What returns will he achieve and what risk will he face?

We will use the following notation.

r_m = returns expected from investing in the **market portfolio** (a portfolio representative of the whole stock market, eg a tracker fund)

r_f = returns from risk-free investments

β = proportion of his funds invested in the market portfolio

Now, the proportion of money invested in the market portfolio β will return r_m, and the remainder invested risk free $(1 - \beta)$ will generate r_f. Using the formulae we established for portfolio theory, the expected return and risk of this portfolio can be calculated as:

Return

$$r_{a+b} = p_a r_a + p_b r_b$$

ie:

$$r = \beta r_m + (1 - \beta) r_f$$

which can be algebraically rearranged, giving:

$$r = \beta r_m + r_f - \beta r_f$$

or:

$$r = r_f + \beta (r_m - r_f)$$

Risk

Using:

$$\sigma_{a+b}^2 = p_a^2 \sigma_a^2 + p_b^2 \sigma_b^2 + 2 p_a p_b \sigma_a \sigma_b \text{Cor}_{ab}$$

The risk that he will face (systematic only since he is diversified) will be:

$$\sigma_s^2 = \beta^2 \sigma_m^2 + (1 - \beta)^2 \sigma_f^2 + 2\beta(1 - \beta) \sigma_m \sigma_f \text{Cor}_{mf}$$

Now $\sigma_f = 0$ since it is risk-free, hence:

$$\sigma_s^2 = \beta^2\sigma_m^2 + 0 + 0 = \beta^2\sigma_m^2$$

$$\sigma_s = \sqrt{\beta^2\sigma_m^2}$$

The level of systematic risk faced will therefore be:

$$\sigma_s = \beta\sigma_m$$

where:

σ_s = the systematic risk in the portfolio

σ_m = the risk (systematic) in the market portfolio

In practical terms, this means that the risk of the portfolio is a function of the proportion of funds invested in the market portfolio (exposed to risk) and the scale of the risk of that market portfolio, since the other investment is risk-free.

NB: So far, we have talked about β as the proportion of funds invested in the market portfolio. It can also be more usefully viewed as the proportion of market portfolio **risk** that we are willing to face, since a simple rearrangement of the above equation gives:

$$\beta = \frac{\sigma_s}{\sigma_m}$$

It is this latter way of viewing β, as the proportion of the market portfolio risk, that is going to give us the relationship we need between risk and return.

4.2.2 Relevance

Considering the above equations, for any given level of risk in relation to the market portfolio $\left(\beta = \frac{\sigma_s}{\sigma_m}\right)$, the return an investor can achieve by a broad investment in the stock market and risk-free investments is given by:

$$r = r_f + \beta(r_m - r_f)$$

As a result, he would only consider an alternative investment opportunity with the same level of systematic risk if it offered a higher return. Hence, this relationship gives the minimum acceptable return for an investment based on its level of systematic risk.

Plotting this relationship on a graph gives the Securities Market Line (SML), as follows, which clearly shows the relationship between relative levels of risk (β) and corresponding expected returns.

3: RISK AND RETURN

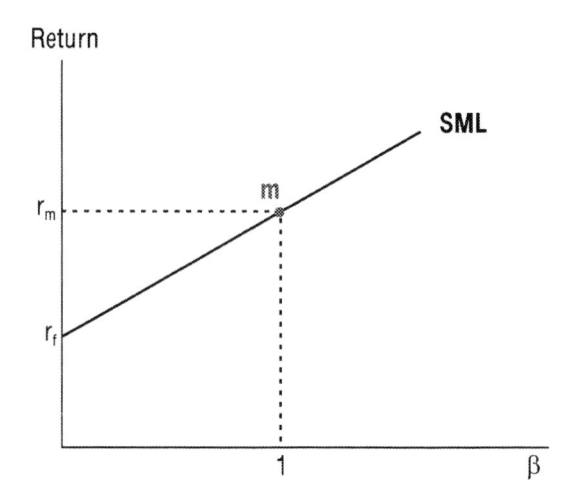

[Graph: Return vs β, showing the SML (Security Market Line) starting from r_f on the Return axis, passing through point m at β = 1 with return r_m.]

4.2.3 Conclusion

For an investment whose risk relative to the market portfolio is given by β, the required (minimum acceptable) return is given by the Capital Asset Pricing Model (CAPM) formula:

$$r = r_f + \beta(r_m - r_f)$$

where:

r_m = the return expected from the market portfolio

r_f = the return offered by a risk-free security

β = the risk of the investment opportunity relative to that of the market portfolio (systematic risk only)

That is, the investor can expect to achieve the risk-free return (r_f) plus a proportion of the **market risk premium** ($r_m - r_f$) based on the levels of relative risk (β) he is willing to face.

Example

For example, suppose that the risk-free rate of return is 6%, and the market is expected to return 14%, what return would a diversified investor require from an investment with a β of the following?

- 0
- 0.5
- 1
- 1.5

Solution

Using:

$$r = r_f + \beta(r_m - r_f)$$

Gives:

β = 0

$r = 6\% + 0 \times (14\% - 6\%) = 6\%$

β = 0.5

$r = 6\% + 0.5 \times (14\% - 6\%) = 10\%$

β = 1

$r = 6\% + 1 \times (14\% - 6\%) = 14\%$

β = 1.5

$r = 6\% + 1.5 \times (14\% - 6\%) = 18\%$

4.2.4 Investment appraisal under CAPM

Investment appraisal under CAPM amounts to plotting investments' expected returns and betas on the SML graph as follows.

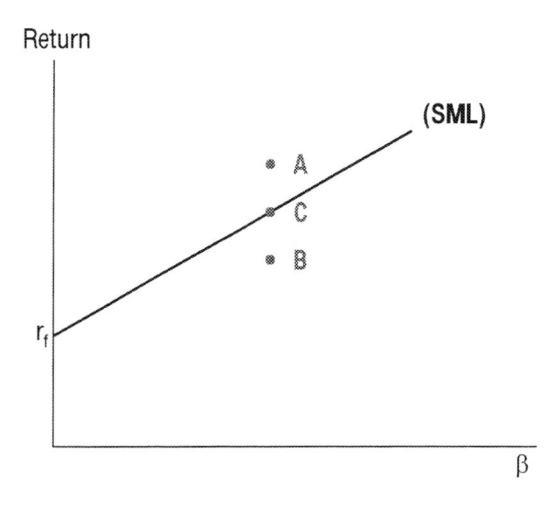

Investment C lying on the SML is currently correctly priced in the market, that is it is offering the expected return for its given risk. An investor should be indifferent to the choice between buying it or not.

Investment A lying above the SML would be accepted by an investor, as it is offering a return higher than that required for its level of risk, ie it is **undervalued**. Such an investment is offering a **positive abnormal return**, ie surplus over what would normally be expected.

Investment B lying beneath the SML would be rejected, as its current return is too low, ie it is **overvalued**. Such an investment is offering a **negative abnormal return**, ie its return is lower than would normally be expected.

4.2.5 Forming portfolios using CAPM

We can use the CAPM to assist in the formation of portfolios where we have determined the degree of risk that the client is willing to face.

An individual seeking a high return would need to take on more risk. Thus, we would need to construct a portfolio with a high β. A portfolio with a β greater than 1 could be expected to give a return greater than that of the market, but at a correspondingly enhanced level of risk.

A young pension fund may be prepared to undertake a similar investment strategy with the view that there will be long-term benefits.

A mature pension fund, on the other hand, is liable to be seeking a safer portfolio and would, therefore, prefer a portfolio with a β less than 1. Clearly, as the proportion of risk-free investments is increased in our portfolio (and the proportion of equities reduced), the portfolio β reduces towards 0.

4.3 Betas

4.3.1 Introduction

What it means

The beta of an investment is a relative measure of the **systematic risk** of that investment.

In general terms:

- The sign of the beta (+/−) indicates whether, on average, the investment's returns move with (+) the market, rising and falling when it does, or in the opposite direction (−) to the market.

- The scale or value of the beta indicates the relative volatility.

A beta of 0.5 (or −0.5) for instance, would indicate that, on average, the investment's returns move one-half as much as the market's do in the same (or opposite) direction. If the market fell by 6%, we would expect the investment to fall (or rise) by 3%; if the market rose by 8%, we would expect the investment's returns to rise (or fall) by 4%, etc.

Summary

$\beta > 1$

On average, the investment's returns will move in the same direction as the market's returns, but to a greater extent.

β = 1

On average, the investment's returns will move in the same direction as the market's returns, and to the same extent.

0 < β < 1

On average, the investment's returns will move in the same direction as the market's returns, but to a lesser extent.

β = 0

The investment's returns are uncorrelated with those of the market. This would be the case if the investment were risk-free, but more generally, this situation will arise when all of the investment's risk is unsystematic.

β < 0

On average, the investment's returns will move in the opposite direction to the market, to a lesser extent if β > −1, to the same extent if β = −1, and to a greater extent if β < −1.

4.3.2 Use of betas

We can use the β for an investment to establish from the CAPM formula what the appropriate risk-adjusted required rate of return is in order to appraise an investment.

Example

A new one-year investment opportunity requires an initial investment of $1m and is expected to give a return of $1.2m at the end of the year.

The current market return is 14%, and risk-free return is 6%.

The investment's beta has been estimated at 1.5.

Assuming investors are well diversified, should the investment be accepted and what value would we place on the investment?

Solution

Required rate of return

The required return given by the CAPM would be:

$r = r_f + β(r_m − r_f)$
$r = 6\% + 1.5(14\% − 6\%)$
$r = 6\% + 12\% = 18\%$

Investment's return and appraisal

The return on the investment will be 20% ($1.2m return from a $1.0m investment), hence it should be accepted. It is offering a better level of return for its level of (systematic) risk than can currently be obtained elsewhere on the market.

3: RISK AND RETURN

Value of investment

To value the investment, the investors will use the required rate given by the CAPM as a risk-adjusted discount rate to find the present value of its future returns (the usual market value approach), giving:

Time	Cash flow ($'000)	Discount factor	Present value ($'000)
0	(1,000)	1	(1,000)
1	1,200	$\frac{1}{1.18}$	1,017
Net present value			17

The $1.017m is the value of the investment's returns to well-diversified investors (hence the market value of the investment). It is the maximum price that they should be prepared to pay for such returns. The investment is accepted because it is worth $17,000 more than it costs.

If capital markets are efficient, then all quoted shares should be correctly valued (any share that was undervalued would be the subject of buying pressure, which would force its price up to the fair value). CAPM shows that a share's market value should be that which equates the actual return from the share with the expected return for the share's beta.

4.3.3 Mathematical derivation

Systematic risk

To get a beta, we need to know the systematic risk element of the investment we are considering (σ_s).

We have said that systematic risk is that part of the total risk that is related to movements in the market portfolio. The correlation coefficient between two investment opportunities is a measure of this relationship, hence:

$$\sigma_s = \sigma_i cor_{im}$$

where:

σ_s = the investment's systematic risk

σ_i = the investment's total risk (systematic and unsystematic)

Cor_{im} = correlation coefficient between the returns of the investment and those of the market portfolios

For instance, if an investment was perfectly correlated with the market so that all its fluctuations could be fully explained by fluctuations in the market, then all of its risk would be systematic $\sigma_s = \sigma_i$.

If an investment was uncorrelated to the market, then its systematic risk would be zero, and all its risk would be unsystematic.

Between those extremes come varying proportions of systematic and unsystematic risk, and we have already established that the relationship between these risks (total, systematic and unsystematic) is:

$$\sigma_i^2 = \sigma_s^2 + \sigma_u^2$$

The beta coefficient

Remember that beta is a relative measure (or index number) showing the level of systematic risk of an investment relative to the market portfolio, ie:

$$\beta = \frac{\sigma_s}{\sigma_m}$$

and from $\sigma_s = \sigma_i Cor_{im}$ above we can establish:

$$\beta = \frac{\sigma_s}{\sigma_m} = \frac{\sigma_i Cor_{im}}{\sigma_m} = \frac{\sigma_i \sigma_m Cor_{im}}{\sigma_m^2}$$

$$\beta = \frac{\text{Covariance (i,m)}}{\text{Variance of the market}}$$

If the covariance or correlation coefficient between the investment and the market can be established using our earlier risk measurement ideas, the beta can be calculated. Alternatively, if we establish the systematic risk, we can establish the beta.

4.3.4 Calculation in practice

Beta factors are calculated in practice for all shares quoted on the Stock Exchange and are available from most data providers or the Risk Management Service operated by the London Business School amongst others.

The method of practical calculation is very much based on the above ideas regarding the average variability of the returns from investments relative to those of the market, involving the use of linear regression analysis. If the historical return on the FTSE index (representing the market) over and above the risk-free return is plotted on a scatter diagram against the corresponding returns of a security i, also over and above r_f, then the following might be observed.

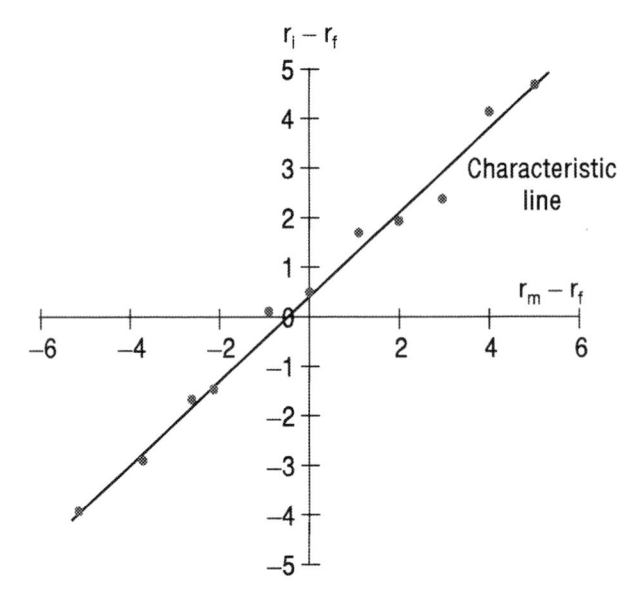

If the line of best fit is found (via linear regression), it will show the average relationship between the two sets of returns. This line is known as the security's characteristic line, and the slope of this line represents the β, as it indicates the volatility of i's return relative to that of the market.

This line also gives the investment's alpha (α) which is given by the intercept (the premium return on the investment when the market premium return is zero).

4.3.5 Betas and risk for portfolios of investments

Portfolio beta

Although any investment must be appraised purely on the basis of its own expected return and beta (without reference, in particular, to the current portfolio), it is possible to work out the impact of accepting the investment on the overall portfolio beta.

When two investments are combined, their combination will have a beta equal to the weighted average (by market values) of the individual betas.

Example

A portfolio has a current market value of $22m, and a beta of 0.8. We are considering an additional investment of $2m to be funded by scaling down the current portfolio. The new investment is expected to yield a net cash inflow of $2.36m in one year, the inflows having a beta of 1.5. The expected return from the market is 14% and the risk-free rate is 6%.

Should the investment be accepted? What will be the new β of the portfolio, assuming that the current portfolio is fairly priced and at equilibrium?

Solution

Required rate of return

From the CAPM formula, we can work out that the appropriate risk-adjusted discount rate to apply to the new investment is:

$r = r_f + \beta(r_m - r_f)$

$r = 6\% + 1.5(14\% - 6\%)$

$r = 6\% + 12\% = 18\%$

Investment's return and appraisal

The return on the investment will be 18% ($2.36m return on a $2m investment), hence it is fairly valued and should be accepted. It is offering a fair level of return for its level of (systematic) risk.

New beta

Of the total market value of $22m, $20m is the market value of flows with a beta of 0.8, while $2m is the market value of flows having a beta of 1.5.

The new overall beta will be the weighted average of 0.8 and 1.5, ie:

$\beta_{a+b} = p_a\beta_a + p_b\beta_b$

giving:

$$\frac{\$20m}{\$22m} \times 0.8 + \frac{\$2m}{\$22m} \times 1.5 = 0.864$$

Portfolio risk

Having established the portfolio beta as the weighted average of the stock betas, we can now calculate the portfolio systematic risk, using:

$$\beta = \frac{\sigma_s}{\sigma_m} \text{ or } \sigma_s = \beta\sigma_m$$

If we wish to establish the portfolio's total risk, we will need to either:

- Establish the portfolio's unsystematic risk using the portfolio theory risk combination formula, and hence the portfolio's total risk using $\sigma_i^2 = \sigma_s^2 + \sigma_u^2$; or
- Use the portfolio theory formula to combine total risks.

Note that to achieve either of these will involve the use of the portfolio theory risk combination formula:

$$\sigma_{a+b}^2 = p_a^2\sigma_a^2 + p_b^2\sigma_b^2 + 2p_ap_b\sigma_a\sigma_b Cor_{ab}$$

This formula can be used to combine either the total risks **or** the unsystematic risks as follows.

3: RISK AND RETURN

- If we know the total risks of the individual stocks and how these **total** risks are correlated, then inserting this data will give the total risk of the portfolio.

- If, on the other hand, we know the unsystematic risks of the individual securities and how these **unsystematic** elements are correlated, we can use this to establish the unsystematic risk of the portfolio.

Thus, the portfolio theory formula can be applied to the total risk or any sub-component of it as long as we have the correlations of the appropriate component.

Example

The following securities are contained within a portfolio in the given proportions.

Security	Proportion p	Return %	β	Specific risk %
A	0.2	15	0.7	5
B	0.5	17	0.9	12
C	0.3	18	1.0	10

If the risk of the market portfolio is 20%, calculate the portfolio:

- Return
- Beta
- Systematic risk
- Unsystematic risk (assuming that the unsystematic risk components are uncorrelated)
- Total risk

Solution

Security	p	r (%)	β	σ_u (%)	pr (%)	pβ (%)	$p^2\sigma_u^2$ (%²)
A	0.2	15	0.7	5	3.0	0.14	1
B	0.5	17	0.9	12	8.5	0.45	36
C	0.3	18	1.0	10	5.4	0.30	9
					16.9	0.89	46

Return

The portfolio return is 16.9%, being a weighted average combination of the individual component returns.

Beta

The portfolio beta is 0.89, being a weighted average combination of the individual component betas.

Systematic risk

The portfolio systematic risk can be calculated as:

$$\sigma_s = \beta\sigma_m = 0.89 \times 20\% = 17.8\%$$

Unsystematic risk

Given the correlations between the unsystematic risk components, we can combine these using the portfolio theory formula which for two securities is:

$$\sigma_{a+b}^2 = p_a^2\sigma_a^2 + p_b^2\sigma_b^2 + 2p_ap_b\sigma_a\sigma_b Cor_{ab}$$

Since the unsystematic risk components are uncorrelated, this can be reduced to (for two securities):

$$\sigma_{a+b}^2 = p_a^2\sigma_a^2 + p_b^2\sigma_b^2$$

which for three uncorrelated securities can be simply extended to:

$$\sigma_{a+b+c}^2 = p_a^2\sigma_a^2 + p_b^2\sigma_b^2 + p_c^2\sigma_c^2$$

This has been evaluated in the final column of the above table as:

$$\sigma_{a+b+c}^2 = 46$$

Hence:

$$\sigma_{a+b+c} = 6.78\%$$

Total risk

The total portfolio risk can now be calculated as:

$$\sigma_i^2 = \sigma_s^2 + \sigma_u^2 = 17.8^2 + 6.78^2 = 362.84$$

$$\sigma_i = 19.05\%$$

4.3.6 Assessing the degree of diversification — R^2

R^2 is the square of the correlation coefficient and indicates the proportion of the total risk of a portfolio that is systematic, ie cannot be diversified away and hence the degree of diversification achieved. This can be seen from one of our earlier relationships:

$$\sigma_s = \sigma_i Cor_{im}$$

From which it follows that:

$$Cor_{im} = \frac{\sigma_s}{\sigma_i}$$

Hence:

$$R^2 = Cor_{im}^2 = \frac{\sigma_s^2}{\sigma_i^2}$$

The closer this is to one, the better the diversification of a portfolio.

3: RISK AND RETURN

Correspondingly, $1 - R^2$ gives the proportion of the total risk that could be eliminated through further diversification, ie the proportion of unsystematic risk. This can be demonstrated as follows.

$$1 - R^2 = 1 - Cor_{im}^2$$

$$= 1 - \frac{\sigma_s^2}{\sigma_i^2}$$

$$= \frac{\sigma_i^2 - \sigma_s^2}{\sigma_i^2}$$

$$= \frac{\sigma_u^2}{\sigma_i^2}$$

Example

A portfolio has a total risk of 13% and a systematic risk of 12%. Assess the level of diversification of the portfolio, ascertaining the proportions of undiversifiable and diversifiable risk.

Solution

Using:

$$\sigma_i^2 = \sigma_s^2 + \sigma_u^2$$

gives:

$$13^2 = 12^2 + \sigma_u^2$$

Hence:

$$169 = 144 + \sigma_u^2$$

$$\sigma_u^2 = 25$$

$$\sigma_u = 5\%$$

The proportion of undiversifiable risk is:

$$R^2 = \frac{\sigma_s^2}{\sigma_i^2} = \frac{12^2}{13^2} = \frac{144}{169} = 0.852 \text{ or } 85.2\%$$

The proportion of diversifiable risk is:

$$\frac{\sigma_u^2}{\sigma_i^2} = \frac{5^2}{13^2} = \frac{25}{169} = 0.148 \text{ or } 14.8\%$$

which corresponds to:

$$1 - R^2 = 1 - 0.852 = 0.148 \text{ or } 14.8\%$$

4.4 Assumptions and limitations of CAPM

4.4.1 The assumptions

There are a number of assumptions underlying CAPM:

- Investors are rational and risk-averse.
- Investors are diversified and therefore, are only concerned with a security's expected return and its systematic risk.
- The capital market is perfect and in equilibrium, which means in particular:
    - It is not dominated by any individual investors
    - There are no transaction costs, for instance commissions or taxes, or other imperfections
    - All securities are fairly valued, hence r_m is a realistic return
- All investors have the same expectations regarding the probability distributions of returns from each security, thus they have the same opportunity set and efficient frontier.
- There exists a single risk-free rate at which all investors may borrow or lend without limit. Furthermore, investors can buy (invest in) or sell (go short) the market portfolio without limit.

4.4.2 The limitations

Aside from the limitations stemming from the CAPM's assumptions, the following limitations of CAPM are worth considering.

Single-period (one year) model

The required rate of return derived from the model is only valid as long as the inputs (r_m, r_f, β) are valid. As a result of annual budgets, which tend to affect tax rates and interest rates (through the Public Sector Net Cash Requirement – PSNCR), we can expect that one or more of these factors will change over a year. As such, the returns that we consider when using CAPM are the holding period returns over that time, which we cover later.

Few investment opportunities last for one year only. However, we can extend the model to more than one time period if we assume that all relevant factors (such as risk-free rate and market rate) remain constant over the period covered.

Only applicable to diversified portfolios

The model assumes that the overall portfolio held is diversified and equates to the market as a whole. If we were dealing with a small undiversified portfolio, then this approach would not be appropriate. We would need to consider Modern Portfolio Theory from which CAPM was developed.

Difficult to estimate the β factor for an investment

To calculate a β factor for an investment, we need to estimate the future returns under different economic conditions. Obviously, this will be extremely difficult to achieve in practice. One solution could be to look at a similar investment that had been accepted in the past and calculate its β factor with the benefit of hindsight.

4.4.3 Non-standard forms based on more realistic assumptions

The realism and relevance of many of the above assumptions and limitations may be questioned. The first two assumptions are probably not too unreasonable (though irrational and undiversified investors do exist, they represent a very small minority of the market). In addition, certain of the perfect competition assumptions are quite realistic within many major capital markets.

Criticism can, however, be levelled at the other assumptions, some of which are clearly invalid, and these, along with the single period limitation, have attracted further investigation. The question is, are the effects of these invalid assumptions significant enough to invalidate the whole theory, or do they just produce minor distortions that can be dealt with separately?

It is worth noting that extensions have been made to CAPM that seek to relax these strict basic assumptions and establish the extent to which it is valid. The model has proved surprisingly resilient to such testing, and it seems that β is a valid and fairly complete measure of risk.

Looking at some of these points in turn.

Capital markets are in equilibrium and no-one can influence the market

CAPM assumes that investors are price-takers, deriving prices from the equilibrium market, though major institutions may well find or believe that their actions can influence the market. Studies have shown that an equilibrium price will still be found under such circumstances with the relevant institution maximising its utility given the equilibrium price that will result from its decision. The result is that this institution will tend to hold less of the risk-free asset and more of the market portfolio given its ability to influence the market, with other price-taking investors unaffected.

No tax

Another assumption of CAPM is that capital markets are perfect, which inherently assumes no tax. Models that attempt to incorporate the effects of tax are made awkward because of the differing tax treatments of income and gains (eg taper relief in the UK).

In general, income components of any return are taxed at higher rates than the gain components, placing pure income products such as a risk-free asset (a money market deposit, say) at a comparative disadvantage against gain-returning assets (eg shares).

When these tax effects are included, the CAPM relationship becomes:

$$r = r_f + \beta[(r_m - r_f) - \tau(d_m - r_f)] + \tau(d_i - r_f)$$

where:

τ = a composite tax rate reflecting the excess tax on income over that on gains
d_m = dividend yield on the market
d_i = dividend yield on the relevant stock

What this shows is that for the same β, a stock yielding a higher dividend will have a higher required return, hence a lower value. Consequently, lower yielding stocks will have higher values and be considered preferable to investors.

The conclusion from this is that the basic ideas still hold true. However, investors will hold more of the tax efficient market portfolio than would be the case in the basic no tax model.

Dealing costs and liquidity

A further consequence of the assumption of perfect capital markets is that there are no dealing costs and there is perfect liquidity. Less liquid stocks tend to have higher dealing spreads and, in the extreme, may be very difficult to sell. Less liquid stocks therefore subject the investor to an additional undiversifiable risk that is not related to the market, and the Securities Market Line needs to be extended to a Securities Market Plane to factor in this second undiversifiable risk dimension as follows.

$$r = r_f + \beta_m(r_m - r_f) + \beta_l(r_l - r_f)$$

where:

$(r_l - r_f)$ = premium return required to compensate for low liquidity
β_l = exposure to illiquidity for this stock

What we have here is our first example of a multi-beta version of CAPM. Such models try to cater for additional undiversifiable risks, and we will see further examples below.

Homogeneity of investor expectations

Another of the assumptions of CAPM is homogeneity of expectations. Where investors do not have the same expectations regarding security returns, risks and correlations, studies have shown that they will face efficient frontiers that are unique to them. They will, therefore, have a 'unique SML' based on their expectation with the market SML being the aggregate of the individual 'unique SML's'. The expected return from a security will be a weighted average of all investor expectations, and the consensus expected return will still be a linear function of the aggregate SML, positively related to beta.

Can freely lend or borrow at the risk-free rate

One of the most obvious invalid assumptions of CAPM is the ability to freely lend or borrow at the same risk-free rate. This has been shown diagrammatically as:

3: RISK AND RETURN

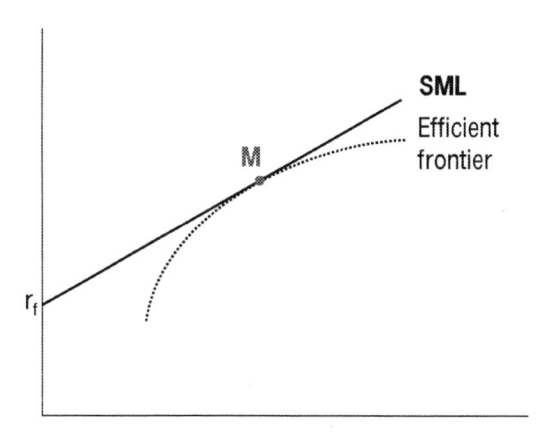

[Graph showing SML as a straight line tangent to the Efficient frontier curve at point M, starting from r_f on the y-axis]

Clearly, this is not realistic and a spread exists between deposit and borrowing rates. Building in this practical reality slightly alters the slope of the SML above the market portfolio, reducing its gradient (and slightly altering the market portfolio, moving along the efficient frontier) where investors may be borrowing at this higher rate to gain additional exposure.

If:

r_l = lending/deposit rate (the lower rate in the spread)
r_b = borrowing rate (the higher rate in the spread)

Then, our SML becomes:

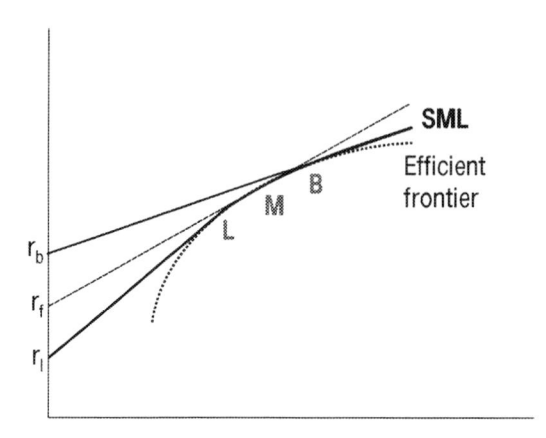

[Graph showing modified SML with two tangent lines from r_b and r_l touching the efficient frontier at points B and L respectively, with M between them]

Lenders will now choose to invest in a portfolio on the efficient frontier L, and borrowers will invest at B. The market portfolio M must lie on the efficient frontier between B and L, since it represents the average holding of the entire market.

Furthermore, investors may be able to invest unlimited sums at the risk-free rate, however they are liable to face an increasing borrowing cost as borrowing levels rise. If borrowing rates increase at higher borrowing levels, this causes the SML slope to shallow further, leading to a curved SML above the market portfolio. As a consequence, this practical reality does slightly alter the SML shape and impact on the market portfolio.

Unlimited short selling

Unlimited short selling is the CAPM assumption that investors can sell shares they do not own to any level. This assumption simplified the original underlying maths, but has proved to be an unnecessary one. If markets are at equilibrium with investors holding the market portfolio, then no investor sells any security short, and limiting short selling will not alter this position.

Single period model

Though the standard CAPM model assumes single period investment horizons (a common single period for all investors), models have been developed to extend this further into a multi-period model. These models include:

- **The consumption CAPM** – The assumption here is that in the long term, investors seek to maximise their utility of lifetime consumption (have what they consider to be the best/most comfortable life in the long run). Based on this, studies have shown that the return on an asset should be linearly related to the growth rate of aggregate consumption in the long term, meaning that the single period model is, in fact, valid for longer periods.

- **CAPM including inflation** – Studies have shown that an equilibrium return from an asset can still be found with uncertain levels of inflation, but that asset risk will be a function of both market risk and inflation risk, ie:

$$r = r_f + \beta_m(r_m - r_f) + \beta_i(r_i - r_f)$$

    where:

    β_m = sensitivity to market
    β_i = sensitivity to inflation
    r_i = return required to compensate for inflation

- **Multi-beta CAPM** – adding additional beta factors to incorporate for inflation and other non-diversifiable risks. These risks may include future earnings, future inflation, default risk, term structure risk, future investment opportunities, etc (the factors are not specified by the model). The model then becomes:

$$r = r_f + \beta_m(r_m - r_f) + \beta_{i1}(r_{i1} - r_f) + \beta_{i2}(r_{i2} - r_f) + \cdots$$

    where:

    β_m = sensitivity to market
    β_{in} = sensitivities to n^{th} other risk factor
    r_{in} = return required to compensate for the nth other risk factor

4.5 International CAPM

We can use this multi-beta CAPM approach to deal with CAPM on an international basis, ie international CAPM.

When appraising an international investment, investors will be primarily concerned by the possible returns and risks as measured in their domestic currency, irrespective of the currency in which the investment is denominated. What we will therefore have is:

3: RISK AND RETURN

$$r = r_f + \beta_m(r_m - r_f) + \beta_{FX1}(r_{FX1} - r_f) + \beta_{FX2}(r_{FX2} - r_f) + \cdots$$

where:

r_f	=	domestic currency risk-free rate
r_m	=	expected return in domestic currency terms on the world market
r_{FXj}	=	expected return in domestic currency terms from currency j
β_m	=	sensitivity of the domestic value of asset i to the world market
β_{FXj}	=	sensitivity of the domestic value of asset i to exchange rate movements on currency j

Example

A UK investor is considering investing in a European stock. The sterling risk-free rate is 5% and the world index offers a 10% sterling return. It is thought that an investment in euros will yield 6% in sterling terms over the coming year. The investment has a sensitivity to the world index of 0.9, and a sensitivity to foreign exchange movements of 0.3. Calculate the expected sterling return.

Solution

$$\begin{aligned} r &= r_f + \beta_m(r_m - r_f) + \beta_{FX1}(r_{FX1} - r_f) \\ &= 5 + 0.9(10 - 5) + 0.3(6 - 5) \\ &= 5 + 4.5 + 0.3 = 9.8\% \end{aligned}$$

4.6 Specific examples of multi-beta models

4.6.1 Fama and French three-factor model

CAPM was developed by Sharpe, Lintner and Mossin in the 1960s from the original work of Markowitz on Portfolio Theory.

Fama and French worked on the original single factor CAPM model and developed a three-factor model (1993). They noticed that small cap stocks and stocks with a high book/market value, tended to produce greater returns than the market as a whole and incorporated these factors into the following model.

$$r = r_f + \beta_1(r_m - r_f) + \beta_2 SMB + \beta_3 HML$$

where:

SMB = Small cap – Big (large cap), ie the historical excess returns on small cap stocks over those of large cap stocks.

HML = High book/price – Low, ie the historical excess returns on high book/price stocks over those of low book/price stocks.

β_2 = takes a value between 0 and 1, 0 being a portfolio that mirrors that market, 1 being a small cap portfolio.

β_3 = takes a value between 0 and 1, 0 being a portfolio that mirrors that market, 1 being a value portfolio

4.6.2 Carhart four-factor model

Carhart (1997) then took this three-factor model and made it into a four-factor model by adding momentum. He noted that returns on a share that had a record of recent historically good returns were better than those on shares that had performed poorly in the recent past. To cater for this, he incorporated a term for momentum.

$$r = r_f + \beta_1(r_m - r_f) + \beta_2 SMB + \beta_3 HML + \beta_4 WML$$

where:

WML = Winners − Losers, reflecting the momentum of returns. It is the historical excess returns on an equally weighted portfolio of stocks with the highest 30% of returns, over the return of an equally weighted portfolio of stocks with the lowest 30% of returns across the last year.

β_4 = Takes a value between 0 and 1, 0 being a portfolio that mirrors the lowest 30% portfolio, 1 being a portfolio that mirrors the highest 30% portfolio.

5 ARBITRAGE PRICING THEORY

5.1 Introduction

Arbitrage Pricing Theory (APT) represents an alternative pricing model to the basic CAPM in which the expected return from a security is determined as a function of several influential factors rather than simply a function of the market risk premium. The basic idea of APT is that the market itself is influenced by many factors (such factors as GDP, inflation, exchange rates, etc), hence the market risk will be made up of the risk of those separate systematic factors. APT is therefore referred to as a multi-factor model.

Like CAPM, APT is for diversified investors who have eliminated the unsystematic risk of their portfolios and are only concerned with the systematic risk (now analysed into several factors).

APT also provides a basis for portfolio strategies where the portfolio is only sensitive to certain of those factors.

Also like with CAPM, APT may also be used as a basis for performance measurement.

In contrast to CAPM, however, APT does not assume that investors evaluate alternatives on the basis of return and risk, only that investors prefer more wealth to less.

5.2 Returns

As noted above, CAPM and APT both give the expected return from a security and it is useful to compare the two ideas.

3: RISK AND RETURN

5.2.1 CAPM

Using basic CAPM, the expected return from a security is given by:

$$r = r_f + \beta(r_m - r_f)$$

where:

r_f = risk-free rate

$r_m - r_f$ = market risk premium, ie the premium return available from market investment

β = beta factor or sensitivity to market movements

That is, CAPM suggests that a security or portfolio is sensitive to just a single factor, the market, and to determine the expected return, we need to know how sensitive we are to this factor (the β) and the premium return associated with this factor ($r_m - r_f$).

We could restate CAPM as:

$$r = r_f + \beta F$$

Where:

r_f = risk-free rate

F = the factor to which we are sensitive, or more particularly the premium return on the factor to which we are sensitive, ie ($r_m - r_f$)

β = beta or sensitivity to that factor

CAPM can, therefore, be viewed as a single-factor model.

5.2.2 APT

The expected return under APT from a security is:

$$r = r_f + b_1 F_1 + b_2 F_2 + b_3 F_3 + ...$$

where:

r_f = risk-free rate

F_1, F_2, F_3 = the factors to which we are sensitive or, more particularly, the premium return on those factors which, ideally, should be uncorrelated

b_1, b_2, b_3 = beta or sensitivity measures to those factors

5.3 Risks

As noted above, APT may be viewed as being an extension of CAPM that considers several factors rather than simply one factor (the market return). This analogy may be extended to cover risks as well as returns.

From basic CAPM, we had:

$$\sigma_i^2 = \sigma_s^2 + \sigma_u^2$$

and:

$$\sigma_s = \beta\sigma_m$$

giving:

$$\sigma_i^2 = \beta^2\sigma_m^2 + \sigma_u^2$$

where:

σ_u = the unsystematic risk of the investment
σ_m = the systematic risk of the factor to which the investment is sensitive
β = measure of sensitivity to that factor

For APT, assuming that all of the systematic risk factors (F_1, F_2, F_3) that we are using are unconnected/ uncorrelated, we have:

$$\sigma_i^2 = \sigma_{s1}^2 + \sigma_{s2}^2 + \sigma_{s3}^2 + \sigma_u^2$$

and:

$$\sigma_{s1} = b_1\sigma_{m1}$$

$$\sigma_{s2} = b_2\sigma_{m2}$$

$$\sigma_{s3} = b_3\sigma_{m3}$$

giving the risk under APT as:

$$\sigma_i^2 = b_1^2\sigma_{m1}^2 + b_2^2\sigma_{m2}^2 + b_3^2\sigma_{m3}^2 + \sigma_u^2$$

where:

σ_u = the unsystematic risk of the investment
σ_{mi} = the systematic risk of factor i to which the investment is sensitive
b_i = measure of sensitivity to that factor

5.4 Factors

One of the limitations of APT is that it does not specify the factors to which the investment is sensitive, however, examples of sensitivity factors to which a security is sensitive may include the following.

3: RISK AND RETURN

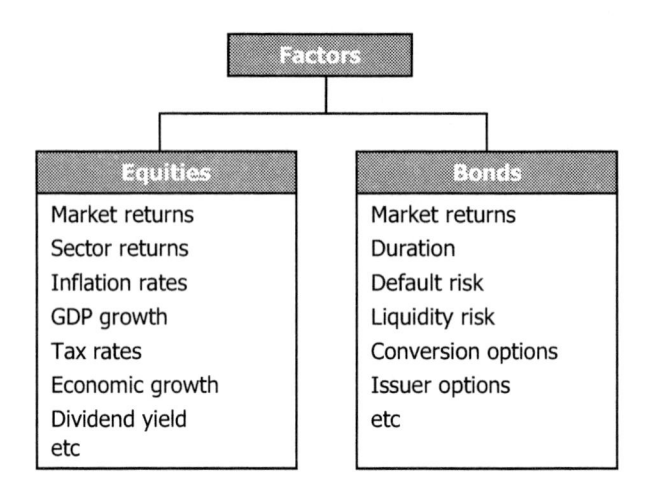

Factors

Equities	Bonds
Market returns	Market returns
Sector returns	Duration
Inflation rates	Default risk
GDP growth	Liquidity risk
Tax rates	Conversion options
Economic growth	Issuer options
Dividend yield	etc
etc	

5.5 Portfolios and APT

When combining securities in a portfolio using CAPM, the portfolio beta is a weighted average of the individual stock betas, which may be expressed as:

$$\beta_p = p_a\beta_a + p_b\beta_b + \ldots + p_n\beta_n$$

Combining beta factors for a portfolio under APT is similarly achieved as a weighted average for each beta factor, ie:

$$b_{pi} = p_a b_{ai} + p_b b_{bi} + \ldots + p_n b_{ni}$$

for each factor (i).

5.6 The theory

APT suggests that based on the various possible securities available and their factor sensitivities, it should be possible to construct a Pure Factor portfolio, ie a portfolio with unit sensitivity to just a single factor. For example, a pure factor 1 portfolio would have an expected return of:

$$r = r_f + F_1$$

By combining such pure factor portfolios, it will be possible to construct a new portfolio with any level of sensitivity to each of the factors, in particular, we will be able to construct a portfolio with the same sensitivity to each factor as any selected security.

If this is achieved, then given that the portfolio and the security have the same risks, they should offer the same returns, otherwise an arbitrage opportunity would exist. As a result, the model gives the expected return from that security for the given risk.

APT also suggests that it may be possible to construct a portfolio with zero sensitivity to any of the factors, in which case we have constructed a risk-free substitute.

5.7 Use of APT

The uses of APT are that we can:

- Construct portfolios with selected sensitivities to certain of the factors.
- Manage the fund to our strengths, optimising the sensitivity to factors that we can predict.
- Immunise the portfolio against uncontrollable/unpredictable factors.

5.8 Assumptions of APT

The assumptions of APT are that:

- Investors prefer higher wealth to lower wealth.

5.9 Limitations of APT

The limitations of APT are:

- APT does not specify the factors to use.
- The problem of determining the relevant beta factors for any security and the stability of those factors.
- The possibility that pure factor portfolios, or a risk-free substitute, may in fact be impossible to construct from the securities available.

3: RISK AND RETURN

Executive Summary

Calculating return

- Arithmetic mean $\bar{r} = \sum pr$ where p is probability of return r.

  $$\bar{r} = \frac{\sum fr}{n}$$ where we have n items.

  Both formulae are best calculated in a table.

  Arithmetic mean is appropriate where we are looking to determine the expected return for a single future period.

- Geometric mean $(1 + r) = \sqrt[n]{(1 + r_1)(1 + r_2)\ldots(1 + r_n)}$

  Geometric mean is appropriate when we are looking to establish or are given the cumulative return R over a longer period.

Calculating risk

- Standard deviation $\sigma = \sqrt{\sum p(r - \bar{r})^2}$ or $\sigma = \sqrt{\dfrac{\sum f(r - \bar{r})^2}{n}}$

- Sample standard deviation $\sigma = \sqrt{\dfrac{\sum f(r - \bar{r})^2}{n - 1}}$

  Either of which is best calculated in a table.

- Variance $= \sigma^2$
- Semi-deviation = Standard deviation of the below-average returns

Correlation

- You need to appreciate the importance of correlation and its relevance to the principle of diversification.

  $$Cor_{ab} = \frac{Cov_{ab}}{\sigma_a \sigma_b}$$

  $$Cov_{ab} = \sum p(r_a - \bar{r}_a)(r_b - \bar{r}_b)$$

3: RISK AND RETURN

Indifference curves

- You need to understand why indifference curves slope upwards with an increasing gradient.
- How to use them to make decisions.
- That they are unique for each individual.

Markowitz Portfolio Theory

- Expected return of a portfolio of two securities.

$$r_{a+b} = p_a r_a + p_b r_b$$

- Total risk (variance) of a portfolio of two securities.

$$\sigma_{a+b}^2 = p_a^2 \sigma_a^2 + p_b^2 \sigma_b^2 + 2 p_a p_b \sigma_a \sigma_b \text{Cor}_{ab}$$

- If $\text{Cor}_{ab} = 1$ then:

$$\sigma_{a+b} = p_a \sigma_a + p_b \sigma_b$$

- If $\text{Cor}_{ab} = -1$ then risk will be eliminated when:

$$\frac{p_a}{p_b} = \frac{\sigma_b}{\sigma_a}$$

CAPM

- You need to understand derivation of the:
  - Efficient frontier
  - Capital market line
  - Market portfolio

- Total risk (variance) of an investment:

$$\sigma_i^2 = \sigma_s^2 + \sigma_u^2$$

- Expected return from a fully diversified portfolio:

$$r = r_f + \beta(r_m - r_f)$$

- $\beta = \dfrac{\sigma_s}{\sigma_m} = \dfrac{\sigma_i \text{Cor}_{im}}{\sigma_m} = \dfrac{\text{Covariance of investment and market}}{\text{Variance of market}}$

  You need to be able to describe how β may be calculated in practice.

- Degree of diversification:

$$R^2 = \frac{\sigma_s^2}{\sigma_i^2}$$

- You need to be:
  - Aware of the assumptions and limitations of CAPM
  - Able to describe extensions to the basic model
  - Outline APT

3: RISK AND RETURN

4 Fixed Income Securities

Contents

1. What is a Bond?..124
2. Pricing Bonds...161
3. Returns Measures – The Yield...170
4. Yield Curve and Term Structure of Interest Rates........................174
5. The Risks of Holding a Bond..180
   Executive Summary...195

4: FIXED INCOME SECURITIES

1 What is a Bond?

1.1 Definition and development

> A bond may be defined as a negotiable debt instrument for a fixed principal amount issued by a borrower for a specific period of time, making a regular payment of interest/coupon to the holder until it is redeemed at maturity, when the principal amount is repaid.

Historically, bonds began as very simple negotiable debt instruments, paying a fixed coupon for a specified period, then being redeemed at face value – a 'straight bond'. In the 1960s and 1970s, bond markets were seen as being investment vehicles for 'widows and orphans'. They were thought to be dull markets with predictable returns and very little in the way of gains to be made from trading.

The bond markets emerged from this shadow during the mid-1970s, when both interest rates and currencies became substantially more volatile. Bonds have emerged since then to be much more complex investments, and there are now a significant number of variations on the basic theme.

While it is perhaps easy to be confused by the variety of 'bells and whistles' which have been introduced into the market in recent years, one should always bear in mind that the vast majority of issues are still straight bonds. The reason for this is that investors are wary of buying investments which they do not fully understand. If an issue is too complex, it will be difficult to market.

1.2 Who issues bonds and why?

Bonds are used by a number of 'individuals' as a means of raising finance. Major bond issuers include the following.

- **Sovereign governments** – who need to raise finance to help them cover any national debt or budget shortfall.
- **Local authorities** – who need to raise finance to help them cover any local budget shortfall.
- **Companies** – who need to raise cash to help them finance business requirements.

Regardless of who the issuer is, there are a number of general characteristics that any bond is likely to have which we will examine next.

1.3 General characteristics

Examining the above definition in a little more detail reveals the general characteristics that a bond may have.

1.3.1 Negotiable instrument

Negotiability means that it is a piece of paper which can be bought and sold. For certain types of bonds, this is easier than for others. Major market government bonds tend to

4: FIXED INCOME SECURITIES

be highly liquid, ie very easy to buy or sell, whereas certain corporate bonds are almost illiquid and are usually held to maturity by the initial buyer.

1.3.2 Nominal value

As we noted above, all bonds are issued for a fixed principal amount or nominal value, which historically represented the amount invested. On most bonds, it is normal to consider a nominal value of $100 (where $ represents the primary unit of currency, $, ¥, €, $ etc) and bond prices are quoted on this basis. Some bonds, however, are quoted in $1,000s so care needs to be taken in the market concerned. This nominal value serves two important purposes:

- Determining the scale of the coupon payments.
- Determining the value of the redemption proceeds.

We discuss both of these purposes below.

1.3.3 Maturity

Initially, all bonds were redeemable at a specific maturity date, which determines when the principal is due for repayment. However, there are now a number of variations we will need to consider. We can subcategorise bonds between:

- Redeemable bonds.
- Irredeemable/Perpetual bonds.

Redeemable bonds

The majority of bonds fall into this category, though there are some subsets we will also need to consider.

- **Single-dated bonds** – bonds which mature at a pre-set date only.
- **Double-dated bonds** – bonds that can be redeemed by the issuer between the specified dates. On a double-dated bond, the earlier date specifies when the issuer may redeem, the later date specifies when the bond must be redeemed.
- **Callable bonds** – where the issuer of the bond is able to redeem the bond at an earlier date, should they wish to do so. Double-dated bonds may be considered as a subset of callable bonds, though callable bonds may have many other features (eg call premiums) and may be callable throughout their lives.
- **Putable bonds** – a more recent innovation which gives the holder the ability to sell the bond back to the issuer at a premium over the face value.

Irredeemable bonds

On irredeemable or perpetual or undated bonds, there is no maturity date and the issuer is under no obligation to redeem the principal sum, though he may have the right to do so if he wishes. On these bonds, the coupon will be paid into perpetuity.

1.3.4 Coupon

The basis for the determination of the coupon on a bond is set before issue, though this does not mean that the value is known at that date. While the vast majority of bonds

4: FIXED INCOME SECURITIES

issued are straights (ie a fixed coupon), there are a number of variants on this theme. In addition, there are bonds whose coupons vary with economic factors. We may, therefore, categorise bond coupons between:

- Pre-determined; and
- Variable.

However the amount is calculated, the full coupon for the period will be paid to the holder of the bond on the ex-dividend date.

Pre-determined coupons

As we have already stated, this category includes, the vast majority of bonds. On these bonds, the gross annual coupon (ie the amount due to be paid in a one-year period, irrespective of the frequency of payment) is specified as a percentage of the nominal value of the bond. Sub-classes here include:

- **Straight/Fixed coupon bonds** – where the coupon is fixed at a set level for the entire life of the bond.
- **Stepped coupon bonds** – where the coupon increases in steps to pre-specified amounts as the bond moves through its life.
- **Zero-coupon bonds** – bonds that carry no coupon and simply redeem at face value at maturity. With such bonds, the investors realise a return since they pay only a fraction of the face value on issue.

Variable coupons

This category includes:

- **Floating rate bonds** – where the coupon varies as interest rates vary.
- **Inflation-linked bonds** – where the coupon and redemption proceeds figures get scaled for the effects of inflation.

1.3.5 Coupon frequency

The frequency of the payment of the coupons is predetermined before issue, normally following the local market conventions. As a result, all investors will be (or should be) aware of those dates.

Conventions regarding the frequency of payment differ between the various bond markets. Some markets have a convention of paying semi-annual coupons, as is the case in Japan, the UK and the US, whereas other markets, in particular the Eurobond market, France and Germany, pay coupons on an annual basis.

1.3.6 Recipient

The norm is that the holder of the bond receives all of the asset flows from that bond throughout its life to the maturity date. There are, however, some markets where it is possible to strip the coupons and the bond apart so that the holder of the underlying bond may receive the redemption proceeds, while the coupons (the 'tint') are paid to another party.

4: FIXED INCOME SECURITIES

1.3.7 Redemption at maturity

As we noted above, it is possible for bonds to be issued which will not redeem at maturity, known as irredeemables. Most bonds are, however, redeemed though, once again, there are a few variations to be aware of. The primary consideration here is the form that the redemption proceeds takes which may be either:

- Cash; or
- Other assets.

Cash redemption proceeds

Once more, the vast majority of bonds fall into this category whereby the bonds are redeemed in cash at maturity. This redemption may be:

- **At par value** – redeemed at the nominal value of the bond at the redemption date.
- **At a premium** – redeemed at a specified premium above the nominal value of the bond at the redemption date.

Other assets

Instead of obliging the issuer to repay cash at maturity, the bond may offer the holder the choice between normal cash redemption proceeds and some other asset, such as:

- An alternative bond of a later maturity.
- Shares issued by a corporation.

1.4 The Non-Euroland Markets

1.4.1 Australian bond markets

Introduction

Segmentation of the Australian bond market

- State government 34%
- Corporates and Kangaroos 20%
- Central government 46%

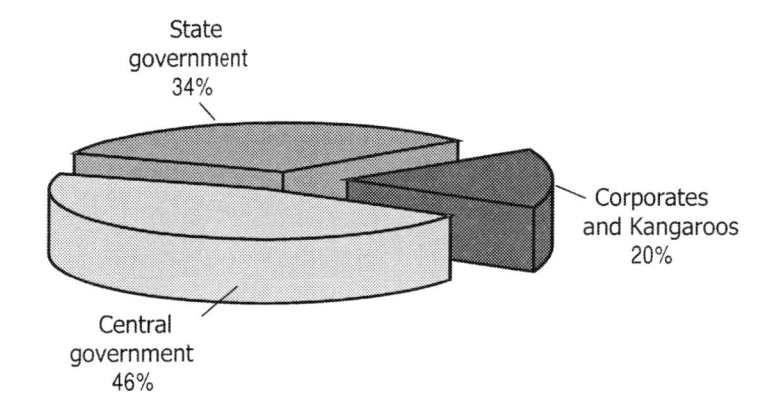

4: FIXED INCOME SECURITIES

The government bond market

The Australian Office of Financial Management (AOFM) manages Australian government debt and cash balances via the Reserve Bank of Australia.

Types of issue

The main types of issue are:

- **Treasury notes** – short-term discount instruments with maturities less than one year.
- **Treasury bonds** – coupon-paying securities with maturities up to 15 years.

By convention the coupon frequency is semi-annual and accrues on an Actual/Actual basis.

In addition to the conventional bonds, there are also Treasury Indexed Bonds (TIBs), which are capital-indexed bonds. In this case, only the capital balance is affected by the actual indexation process. The coupon is simply then calculated on the basis of the set rate as applied to the adjusted capital value. These bonds pay their coupon quarterly. As with most index-linked markets, the liquidity is relatively low.

In addition, there are also Treasury Adjustable Rate Bonds (TABs). These are floating rate instruments and are issued normally with relatively short-dated maturities (three- and five-year issues are conventional).

Primary market

The debt is issued by way of a monthly competitive public tender. While relatively large in the past, the sales of these issues have reduced due to the strength of the government's fiscal position.

Secondary market

The secondary market is relatively unstructured with no formal market makers.

As in the UK, the introduction of a full repo market has diminished the level of activity in these contracts, which at one stage was greater than the cash market.

Trading, settlement and holding tax

Settlement is normally on a T + 3 basis. There is still a withholding tax of 10% applicable to overseas residents. This withholding tax is zero for UK and US financial institutions.

Other bond markets

State government bonds

State governments are also significant borrowers in this market. The range of products that they use is very much the same as the Commonwealth government, including the use of index-linked bonds. The States were the main instigators of the surge in asset-backed

4: FIXED INCOME SECURITIES

bonds in the 1980s as they used bonds to finance projects such as State housing schemes. Each State has its own Central Borrowing Authority or CBA.

In addition to closed auctions (to a restricted panel of bidders), the debt is released by way of taps into the secondary markets and placements.

The secondary market in these securities is relatively limited with only modest activity levels.

Corporate bond markets

The corporate bond market has remained relatively small, however, with the decline in the financing requirements of the government there are signs of a resurgence in corporate bond issuance. In particular, there has been a buoyant market in asset-backed securities.

The Australian equivalent of the Yankee bond market is Kangaroos. These bonds are issued by non-Australian borrowers and are exclusively sold to Australian investors. In addition to Kangaroos, there are Matildas. Matildas are bonds issued by overseas borrowers into the Australian and international markets simultaneously, in essence a global bond issue.

Bond derivatives

The Sydney Futures Exchange offers both futures and options on both the three-year and ten-year bonds.

1.4.2 Canadian bond market

Introduction

Segmentation of the Canadian bond market

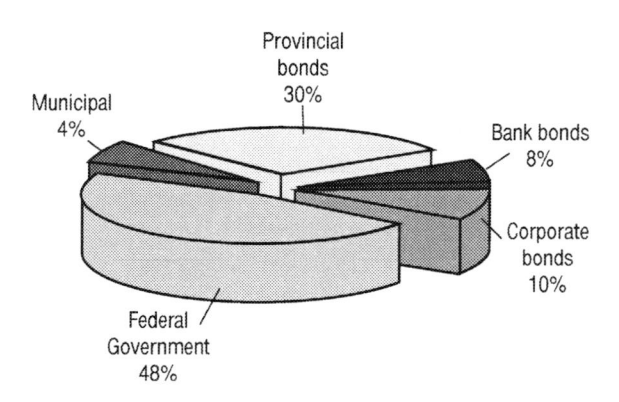

- Provincial bonds 30%
- Municipal 4%
- Bank bonds 8%
- Corporate bonds 10%
- Federal Government 48%

The government bond market

The Canadian government bond market is relatively small compared to other members of the G7. The principal reason for this is that the Canadian system operates on a much more decentralised basis than most other countries. In essence, the Provinces act as clearly distinct economic units with their own tax-raising and borrowing powers.

Types of issue

The two major types of issue are:

- **Government of Canada Treasury Bills** – short-term discount instruments.
- **Government of Canada Marketable Bonds** – coupon-paying bonds typically issues with maturities of 2, 5, 10 or 30 years.

The bonds are quoted on a clean price basis with accrued interest on the semi-annual coupon calculated Actual/Actual.

In line with many countries who have had a problem with inflation, the Canadian government has issued Real Return (index-linked) bonds. These bonds track the Canadian CPI (Consumer Price Index), pay coupons semi-annually and trade on dirty prices. The inflation time delay is three months, making these bonds an effective hedge against inflation.

Primary market

Bonds are issued by auction, administered by the Bank of Canada on behalf of the Department of Finance.

There is an effective 14-day ex-coupon period. However, all trades are done on a cum coupon basis. Therefore, any seller of bonds during the ex-period must deliver not only the bond, but also a post-dated cheque for the coupon payment.

Secondary market

Given the size of the outstanding market, the secondary market is perhaps surprisingly liquid.

Trading, settlement and withholding taxes

Bonds are settled on a T+3 basis. A withholding tax of 10% is applicable to most major overseas investors.

Other bond markets

As mentioned above, a large proportion of finance for the Canadian State is provincial debt raised by the quasi-autonomous provinces. Much of this has in the past been raised via the Euromarkets. In particular, the larger borrowers such as Quebec have issued global bonds that qualify as domestic and euro securities.

Derivatives

The Montreal Exchange trades futures on the two-year and ten-year Government of Canada bonds with notional coupons of 4% and 6% respectively. They also trade options on the ten-year bond.

Economic linkage to the US

The Canadian economy has always been regarded as an adjunct to the US market, and given the size of the US economy and the strong trading links between the two economies, there will always tend to be a relatively high correlation.

1.4.3 Japanese bond market

Introduction

Segmentation of the Japanese bond market

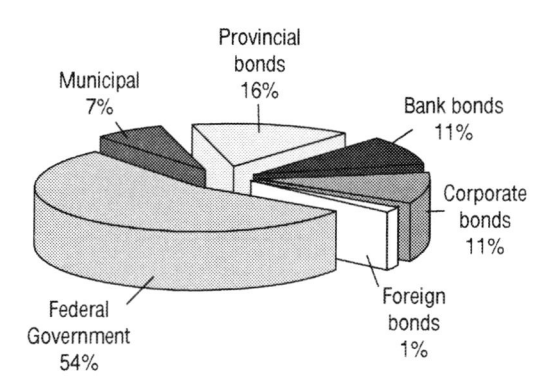

- Municipal 7%
- Provincial bonds 16%
- Bank bonds 11%
- Corporate bonds 11%
- Foreign bonds 1%
- Federal Government 54%

The Japanese government bond market

The Japanese government bond market is the second largest in the world. The market has basically grown from nothing in the early 1960s to its current size. From that point on, the government has consistently borrowed money initially to finance investment in the nation's infrastructure.

However, more recently the poor economic conditions within Japan have led to a need to borrow in order to finance fiscal injections into the economy.

The Japanese bond market is dominated by government bonds. This domination is not in terms of volume, where Japanese Government Bonds (JGBs) account for only half of the market, but in the secondary market where they account for the majority of the secondary market trading.

Initially, the market was dominated by domestic investors, however, due both to the size of issuance and the growing importance of the yen, the market has attracted increasing numbers of overseas investors. To aid this internationalisation of the market the government has introduced a number of liberalising measures, though it is still impossible to settle and deliver JGBs outside Japan.

The Japanese market has in the past been regarded as one of the least developed and most 'investor unfriendly' markets amongst the major government bond markets. The Bank of Japan was, until recently, one of the least independent of all the central banks. However, steps have been taken in order to bring the market into line with the other major markets. These steps have included a greater level of say for the BoJ in the establishment of policy.

It is still the case that many international investors regard the Japanese market as a hostile environment and therefore tend to avoid it. Only 5% of JGBs are owned by non-Japanese citizens.

Types of issue

There are three main types of instrument issued.

- **Treasury bills** – Issued with three- and six-month maturities, these are discount securities issued via public auction twice a month. The market is not active and external investors only have limited access.
- **Medium term Notes** – These are two-year maturity notes that are issued via an auction every two months.
- **Government bonds** – These are conventional debt securities predominantly with a maturity of ten years. The government does issue 'super longs' that have a maturity of 20 years. The Ministry of Finance has also placed a number of 30-year zero-coupon bonds in the past.

All prices are clean and accrued interest on the semi-annual coupon is calculated on the Actual/365 convention. While JGBs do not trade ex-dividend as such, it is not possible to settle in the 14 days prior to coupon payment dates.

In March 2004, Japan issued inflation-linked bonds (ten-year). They are structured similarly to UK ILGs, with a three-month inflation lag. They are not available to overseas investors.

The JGBs are referred to as:

- **Construction** – these are bonds used to finance development of the infrastructure.
- **Refinancing** – bonds issued to repay maturing debt.
- **Deficit financing** – bonds issued to cover a budget deficit.

In essence, they are all the same semi-annual government bonds. The only difference is that the deficit financing stocks must be approved by the parliament. All new issues now pay their interest on set dates. JGBs can be in either registered or bearer form, and can be converted within two business days.

Primary market

The issue process is more complex than the structure used in most markets with a monthly auction/syndicate issue. In Japan, the syndicate (still dominated by the large investment banks) is allocated 40% of the issue, with 60% sold via public auction. The terms of the issue are set by the Ministry of Finance having taken soundings in the market from the syndicate.

4: FIXED INCOME SECURITIES

Secondary market

JGBs trade on both the Tokyo Stock Exchange and the Broker Broker (OTC) market settling on a T+3 basis. The market does tend to focus on the 'benchmark' issues, with occasionally 90% of the volume taking place in that stock. However, any issues that are deliverable into the JGB future will possess a fair degree of liquidity.

While a form of repo market ('Gensaki') does exist, it is not as liquid or as important as in many other markets.

Trading, settlement and tax

TSE transactions settle after three days with the OTC taking nine days or more, following a complicated settlement timetable. Settlement is conducted through book entry systems. Withholding tax is levied at 10% where tax treaties exist (most major developed countries), 15% where they do not. Recently, in an attempt to encourage more external participation, withholding taxes for overseas owners have been removed.

Other bond markets

There are a number of important issuers other than the government. In the form of 'quasi-government' there are the agencies and municipal stocks (11%). The banks are large borrowers (19%), using the funds raised in this way to lend to their customers.

As the market in JGBs has become more international, some of this interest has filtered through to the other more domestically-oriented markets.

International borrowers are able to access the domestic pool of savings through the issue of Samurai (publicly issued yen bonds) and Shibosai (yen bonds issued via private placement). This is not an important part of the market, with much more being issued in the form of euro-yen (for much the same reasons as the decline of the UK bulldog market).

In addition, there are Daimyo bonds, which are in effect a cross between the Samurai and the euro-yen; domestic bonds with the ability to settle through the normal Eurobond channels. Trading in all of these markets is meagre compared with the volume and liquidity of the JGB market.

Bond derivatives

JGBs Futures are available on the Toyko Stock exchange (TSE) and Eurex.

1.4.4 UK bond markets

Introduction

Segmentation of the UK bond market

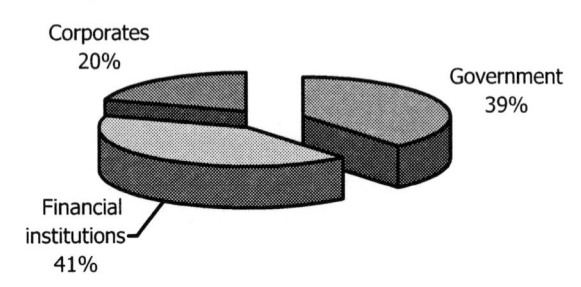

- Corporates 20%
- Government 39%
- Financial institutions 41%

The government bond market

The Bank of England is the central bank in the UK which historically issued and managed gilts on behalf of the government, however this is now undertaken by the Debt Management Office (DMO). The prime role of the Bank of England now is to set interest rates in order to control inflation and to maintain a stable financial system in the UK.

Types of issue

Main issues

There are two main types of instrument issued:

- **Treasury bills** – These normally have a maturity of three months, however occasional issues have been as short as one month and as long as six months.
- **Treasury gilt-edged securities (gilts)** – These are coupon-paying securities and are issued with initial maturities of between five and 30 years.

All UK bonds are quoted on a clean basis. The coupon-paying bonds all pay semi-annual coupons and adopt the Actual/Actual basis for accrued interest.

The majority of gilts in issue pay a fixed coupon that is set at issue, usually reflecting market rates. There are also a number of index-linked gilts in issue whose returns are linked to the RPI. Finally, there have been occasional issues of floating rate gilts whose coupons are based on prevailing interest rates.

Primary market

The prime responsibility of the DMO is to ensure that the government is able to borrow the money it requires to fund the Public Sector Net Cash Requirement (PSNCR). The most important source of financing open to the government is the gilts market.

The DMO is also the lead regulator in the gilts market and its objective is to ensure that the gilts market remains solvent, liquid and, above all, fair.

4: FIXED INCOME SECURITIES

The DMO controls the issue of gilts into the marketplace and uses a variety of methods depending upon the circumstances it faces at any time.

The competitive auction

Since 1987, the primary issuance method became the competitive auctions system.

In a competitive auction investors apply for gilts at a price which they are prepared to pay. The DMO issues the gilts to those investors who apply at the highest prices.

Secondary market

Participants and operation

Central to the operation of the market are the **Gilt-Edged Market-Makers (GEMMs)**. Their role is to ensure that two-way quotes exist at all times for all gilts and these quotes are available through the London Stock Exchange. GEMMs are allowed to enter the market by the Debt Management Office. Once accepted as a gilt-edged market-maker, the firm is obliged to make a market in **all conventional gilts** at a size deemed appropriate by the DMO.

For index-linked stocks, because the market is less liquid, the DMO has authorised a more limited list of market-makers.

The strips market

The strips market in the UK began on 8 December 1997 and all strippable gilts are currently conventional fixed coupon instruments. This followed the successful development of a US strips market in the 1980s.

Trading, settlement and taxes

All bonds are traded on a clean price basis.

Gilt settlement occurs on the business day following the transaction. Market professionals such as GEMMs settle electronically through CREST, a subsidiary of Euroclear UK & Ireland Ltd.

There are no withholding taxes on UK government securities, which makes them particularly attractive to overseas investors.

Other bond markets

Unlike conventional government bonds, which are predominantly redeemed in bullet form, these issues repay a portion of the capital with each coupon payment. In addition to these quasi-governmental organisations, there are also Municipal bonds or 'Muni's' issued by States and districts. These obviously have a higher credit risk and are less liquid. Yields are consequently greater.

4: FIXED INCOME SECURITIES

Domestic corporate bond markets

The biggest issuers of bonds in the UK are financial institutions, though corporate issues are also quite significant. These non-government issues are mainly bought by institutions rather than individuals whose emphasis seems to be in equities.

For domestic bonds there is only a limited secondary market. The majority of issues are never actively traded. Consequently, the market is not particularly structured with very little involvement of market makers.

Bond derivatives

NYSE LIFFE trade futures on a notional 6% long-dated gilt, and options are available on these futures contracts.

1.4.5 US bond markets

Introduction

Segmentation of the US bond markets

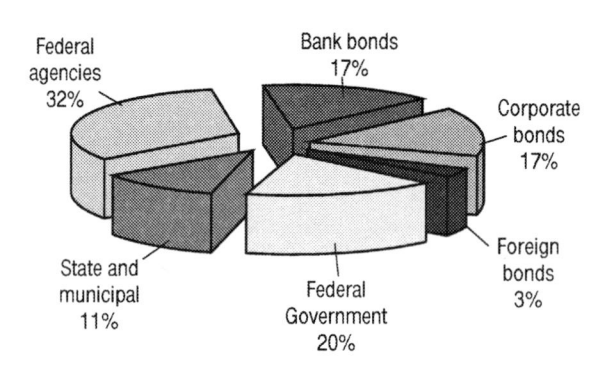

- Federal agencies 32%
- Bank bonds 17%
- Corporate bonds 17%
- Foreign bonds 3%
- Federal Government 20%
- State and municipal 11%

The government bond market

The US government bond market is the largest in the world having expanded rapidly in the 1980s. This size is evident in both the quantity of issuance in the primary market and volumes of activity in the secondary market.

The market is not dissimilar in structure from the UK gilts market. This is due to the UK reforms that have been designed to bring the two markets into line. Indeed, the general direction of all government bond markets has been towards greater 'fungibility' or similarity, with the US being seen as the role model.

The Fed

The key player in the market is the Federal Reserve (the 'Fed'). As the US central bank, the Fed, through **open market operations**, manipulates liquidity to control US monetary policy. The Fed is largely independent, the only political involvement comes in the appointment of the board. To this extent, many argue that the Fed is less independent than the Bundesbank. However, in many ways this possibility of political influence is more apparent than actual. For if a President were to try to 'rig' the Fed, then it is likely that the markets would react unfavourably and the benefits of credibility would be eroded very quickly.

The Fed's own publications summarise the objectives of the Board of Governors and the 12 Federal Reserve banks as being the following.

- Conducting the nation's monetary policy by influencing money and credit conditions in the economy in pursuit of full employment and stable prices. However, the clear focus of policy is towards the latter of these two objectives in the belief that price stability is a prerequisite for higher levels of employment.
- Supervising and regulating banking institutions to ensure the safety and soundness of the nation's banking and financial system and to protect the credit rights of consumers.
- Maintaining the stability of the financial system and containing the systemic risk that may arise in financial markets.
- Providing certain financial services to the US government, the public, financial institutions, and foreign official institutions, including playing a major role in operating the nation's payments system.

The Treasury

The Treasury is part of government and responsible for the issuance of debt in order to fund the deficit.

Types of issue

Main issues

There are three main types of instrument issued:

- **Treasury bills (T-bills)** – These have a maturity of three months to one year and are issued at a discount to face value.
- **Treasury notes (T-notes)** – These are coupon securities and are issued with initial maturities of between two and ten years.
- **Treasury bonds (T-bonds)** – These are again coupon securities and are issued with an initial life of over ten years.

All US bonds are quoted on a clean basis. The coupon-paying bonds all pay semi-annual coupons and adopt the Actual/Actual basis for accrued interest.

There is a tendency for the market to focus into the liquid issues referred to as the '**on-the-run bond**' or '**hot runs**'. These benchmarks are normally the most recent issues; other issues are referred to as 'trade by appointment'.

Treasury Inflation Protected Securities (TIPS)

In 1997, the US government issued Treasury Inflation Protected Securities or index-linked bonds for the first time. In part, this was seen as an unusual decision by the markets, who initially viewed it as a worrying sign with regard to the government's commitment to low inflation. The justification is that, far from undermining the government's commitment to low inflation, it actually reinforces it by ensuring that if inflation does take off, government finance cost will likewise rise in nominal terms.

On TIPS, the principle value is adjusted for changes in the CPI to reflect inflation and the coupon is a fixed rate payable on this adjusted value.

The bonds are semi-annual paying with quotations on a dirty basis.

Primary market

The US Treasury is responsible for the issuance of new securities. Issuance takes place on a regular calendar with weekly issues of three- or six-month Treasury bills, monthly issues of one-year bills and two- and five-year notes, and quarterly issues in set cycles of longer dated stocks. These quarterly issues are referred to as the quarterly refunding. The quarterly refunding simply allows for the Treasury to clarify the current state of the government's finances and to signal changes for the future. The extent of each auction is announced a week in advance of the auction.

In 2001, the government stopped issuing the 30-year T-bond. Ostensibly this was designed to reflect the reduced funding needs of the State. However, increased demands from pension funds and other long-term investors allied with low long-term yields led to their reintroduction in 2006.

T-bonds are issued through competitive auction. Two- and five-year T-notes are issued using a uniform price auction, or tender, where each bidder pays the highest accepted yield (ie the lowest accepted price).

The competitive auction

The competitive auction in the US is basically the system that was introduced into the UK in 1987. The principal differences are that, in the US, the primary dealers are obliged to bid for stock and bids are on a yield basis (rather than price in the UK). Non-competitive bids are accepted and they **will** be allocated stock at the average of the successful competitive bids.

The lowest accepted bid is known as the '**stop-out yield**' and the difference between this and the average price is the '**tail**'. The amount by which bids exceed the issue is referred to as the '**cover**'.

Secondary market

Participants and operation

Central to the operation of the market are the **primary dealers**. These firms are the market-makers. They are authorised to conduct trades by the Fed and are obliged to make markets in all issues. As with the UK, there are inter dealer brokers (IDBs) to facilitate the taking and unwinding of large positions. There are no money brokers, but there is a full repo market.

While the stocks are listed on the New York Stock Exchange, the market is effectively an over-the-counter market. The market is perhaps the most truly global market and has deep liquidity across the maturity range.

The strips market

The development of a full strips market in the US during the early 1980s has enabled the investors in the US Treasuries market to create highly structured strategies based on the movement of the yield curve, and achieve more precise matching of asset and liability cash flows.

Trading, settlement and taxes

All bonds are traded on a clean price basis excepts for TIPS.

Settlement takes place predominantly through the Fed's wire (book entry system). Settlement is by convention for the next business day, although same day settlement is possible.

There are no withholding taxes on US government securities, which makes them particularly attractive to overseas investors.

Other bond markets

Federal agencies

These are quasi-governmental institutions established to fill gaps in the US financial markets. They are backed by the guarantee of the US government via the Fed and are therefore riskless. However, they may well trade at a slight premium to the equivalent US government securities principally due to lower liquidity.

The main federal agencies are:

- Federal National Mortgage Association (FNMA) ('Fannie Mae')
- Government National Mortgage Association (GNMA) ('Ginnie Mae')
- Federal Home Loan Mortgage Corporation (FMLMC) ('Freddy Mac')
- Federal Home Loan Bank System (FMLB)
- Federal Farm Credit Bank (FFCB)

Prior to its privatisation in 2004, a further federal agency was the Student Loan Association (Sallie Mae), now the SLM Corporation.

Unlike conventional government bonds, which are predominantly redeemed in bullet form, these issues repay a portion of the capital with each coupon payment. In addition to these quasi-governmental organisations, there are also Municipal bonds or 'Muni's' issued by States and districts. These obviously have a higher credit risk and are less liquid. Yields are consequently greater.

Domestic corporate bond markets

Unlike the UK, the US corporate sector has been able to borrow substantial sums via the issue of debt securities. In part, this has been forced upon them by the highly fragmented nature of the domestic banking market. Equally, however, investors are willing to hold corporate debt as part of their portfolios in a way in which UK investors are not.

Yankee bonds

Ever since 1945, the dollar has been the key international currency, and there has been substantial interest from non-US firms in raising dollar finance.

A Yankee is a dollar-denominated bond issued in the US by an overseas borrower. Given that Eurodollar bonds may not be sold into the US markets until they have **seasoned** (a period of 40 days), there is still a divide between the Euromarket and the domestic market. Apart from the access to a different investor base, the market also allows issuers to raise longer-term finance, since the American domestic investors are prepared to accept longer maturities.

These domestic and international bonds trade in the same way as shares.

US private placement market

In the US, corporates are allowed to issue bonds into the private placement market without seeking full SEC registration. This access to the market is available to both domestic and overseas issuers, though the market is dominated by US domestic issuers who have chosen not to enter the public market.

The buy side of the market is restricted to certain institutional investors (primarily insurance companies) who are predominantly 'buy and hold' investors. The market is therefore less liquid than the full domestic market, since issues tend to be held to redemption, thereby limiting the secondary market. This thin secondary market is itself a discouragement to potential investors such as the mutual investment funds.

Reflecting the nature of the market as in effect a one-to-one contract, new issue terms are negotiated between the issuer and the lender. This process can take up to eight weeks to complete. Equally, as a consequence, borrowers tend to have to pay a premium over the public market yields. However, they do not have the cost of seeking a credit rating, nor are they bound by the rules of the SEC.

Bond derivatives

CBOT trade futures on the two-year, five-year, ten-year and thirty-year bonds/notes, and options are available on the five-year, ten-year and thirty-year notes/bonds via CBOE.

1.5 The Euroland bond markets

With effect from 1 January 1999, the separate bond markets of those nations participating in the first wave of EMU became one single market. This market ranks on as the third biggest market in the world.

4: FIXED INCOME SECURITIES

Relative share of the Euroland bond market

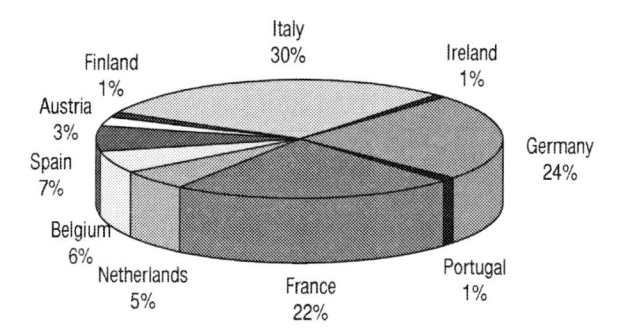

- Italy 30%
- Finland 1%
- Austria 3%
- Spain 7%
- Belgium 6%
- Netherlands 5%
- France 22%
- Portugal 1%
- Germany 24%
- Ireland 1%

The immediate impact of this was that debt previously denominated in individual currency units was redenominated into euros.

Initially, the markets continued much as they had done before, although all of them now share the same currency.

However, reforms rapidly pushed the markets towards greater levels of harmonisation with regard to the structures of the individual markets. All nations moved to the Actual/Actual basis for accrued interest.

1.5.1 Dutch bond market

Introduction

Segmentation of the Dutch bond market

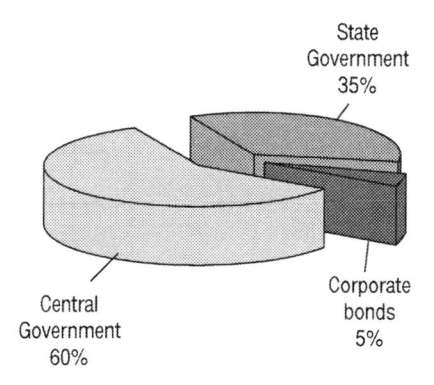

- State Government 35%
- Central Government 60%
- Corporate bonds 5%

Government bonds

The Dutch domestic market in bonds is dominated by the Dutch government bond issues, which represent over 60% of the total outstanding amount.

4: FIXED INCOME SECURITIES

Types of issue

There are two primary issues:

- **Dutch Treasury Certificates (DIC)** – short-dated discounts instruments.
- **Dutch State Loans (DSL)** – longer-term coupon-paying bonds.

The coupon-paying bonds pay an annual coupon and apply the Actual/Actual basis for accrued interest.

Primary markets

All new issues are undertaken by the Dutch State Treasury Agency in the form of bullets. The main insurance method is via an auction though smaller issues may be by direct tap into the secondary market.

Secondary market

The government issues trade freely on both the Amsterdam Exchange (ASX) and the Amsterdam Interprofessional Market (AIM).

Trading, settlement and withholding tax

The settlement convention is three business days with all stock being held in dematerialised form. Interest is paid on an annual basis on either the 1st or 15th of the month. There is no withholding tax for overseas investors.

Other bonds

Local authorities are also substantial borrowers in the capital markets. In addition, the banks issue a variety of bonds into the debt market. These tend to dominate the non-government bond market by virtue of their high credit rating. While other corporates do issue bonds, they represent only a small proportion of the market.

1.5.2 French bond market

Introduction

Segmentation of the French bond market

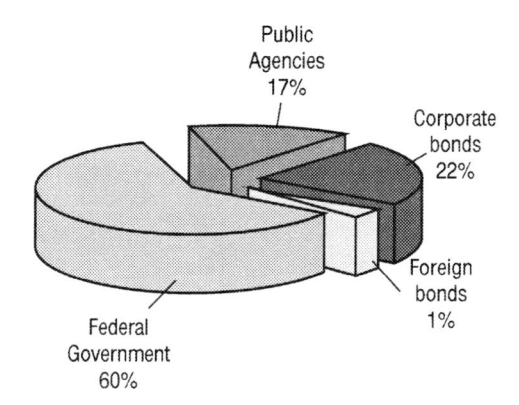

- Public Agencies 17%
- Corporate bonds 22%
- Foreign bonds 1%
- Federal Government 60%

Government bonds

The Banque de France is the central bank in France and the issue of French government bonds is undertaken by the Agence France Tresor, the French debt agency.

Types of issue

There are three main types of instrument issued:

- **Bons du Trésor à Taux Fixe (BTFs)** – These are the French T-bills, issued at a discount to face value and with maturities of 13, 26 and 52 weeks.
- **Bons du Trésor à Taux Fixe et Intéret Annuel (BTANs)** – These are fixed rate coupon-paying Treasury notes issued with maturities of between two and five years.
- **Obligations Assimilables du Trésor (OATs)** – These are the conventional coupon-paying government bonds with maturities of between seven and 30 years.

The coupon paying bonds all pay annual coupons and adopt the Actual/Actual basis for accrued interest.

Variable rate OATs are also available and these are linked to either long- or short-term reference rates. Since the late 1990s the French have been issuing index-linked OATs, once again following the Canadian model, with a three-month delay in the indexation period.

Primary market

Debt is issued by way of monthly auctions to the public. There is, however, a syndicate of banks that the government uses to underwrite issues in particular situations. Issuance takes place in accordance with a preset calendar.

- **BTFs** – Auctioned on weekly basis. The issue is announced on Thursday and the auction takes place on Monday. All bids are on yield basis.
- **BTANs** – Auctions take place on the third working Thursday of the month. The stock to be offered is announced on the Monday preceding the issue. During a six-month period all issues are into the same two- or five-year stock. These stocks are the benchmarks and attract the strongest liquidity. All bids are on a price basis (in basis points).
- **OATs** – Auctions take place on the first Thursday of the month on much the same basis as BTANs. Settlement of the stock purchased in the auction takes place on the 25th of the month.

Secondary markets

The market is focused around market makers who are obliged to make continuous two-way prices in all stock and participate in the auctions. Only the OATs are listed on the Bourse. A substantial amount of trading takes place on the over-the-counter market.

There is an active repo market in French government debt. In addition, the French market has a liquid and efficient strips market.

Trading, settlement and tax

All issues are now in book entry form with no physical delivery. The records are maintained either through RELIT, the domestic system, or Euroclear or Clearstream. Settlement is on a three-day basis.

Settlement is either cash or, for external holders of the bonds, follows the normal Euroclear and Clearstream timetable. Full facilities are available for investors to hold French government debt through Clearstream and Euroclear. BTANs settle on the T+1 basis for domestic holders.

There are no withholding taxes applicable to overseas investors for French bonds.

Other bonds markets

As noted above, over half the market is made up of debt issues from the public corporations. These stocks are not, for the most part, guaranteed by the government, but the corporations concerned do possess strong credit ratings. They have established their own market structure in order to facilitate trading in their stocks. All issues are by way of a placing through a syndicate of mainly local banks.

Gradual deregulation is easing up the market. The removal of stock queues should have the effect of allowing faster access to the market and therefore enable firms to exploit swap opportunities.

4: FIXED INCOME SECURITIES

1.5.3 German bond market

Introduction

Segmentation of the German bond market

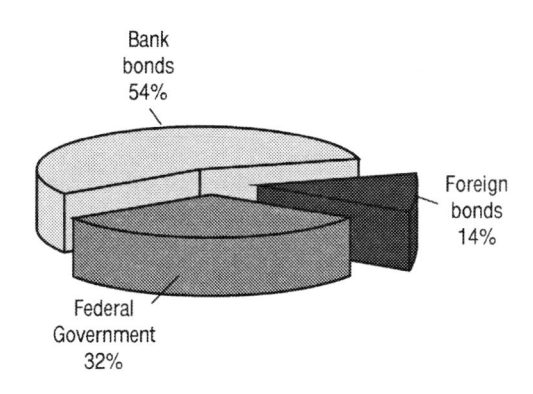

- Bank bonds 54%
- Federal Government 32%
- Foreign bonds 14%

The government bond market

The German bond market, including government bonds, domestic bonds and Eurobonds, is one of the largest in the world. In contrast to the UK, the Germans have a strong corporate debt market and a much weaker equity market. The bulk of finance for industry is provided through the banks, either as lenders or shareholders, with debt securities other than Eurobonds being less significant. Within the context of debt issuance, it is the banks that issue bonds and then lend on the money to the corporate sector.

The key participant is the Bundesbank (Buba), the German central bank. Unlike many of the other central banks, Buba is totally outside political control. The role of Buba is to generate price and currency stability and the politicians have to operate within any constraints that this creates. The Bundesbank is obliged to support the overall direction of Federal Government policy to the extent that this does not conflict with price stability.

Types of issue

There are four main type of instruments issued:

- **BU-Bills** – six-month bills issued at a discount to face value.

- **Bundesschatzanweisungen (Schatze) and Kassenobligationen** – coupon-paying bonds with maturities of between two and six years.

- **Bobls (Bundesobligationen)** – These are medium-term issues with lives of up to five years. Initially designed for the domestic market, they have been opened to foreign investment since 1989.

4: FIXED INCOME SECURITIES

- **Bunds (Bundesanleihen)** – coupon-paying bonds with normal maturities of ten years.

Primary market

Primary issuance of bunds is achieved by way of competitive auction.

The primary market in Bobls is still restricted to domestic purchasers and takes the form of a **tap** directly into the secondary market. Once the stock has been listed, then the market is open to all investors.

Secondary market

There are three main domestic routes for trading:

- The domestic stock exchanges (mainly Frankfurt).
- The over-the-counter market.
- The domestic computerised market known as IBIS.

The market is focused on those stocks that are deliverable into the futures contracts of Eurex.

In May 1997, the Bundesbank introduced a domestic strip facility with regard to the Bund market. In addition there is an active domestic repo market.

Trading, settlement and withholding taxes

Settlement date for domestic bond deals is three banking days after the day of dealing. There are no withholding taxes applicable to overseas investors.

Other bond markets

The bulk of the banking sector bond issuance comes in the form of Pfandbriefe. These are effectively bonds collateralised against portfolios of loans. Offenliche Pfandbriefe are backed by loans to the public sector and Hypotheken Pfandbriefe are backed by mortgages. Traditionally, while being very secure, they have offered higher yields than bunds by virtue of their illiquidity. This is beginning to change.

The domestic bank bonds are normally issued via placings. A substantial proportion of the market is comprised of Pfandbriefe (mortgage bonds) and Offentliche Pfandbriefe (municipal bonds). The yield spreads on these issues are more a reflection of the liquidity in the market than credit.

Bond derivatives

Eurex trades futures and options based on the Schatze, Bolb and Bund. These are effectively bond derivatives for the entire Euro zone.

1.5.4 Italian bond market

Introduction

Segmentation of the Italian bond market

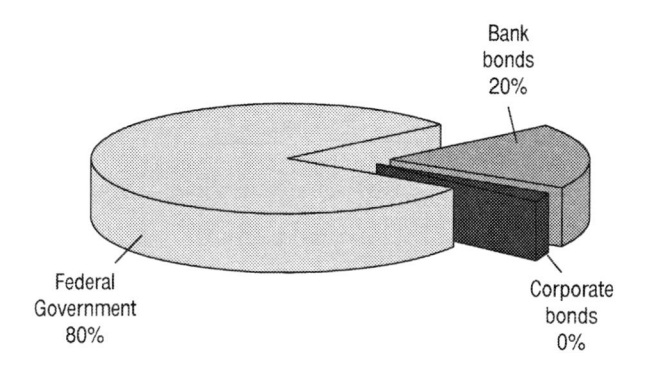

- Federal Government 80%
- Bank bonds 20%
- Corporate bonds 0%

Government bonds

Italian government bonds are issued by the Dipartimento del Tesoro, the Italian debt management agency.

Types of issue

There are three main types of issue:

- **Buoni Ordinari del Tesoro (BOT)** – discount instruments with maturities of three, six and twelve months.

- **Buoni del Tesoro Poliennari (BTPs)** – coupon-paying bonds issued into the five- to seven-year maturity ranges, although some maturities of ten years have now been issued with limited issuance at the 30-year mark.

- **Certificati di Credito del Tesoro (CCTs)** – a form of floating rate notes. The coupon rate is established by adding a fixed margin to the BTP yield, as determined in the market. The normal maturity of these issues is between five and ten years.

The coupon-paying bonds all pay a semi-annual coupon and adopt the Actual/Actual basis for accrued interest.

While the BTPs and CCTs are bullets, the government has also issued Certificati del Tesoro con Opzione (CTOs), which are six-year bonds with an optional redemption after three years. The redemption is at par multiplied by the difference between 100 and the issue price.

In common with the UK, the Italian authorities have also issued index-linked CTRs. In 1995, the authorities commenced the issuance of zero-coupon bonds targeted primarily at the retail sector called Certificati del Tesoro, a zero coupon (CTZs).

4: FIXED INCOME SECURITIES

Primary market

BOTs are auctioned twice monthly, at the middle and end of the month. The auction is run on a competitive basis, unlike the issue of BTPs, which is conducted through a monthly uniform price auction or tender.

Secondary market

Trading takes place through one of three markets. The Stock Exchange is by far the smallest of the three and lists the issues on call. In response to the inadequacy of the stock market, an OTC market was established using Reuters screens to display price information. This too has proved to be unsuccessful and now the market has switched to the Telematico market, where primary dealers focus the liquidity of the market. Maximum liquidity is generated in the new issues immediately post-issue.

Trading, settlement and tax

Settlement takes place on the basis of three business days for domestically settled trades. Settlement takes place in book entry form through specified accounts held at the Bank of Italy. As with most European bond markets, settlement facilities are available through Euroclear and Clearstream on a T + 3 basis.

There are no withholding taxes on Italian government bonds.

1.5.5 Spanish bond market

Introduction

Segmentation of the Spanish bond markets

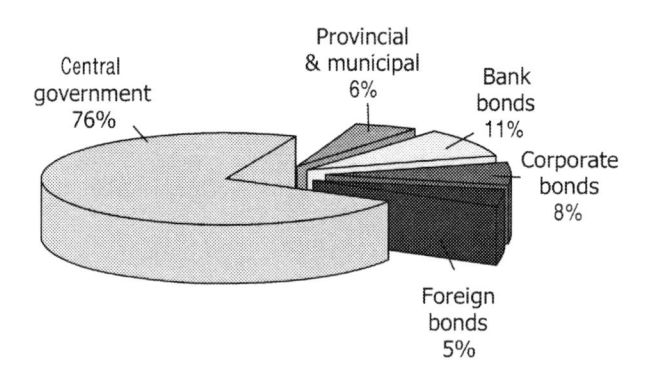

- Central government 76%
- Provincial & municipal 6%
- Bank bonds 11%
- Corporate bonds 8%
- Foreign bonds 5%

Government bonds

The Tesoro Publico undertakes the issue of Spanish government bonds. The majority of the issues are Euro denominated, though there are small non-euro issues, mainly in US dollars and sterling.

4: FIXED INCOME SECURITIES

Types of instrument

There are three types of instrument:

- **Letras del Tesoro (Treasury bills)** – zero-coupon bonds issued at a discount to their face value with a maximum life of 18 months, to date they have only been issued with maturities of three and 12 months.

- **Bonos del Estado (Bonos)** – These are coupon-paying bonds with lives of three to five years.

- **Obligaciones del Estado** – These are coupon-paying bonds with a maturity over five years, usually 10 years and 30 years.

All maturities pay annual coupons, are issued as bullets and are redeemable at par. Prices are quoted clean with accrual interest calculated on a Actual/Actual basis.

Primary markets

All bonds are now issued through monthly auctions. These issues take place on a set calendar announced at the start of the year. The coupon for the next three issues is announced prior to each auction. In line with most markets, issuance tends to focus into the reopening of existing bonds in order to deepen liquidity.

Secondary market

The secondary market functions around a market maker 'blind' (anonymous) system. Trading is conducted electronically without knowledge of the identity of the counterpart. There is a second level market that deals with smaller orders on a named basis.

Both Repos and strips are traded on the secondary market.

1.5.6 Trading, settlement and withholding tax

Bonds settle on a T+3 basis. There are no withholding taxes on Spanish bonds.

4: FIXED INCOME SECURITIES

1.6 Summary of major international government bond markets

	French OAT	German Bund	Italian BTP	Japan (JGB)	UK Gilt	US T-Bond
Coupon frequency	Annual	Annual	Semi-annual	Semi-annual	Semi-annual	Semi-annual
Settlement	3 business days	3 business days	3 business days	3 business days	Same/next day	Same/next day
Registered or Bearer	R	R	R or B	R or B	R	R
Normal life	Issued with lives of between 7 and 30 years	Mostly 10 years	Usually 5 to 7 years, but have been as long as 10 years	10 years, some super longs with life of 30 years	Varied	Life of over 10 years
Quotation	1/100	1/100	1/100	1/100	1/100	1/32 Converting to 1/100
Withholding tax (for overseas investors)	None	None	None	None	None	None
Medium-Term Debt	BTAN life of 2 to 5 years	Bobls with lives of up to 5 years and Schatz with lives of 2 to 6 years	CTOs with lives of up to 6 years	–	–	T-note life of 2 to 10 years
Settlement agencies	Relit, Sicovam and Euroclear and Clearstream	Kassenvereine and Euroclear and Clearstream	Bank of Italy, Euroclear and Clearstream	Tokyo Stock Exchange	CGO/CREST, Euroclear, Clearstream and RBNY.	Federal Reserve
Accrued interest convention	Actual / Actual	Actual / Actual	Actual / Actual	Actual / 365	Actual / Actual	Actual / Actual

1.7 Emerging bond markets

The risk-reward payoff

The bull market of the 1990s reduced yields in the developed markets to such a level that investors began to look outside the traditional markets for higher returns. Higher returns will only come with higher risk, but in a diversified portfolio this level of risk might be acceptable. In this light, the emerging bond markets offer an attractive investment opportunity. Indeed, many saw the market as significantly undervalued offering attractive returns.

4: FIXED INCOME SECURITIES

The risks involved in emerging markets

Political risk

Unstable governments create a number of risks for potential investors. Included amongst these are default risks on government bonds, nationalisation and the potential expropriation of assets held within the economy. The move towards democratic regimes in Latin America was one of the key prerequisites for the development of international activity. The recent experience of the Russian market, however, highlights the possibility of default.

The imposition of exchange controls is also a potential threat with the risk that the currency will be **closed**, effectively blocking the ability of remitting the capital back to the investor's country.

Exchange risk

Where these currencies are subject to market forces, they are often prone to extreme fluctuations as market sentiment moves. These fluctuations are often so extreme as to remove the profit that the investor has made in local currency.

Corporate risk

As with any investment into a company, the investor must assess the risk of the company concerned. This is often more difficult in emerging markets due to the lack of formal information and the absence of credit rating agencies.

This is often exacerbated by the risk that the information that is available is either false or inaccurate. Once again, this will serve to heighten the risks that are faced by the investor and will obviously discourage many.

Local market risk

There is obviously a risk in using the local market. For example, potential loss through the failure of an undercapitalised local brokerage, or inefficient systems resulting in delayed settlement.

In addition, there are other risks associated with local settlement and custodial arrangements, all of which must be addressed prior to large-scale institutional inward investment.

Market inefficiencies

Arguably a benefit as opposed to a risk, in these markets knowledge and expertise can be fairly thinly spread. Consequently, it may be possible to pick up bargains that in more mature markets either would not or should not appear.

These risks were reflected in the Mexican peso crisis of 1994 and very strongly in the Asian bond market crisis of 1997/8.

The Brady bonds

A particular sub-niche of the emerging market comprises Brady bonds created in 1989.

4: FIXED INCOME SECURITIES

The Brady plan

The Brady plan has also acted as a promoter of growth and activity in the emerging bond markets. Brady plans reflect the fact that the debtor nations would never be able to repay their existing debt, built in the 1970s and that it is better to get something out of this than to persist in the belief that the debt has some value. Accordingly, the creditors agreed to forgo some of the debt in order to restructure the debt into a more tradable form.

The basis of any Brady plan was the adoption and approval by the IMF of domestic policies which would, in the IMF's view, stabilise the country's economy. Once the economic plan had been agreed, the IMF/IBRD would lend the nation enough money, together with its own reserves, to buy specially created US Treasury zero-coupon bonds. These zeros were lodged in New York and represented the collateral for the capital value of the bonds.

Those investors holding debt were then invited to surrender their debt in return for these collateralised bonds issued by the debtor nation. To reflect the fact that the original loan was unsustainable, the investors surrendering the debt received either bonds representing a proportion of the debt surrendered or the full value of the debt in bonds with a coupon below the market rate.

The creditor now had an asset which it was able to trade and the nation had a debt burden it could service.

If all else failed, then the holders of the bonds knew that the bond they were holding was backed by a US Treasury zero-coupon bond. Indeed, most plans also collateralised the coupon stream for the next 12 to 18 months using other investment grade bonds.

This arrangement between the debtor nations and the holders of the debt reflects economic rationality, a rationality many argue that was not present in the initial loans.

Conclusions

Emerging markets are undoubtedly more volatile and consequently offer the attraction of higher returns in order to compensate for the greater risks involved. The key risk to monitor is credit risk with the additional factor of significant currency risk when the bonds are denominated in the local currency.

As ever with credit risk, the fundamental truths apply. The risk is determined by the likelihood of default coupled with the severity of loss in the event of default and the likely timing of any default. This will always make the pricing of this debt more problematic than the debt of the developed nations where these factors are to an extent more predictable.

1.8 Islamic bond markets

Introduction

Islamic bonds or Sukuk are bond issues that satisfy Islamic principles and have gained Sharia approval. Western-style bonds do not satisfy certain Islamic principles, in particular, the prohibition of speculation and the payment of interest or any charge simply related to time. Much effort has been made in the Islamic world to structure acceptable financial arrangements.

4: FIXED INCOME SECURITIES

Though Islam frowns on speculation, it does approve of partnerships and risk-sharing and Sukuk are based on partnership risk-sharing ideas. When investing in such bonds, the Sukuk holder is effectively becoming a part owner of the asset being financed, sharing in profits it generates or losses it incurs. The arrangement is achieved through a special purpose vehicle (SPV) which buys the asset to be financed with the funds raised and acts on behalf of all the Sukuk investors.

In any partnership there are at least two parties involved who may contribute capital, skill and effort, or both. With Sukuk, we have the following parties:

- Rab al Mal – provides capital
- Mudarib – provides skill and effort

Types of issue

The main types of issue are:

- **Mudaraba Sukuk** – This is the primary type of Sukuk contract where the SPV is the Rab al Mal and company needing finance is the Mudarib. In such an arrangement, all profits are shared as defined in the Sukuk contract, all losses are absorbed by the Rab al Mal. As part of the contract it is normal for the Mudarib to contract to buy the financed asset at maturity in order to redeem the Sukuk holders. The result of this arrangement can be very similar to that of Western asset-backed bonds depending on how the profit-sharing arrangements are structured.
- **Musharaka Sukuk** – Where all parties contribute both capital and effort. All profits are shared as defined in the Sukuk contract, all losses are absorbed in proportion to capital introduced. This is totally unlike Western bonds, Western bond-holders would not expect to contribute anything other than capital.
- **Salam Sukuk** – Has a structure similar to a short-term zero-coupon bond which is achieved through a combination of spot and deferred payment sales.
- **Istisn'a Sukuk** – Used in construction contracts where the profits are generated from rents received and the ultimate sale of the property constructed.
- **Ijara Sukuk** – Has a structure similar to a leasing arrangement.

Primary market

Sukuk markets are relatively new and are not yet as developed and standardised as Western markets. They were originated by government entities, particularly that of Malaysia, and government entities still dominate the market, though corporate issues are gaining in importance.

Issuance is achieved in a similar manner to corporate bond issues in the UK, with investment banks underwriting and managing the issues.

Secondary market

Sukuk other than the short-term Salam Sukuk are traded by being listed on stock exchanges, though liquidity levels are currently quite low and many issues are held to maturity.

1.9 Corporate bonds

1.9.1 Loan stock

Loan stock represents a written acknowledgement of debt which, as such, can often be traded. Loan stock may be furnished with some security by the borrower; when there is no security being provided, the stock is referred to as unsecured loan stock (ULS).

There is no obligation for a company to give security on any loan. However, the consequence of not giving security will be that the coupon it is obliged to pay will be higher. Many companies have issued unsecured loan stock, but major issues tend to be only those companies with, in general, a high credit rating or status.

1.9.2 Credit risk

Corporate bonds are exposed to a greater degree of credit risk than gilts. Credit risk covers the risk that the issuer will default on his obligations to pay interest and capital, and is measured by the rating agencies.

1.9.3 Choice of market

The corporate borrower has a choice as to which market to issue into. Large multinational firms with high credit ratings are able to access the Eurobond or international market. Smaller companies will be constrained to use the less active domestic corporate bond market.

A **Eurobond** could be defined as an international bond issue, underwritten by a syndicate of banks, and sold principally in countries other than that of the currency of denomination.

However, the instruments are essentially the same, the only difference being that the pace of innovation is greater in the Euromarkets.

1.9.4 Legal form

Most Eurobonds issued are in bearer form, whereas domestic issues may be obliged to be in registered form.

1.9.5 Rating agencies

The credit risk of bonds is assessed by the various rating agencies, such as Moody's and Standard & Poor's. They will ascribe bonds with a credit rating. Should they decide to downgrade this rating, the return investors' demand will increase (the discount rate), causing the price to fall. Alternatively, a rating upgrade will reduce the required return of investors causing the price to rise.

1.9.6 Credit ratings

The purpose of credit ratings is credit risk evaluation, ie identifying the probability of default by an issuer. It is not a recommendation to take investment actions, since it does not take into account factors such as price and the preferred investment characteristics of the investor. Ratings are usually assigned to individual issues and hence do not serve as a general purpose of rating the issuer.

4: FIXED INCOME SECURITIES

Credit ratings are calculated from financial history and current assets and liabilities. Rating agencies focus on various accounting ratios such as interest cover, in order to identify the probability of the subject being able to pay back the loan.

It is conventional for issuers in the Euromarkets to have a credit rating. While this does not in itself make the company any more secure, it will mean that potential investors have a clearer perception of quality. Credit ratings are sub-categorised between prime/investment grade and junk/non-investment grade, and we need to be aware of the cut-off *points between* these gradings.

Standard & Poor's	Moody's
\multicolumn{2}{c}{Investment Grade (Prime)}
AAA	Aaa
AA+	Aa1
AA	Aa2
AA−	Aa3
A+	A1
A	A2
A−	A3
BBB+	Baa1
BBB	Baa2
BBB−	**Baa3**
\multicolumn{2}{c}{Non-Investment Grade (Non-Prime or Junk)}
BB+	**Ba1**
BB	Ba2
BB-	Ba3
B+	B1
B	B2
B-	B3
CCC	Caa
CC	Ca
C	C
D	

1.9.7 Security

Companies have the ability to issue debt which is secured against the company's assets. The alternatives and legal consequences are country-specific and are not covered here.

1.9.8 Redemption

Corporate bonds can have a variety of redemption terms.

Bullets

The vast majority of bonds issued are still in the form of bullets. A bullet issue has a single redemption date. There has been a tendency to issue callable bonds, or indeed putable bonds, where the holder has the right to call for early redemption, but the complications involved in analysing these issues often dissuade investors from purchasing them. This shift away from unorthodox redemption patterns is particularly true for the next two potential repayment schemes that are now rarely used.

Sinking funds or sinkers

This is a process whereby a proportion of the bonds in issue are redeemed each year. The bonds to be redeemed are selected by the process of 'drawing' the serial numbers which are then published and the holders submit the bonds to the paying agent for redemption at par. The final repayment is normally larger than the others and is referred to as the balance or balloon repayment.

Sinking funds tend to come into operation towards the end of the bond's life and rarely start to redeem from the first coupon date.

Purchase fund

A purchase fund buys back the bonds in the secondary market, and not at par. The obligation to repay is triggered by a condition specified in the offer document, normally the bond trading below par.

Serial notes

A serial note is one where a proportion of the capital is repaid each year together with the interest.

Optional redemption

The option to redeem a bond can be given to either side of the deal. A call right would give the issuer the right to seek an earlier redemption; for example, the double-dated gilts in the UK market, where the government has the right to redeem from the earlier of the two dates, but must redeem by the later date.

1.9.9 Coupons

Zero coupon

Bonds may be issued with zero or a very small dividend. Such bonds would be issued at a discount to their redemption value to provide an acceptable gross redemption yield.

Discounted bonds will be subject to a specific tax regime if their discount exceeds either 0.5% for each year of life or 15% in total. Bonds that exceed these criteria may be referred to as deep discount bonds and the owner will pay income tax on the excess received over cost when realised by sale or redemption.

Most bonds are issued with a fixed coupon. However, a number of variations are possible.

Stepped coupons

A stepped coupon rises over the life of the bond.

Year 1	4%
Year 2	6%
Year 3	8%
Year 4 to Year 10	10%

The advantage to the issuer is that it will not be burdened by the full interest cost in the early years of the debt. However, overall the issuer will be paying a higher coupon rate. It is also possible to issue a reversed stepped coupon with the coupon rate declining progressively over the life of the bond.

Floating Rate Notes (FRNs)

Floating rate notes are ordinary bonds where the coupon level varies in line with some measure of the market rate of interest. The coupon on these bonds comprises two elements. First, the reference or **index rate** and second a **quoted margin** that must be paid above that index rate.

Initially, in this market, the quoted margins were measured in half and a quarter per cent but, with competitive pricing, these have come down to a matter of mere basis points.

The quoted margin is established at the outset of the deal and reflects the borrower's credit rating and the size of the issue, along with the market conditions at the time.

Other conditions may be included. A bond may be a **drop lock** where the coupon is allowed to float but once it reaches its set minimum, the bond locks into being a fixed coupon bond at that minimum interest rate.

These are obviously fairly rigid structures and have been replaced frequently by floors where the bond's coupon level cannot fall below a certain point. For example, the floor of a bond might be 5%. If the index rate and the quoted margin gradually floated down to this level then, at the point of 5%, the coupon will be locked. However, as the index rate begins to pick up, then the coupon may increase beyond 5% unlike a drop lock where, of course, once it touches the floor, the bond is locked until redemption.

The minimum rate or floor is obviously a protection for the investor purchasing the floating rate note. It is possible for the issuer also to take up protection in the form of a ceiling or a cap whereby as interest rates rise, the coupon on the FRN also rises, but not beyond this pre-set ceiling.

It has been common for issuers to offset the costs of establishing a ceiling by including a floor value (**minimax bonds**), which in effect **collars** the interest rate available on the floating rate note.

1.9.10 Currency

There is no need for the currency of the coupon and that of redemption to be the same; it is entirely possible for the two to be different – **dual currency bonds**. For example, a bond may pay coupons in dollars while be redeemed in sterling. The rate of exchange can either be established at the outset or be the spot rate at the time of the transaction.

Bonds have also been issued which contain an option to use a variety of currencies, either at the issuer or holder's choice.

1.9.11 Callable and putable bonds

Callable bonds

Callable bonds are where the issuer has the right to redeem the bonds at an agreed price prior to its maturity. This price may be above the normal redemption price and the extra price paid is referred to as the call premium.

The call provision is valuable to the issuer, but is a disadvantage to the investor, since the issuer will only exercise the call if it suits the issuer to do so. As a result, the price at which a callable bond can be issued will be lower than for a comparable straight bond, and the interest rate it will need to pay will consequently be higher.

A call provision will reduce the expected time to maturity of the bond, since there is a possibility that the bond will be retired early as a result of the call provision being exercised.

Call provisions will be exercised when the issuer can refinance the issue at a cheaper cost due to interest rates having fallen. For example, if a bond was issued when interest rates were 15% and interest rates then fell to 5%, the issuer could issue a new bond at the current low interest rate and use the proceeds to call back the higher coupon bond.

Putable bonds

This is where the investor has a **put option** on the bond, giving him the right to sell the bond back to the company at a specified price (the put price). The put price is typically around par, given that the bond was issued at par.

The benefit to the investor is that if interest rates rise after the bond is issued, they can sell the bond at a fixed price and reinvest the proceeds at a higher interest rate. As a result of the benefit to investors, putable bonds are issued at higher prices or lower coupons than comparable nonputable bonds.

1.10 Eurobonds

1.10.1 The market

The Eurobond market is in effect an international market in debt. Companies issuing debt in the Eurobond market have their securities traded worldwide and are not limited to one domestic marketplace.

The market only accepts highly rated companies, since Eurobonds themselves are unsecured debt.

1.10.2 The instrument

In essence, a Eurobond is simply a debt instrument issued by a borrower (typically, a government or a large company) normally or predominantly outside of the country in whose currency it is denominated. For example, a US dollar Eurobond could be issued anywhere in the world, except for the US. As such, a better name for it might be an 'international bond'. As mentioned above, Eurobonds frequently carry no security other than the high name and credit rating of the issuer. Another important feature of bonds issued in this market is that, for the most part, they are issued in **bearer form**, with no formal register of ownership held by the company.

It should be noted that for a number of pragmatic reasons, the clearing houses in the Euromarkets do maintain a form of register of ownership, but that this register is not normally open either to government or tax authorities. Combined with the feature of being bearer documents, a vital aspect of the Eurobond is that, unlike most government bonds, it does not attract withholding tax. **Eurobonds pay coupons gross** and usually **annually**.

Most Eurobonds are issued in **bullet form**, redeemed at one specified date in the future. However, a number of issues have alternative redemption patterns. Some bonds are redeemed over a number of years with a proportion of the issue being redeemed each year. While Eurobonds are not issued in registered form, each will have an identifying number. A **drawing** of numbers is made every year from the pool of bonds in issue, the numbers drawn are published, and the bonds are called in and redeemed. This redemption process is known as a drawing on a Eurobond.

1.10.3 Dealing and settlement

There is no formal marketplace for Eurobond trading. The market is telephone driven and the houses are based in London. The market is regulated by the **International Capital Markets Association (ICMA)**, which operates rules regulating the conduct of dealers in the marketplace.

Settlement is conducted for the market by two independent clearing houses, **Euroclear and Clearstream**. These clearing houses immobilise the stocks in their vaults and then operate electronic registers of ownership.

Settlement in the Eurobond market is based on a **three-business-day (T + 3)** settlement system. Once again, the important feature about the registers maintained by the two clearing houses is that they are not normally available to any governmental authority, thereby preserving the bearer nature of the documents.

1.10.4 Eurobond issuance

The methods of Eurobond issuance are identical to those of corporate bond issues in the domestic markets.

New issues in the Eurobond market

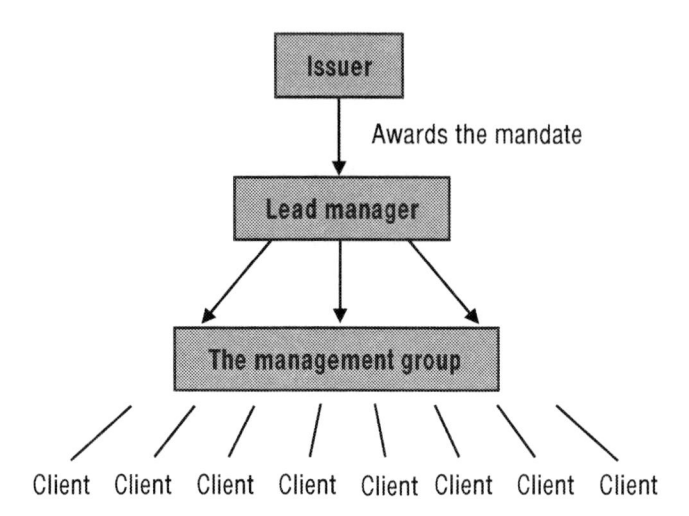

```
                    Issuer
                      │
                      │  Awards the mandate
                      ▼
                 Lead manager
                 ╱    │    ╲
                ▼     ▼     ▼
            The management group
           ╱ ╱ ╱ │ ╲ ╲ ╲
      Client Client Client Client Client Client Client Client
```

The most common form of issue used in the Eurobond market is a **placing**. A traditional method of issuing a Eurobond is for an issuer to appoint a lead manager and award them the mandate. The mandate gives the lead manager the power and responsibility to issue the bond on the issuer's behalf.

A **bought deal** is where the lead manager agrees detailed terms with the issuer including the coupon and the maturity. In normal issues, the lead manager has the ability to amend the terms of the issue as market conditions dictate.

The lead manager may then create a management group of other Eurobond houses. Each house then receives a portion of the deal and places it with its client base. The lead manager may elect to run the entire book alone, and miss out the other members of the management group.

There are a number of variations on these methods of issue. Under **a fixed price re-offer**, the members of the management group are prohibited from selling the bonds in the secondary market at below the issue price until the syndicate has been broken. The syndicate will break when the lead manager believes the bulk of the issue has been placed.

2 PRICING BONDS

2.1 Introduction

Since the cash flow values and timings from a bond are known with such certainty, at least for a straight bond, the application of DCF evaluation techniques is clearly appropriate.

There are, however, two pricing aspects to consider:

- DCF evaluation
- Clean and dirty bond pricing

The first of these ideas is the method that we will primarily use to evaluate a bond, the second is relevant for determining the correct tax treatment.

2.2 Discounted cash flow valuation of straight bonds

2.2.1 Redeemables

A straight redeemable bond pays a coupon to the maturity date, then pays the redemption proceeds at that date. If we know the required return to the bond-holders, we can, using DCF, evaluate this bond. If the bond is of a fairly short maturity, we may consider each cash flow separately. If, however, the bond is longer dated, it would be more convenient to apply the idea and calculation of an annuity.

Example

A bond pays an annual coupon of 9% and is redeemable at par in three years. Evaluate this bond if interest rates are:

- 8%
- 9%
- 10%

Solution

Interest rate at 8%

Time	Cash flow $	DF (8%)	Present value $
1	9.00	$\dfrac{1}{1.08}$	8.33
2	9.00	$\dfrac{1}{1.08^2}$	7.72
3	109.00 (100.00 + 9.00)	$\dfrac{1}{1.08^3}$	86.53
			102.58

Interest rate at 9%

Time	Cash flow $	DF (9%)	Present value $
1	9.00	$\dfrac{1}{1.09}$	8.26
2	9.00	$\dfrac{1}{1.09^2}$	7.58
3	109.00	$\dfrac{1}{1.09^3}$	84.16

4: FIXED INCOME SECURITIES

			100.00

Interest rate at 10%

Time	Cash flow $	DF (10%)	Present value $
1	9.00	$\dfrac{1}{1.10}$	8.18
2	9.00	$\dfrac{1}{1.10^2}$	7.44
3	109.00	$\dfrac{1}{1.10^3}$	81.89
			97.51

Conclusion

This example illustrates two important features about bonds, specifically:

- There is an **inverse relationship between bond prices and interest rates**, i.e. as interest rates rise, market values fall (and *vice versa*).
- When the coupon rate on the bond is equal to the prevailing interest rate, the bond will be valued at par, as illustrated above, when interest rates are 9%.

It is vital that you are aware of, and comfortable with, these two conclusions. Their appreciation is essential for the effective appraisal of a bond investment or the management of a bond portfolio.

This calculation may be expressed mathematically as follows.

$$\text{Redeemable straight bond price} = \frac{C_1}{1+r} + \frac{C_2}{(1+r)^2} + \frac{C_3}{(1+r)^3} + \cdots + \frac{C_n + R}{(1+r)^n}$$

where r = investor's required return.

We shall refer to this formula from time-to-time. However, the above tabular approach to the calculation is probably most convenient.

Example

Calculate the value of the above bond at 10%, assuming it matures in eight years.

4: FIXED INCOME SECURITIES

Solution

This bond will pay its coupon for the next eight years and then be redeemed. Its value will, therefore, be:

Time	Cash flow $	DF (10%)	Present value $
1 – 8	9.00	$\frac{1}{0.10}\left(1 - \frac{1}{1.10^8}\right)$	48.01
8	100.00	$\frac{1}{1.10^8}$	46.65
			94.66

2.2.2 Irredeemables

When we have an irredeemable bond, we are evaluating a perpetuity stream of cash flows.

Example

Evaluate a 9% irredeemable, assuming interest rates are 10%.

Solution

Time	Cash flow $	DF (10%)	Present value $
1 – ∞	9.00	$\frac{1}{0.10}$	90.00
			90.00

This calculation may be expressed mathematically as follows.

$$\text{Irredeemable straight bond price} = \frac{\text{Coupon}}{r}$$

where r = investor's required return.

2.3 Clean and dirty prices

2.3.1 Introduction

A further pricing aspect is clean and dirty pricing. The value of a bond has two elements, the underlying capital value of the bond itself (the **clean price** which is quoted) and the coupon that it is accruing over time (**accrued interest**). Periodically, this coupon is distributed as income to the holders or, more specifically, the individual who was the registered holder on the ex-dividend date specified for the bond.

The **dirty price** calculated above using DCF is the price that is paid for a bond, which combines these two elements. Consequently, ignoring all other factors that might affect the price, a dirty price will rise gradually as the coupon accrues or builds up and then fall back as the stock is marked either ex-dividend or pays the dividend.

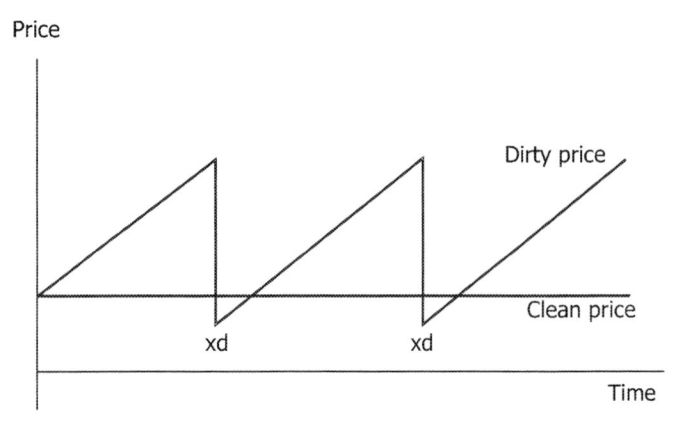

As already noted, however, though the price paid is the dirty price, bond prices are not quoted on a dirty basis but are quoted clean. This is done for the following reasons.

- Coupon income and bond gains are generally taxed differently so splitting the income from the capital component is important.

- As we illustrated above, the full value of a bond drops sharply on coupon date creating a false picture of price volatility. Clean pricing reflects just the value of the principal, and any volatility exhibited in the clean price reflects the underlying economic events and market conditions more realistically.

- Splitting out the interest component results in the remainder of the bond value (the principal, by definition) being much more closely aligned to the changes in the yield.

2.3.2 Cum-dividend bargains

A purchase made before the ex-dividend date is referred to as a cum-dividend bargain. In this situation, the buyer of the bond will be the holder on the next ex-div date and will, therefore, receive the full coupon for the period. The seller, however, has held the bond for part of this period and is therefore entitled to a part of that coupon. To account for this, the purchaser of the bond must compensate the seller for the dividend which he has earned.

4: FIXED INCOME SECURITIES

Example

```
Last coupon                          Next coupon
    |_____•_____|
                     Purchase
```

In this example, the purchaser will pay the clean price plus the interest from the last payment date up to the purchase. On the next payment date, the holder will receive the whole of the interest for the six months. However, on a net basis, they will only have received the interest for the period of ownership.

The formula used is:

$$\text{Dirty price} = \text{Clean price} + \text{Period coupon} \times \frac{\text{Days}}{\text{Days in period}}$$

or:

Price paid = Quoted + Accrued interest from period start

where:

Days = number of days from the **last coupon payment date** up to and including the calendar **day before the settlement** day

Days in period = number of days from the **last coupon payment date** up to and including the calendar **day before the next coupon**

Thus, the period coupon is spread over the number of days in the period, giving a coupon per day, then allocated to the relevant holder on a daily basis.

Example

Semi-annual coupons are paid on 1 April and 1 October. On 10 July, an investor buys $10,000 nominal of an 8% bond @ $101.50 for settlement on 11 July. How much is paid?

Solution

The 8% bond pays a 4% coupon each period (half year) giving:

		$
Clean price	10,000 @ $101.50	10,150.00
Accrued interest	($10,000 × 4% × $\frac{101}{183}$)	220.77
Dirty price		10,370.77

the number of days having been calculated on an Actual/Actual basis (as applied to almost all major market government bonds) as follows.

4: FIXED INCOME SECURITIES

Month		Days	Days in period
April	From last coupon (inclusive)	30	30
May		31	31
June		30	30
July	To day before settlement	10	31
August			31
September	To day before next coupon		30
		101	183

Note: The Actual/Actual basis is used for almost all major market government bonds, hence its use in our illustration here. Some markets do, however, have a different day count basis that we examine in the next section.

2.3.3 Ex-dividend bargains

An ex-div bargain is one occurring after the ex-div date for that stock, but before the coupon is paid. Any person buying the stock after it has been marked ex will not, therefore, be entitled to the interest. Consequently, the pricing must reflect this.

Example

Last coupon ——————————•—————————— Next coupon

Purchase

In this example, the buyer of the bond will be entitled to the coupon for the last few days of the period, but will receive nothing, as this will all go to the seller who held at the ex-div date. He will, therefore, require this to be adjusted in the price.

Accordingly, he pays the clean price as determined by the market less the number of days worth of interest that he is not receiving.

The formula used in this situation is:

$$\text{Dirty price} = \text{Clean price} - \text{Period coupon} \times \frac{\text{Days}}{\text{Days in period}}$$

Price paid = Quoted — Accrued interest to end of period

where:

Days = number of days from the **settlement day** to the calendar **day before the next coupon payment date** (inclusive)

Days in period = number of days from the **last coupon payment date** up to and including the calendar **day before the next coupon**

4: FIXED INCOME SECURITIES

2.4 Day count conventions

2.4.1 Conventions

In the preceding section we needed to be able to deal with the practicality of being part way through a coupon period, and to achieve that we needed to establish what fraction of that period we are either from the start or from the end.

And so the question is, how do we establish the appropriate fraction of the period?

In all of the assessments that we do we will use:

$$\text{Fraction of period} = \frac{\text{Days}}{\text{Days in Period}}$$

Where either:

- Days = number of days from the start of the period (for cum-dev trades)
- Days = number of days to the end of the period (for ex-dev trades)

as appropriate.

But the question is, how do we count the number of days for the top and bottom lines of this fraction?

Unfortunately, there is no single universally applied answer to this question and there are a number of day count conventions that we need to be aware of. What is universally applied, however, is that the reference dates that we count from and to are cash flow dates, ie coupon payment dates, maturity dates or transaction settlement dates. We will always be measuring between cash flow dates.

2.4.2 Actual/Actual

Actual/Actual is the basis used for all Euro, UK and US government bonds and for Eurobonds issued after January 1999.

Under this basis, as we saw above:

- Days = either
  - number of days from the last coupon payment date up to and including the calendar day before the settlement day (Cum Div).
  - number of days from the settlement date up to and including the calendar day before the next coupon. (Ex Div)
- Days in Period = number of days from the last coupon payment date up to and including the calendar day before the next coupon.

These calculations must be done based on exact calendar dates, taking account of leap years where necessary.

2.4.3 Actual/365 and Actual/360

Actual/365 is the convention applied to Japanese government bonds and to the floating rate notes (FRNs) and money-market instruments of the UK, Australia, Canada, New

Zealand and some other commonwealth countries. Actual/360 is the convention applied to most other countries' money markets and FRNs.

On these bases the top line, Days, is counted as above based on specific calendar dates taking account of leap years. However, the Days in Period is set at 365 or 360 irrespective of the actual length of the year.

It should be noted that in such markets, the quoted coupons and yields are those applicable to a 365- or a 360-day period and so, for example, the actual coupon paid for a year may not simply be that expected from the coupon rate.

For example, if we hold $100,000 nominal US money market instrument quoting a 6% coupon, the actual coupon paid in a year would not simply be $6,000, rather it would be:

- Normal year = $100,000 × 6% × $365/360$ = $6,083.33
- Leap year = $100,000 × 6% × $366/360$ = $6,100.00

2.4.4 30/360 and 30E/360

30/360 is the basis used for domestic US bonds (Yankee bonds, federal agencies, corporate and municipal bonds).

30E/360 is the basis applied to Eurobonds issued before January 1999, sometimes referred to as legacy bonds.

Under each of these bases each full month, including February, is assumed to have 30 days, giving 360 for the full year, the Days in Period.

The Days figure for the top line is, as for all such calculations, assessed by reference to cash flow dates. If the cash flow date that starts the period in question is D1/M1/Y1, and the cash flow date that ends the period in question is D2/M2/Y2, then:

$$\text{Days} = 360 \times (Y2 - Y1) + 30 \times (M2 - M1) + (D2 - D1)$$

In undertaking these calculations, however, we must bear in mind:

30/360	If D1 = 31, change to 30
	If D2 = 31, change to 30 but *only* if D1 = 30 or 31
30E/360	If D1 = 31, change to 30
	If D2 = 31, change to 30

Once again, the last day in February is always regarded as day 30.

2.4.5 Others

There are other bases applied in certain markets but these are the main ones that we need to be aware of.

4: FIXED INCOME SECURITIES

Example
A bond has a coupon payment date of 31 December, the number of Days for pricing calculations will be as follow

Settlement date	Days convention		
	Actual	30	30E
28 February	59	58	58
29 February	(60)	(59)	(59)
1 March	60(61)	61(61)	61(61)
24 March	83(84)	84(84)	84(84)

Figures in brackets refer to leap years.

Example
A bond has a coupon payment date of 28 April, the number of Days for pricing calculations will be as follows.

Settlement date	Days convention		
	Actual	30	30E
31 July	94	93	92
1 August	95	93	93
31 August	125	123	122
1 September	126	123	123

2.4.6 Applications

The application of the above day count conventions in the major bond and money markets is as follows.

Country		Bonds	Money markets
Australia		Actual/Actual	Actual/365
Canada		Actual/Actual	Actual/365
Eurozone	– Government	Actual/Actual	Actual/360
	– Eurobonds issued after January 1999	Actual/Actual	–
	– Eurobonds issued pre-January 1999	30E/360	–
	– Sterling Eurodeposits	–	Actual/365
Japan		Actual/365	Actual/360
New Zealand		Actual/Actual	Actual/365
UK		Actual/Actual	Actual/365
US	– Government	Actual/Actual	Actual/360
	– Yankee, federal, corporate, municipal	30/360	–

3 RETURNS MEASURES – THE YIELD

The value of any investment will depend on the return that it generates and the risks inherent in those returns. In bond markets, the single most important measure of return is the yield. There are, however, several different yield measures that we may wish to calculate, each having its own uses and limitations. For each of these measures, we need to know:

- How it is calculated
- Its uses
- Its limitations

3.1 The flat yield

3.1.1 Calculation

The simplest measure of the return used in the market is the flat (interest or running) yield. This measure looks at the annual cash return (coupon) generated by an investment as a percentage of the cash price. In simple terms, what is the regular annual return that you generate on the money that you invest?

$$\text{Flat yield} = \frac{\text{Annual coupon rate}}{\text{Market price}}$$

Example

We hold 10% loan stock (annual coupon) redeemable at par in four years. The current market price is 97.25. Calculate the flat yield.

Solution

The flat yield for the above would be:

$$\text{Flat yield} = \frac{10.00}{97.25} = 0.10283 \text{ or } 10.283\%$$

3.1.2 Uses

This measure assesses the **annual income return** only and is most appropriate when either:

- We are dealing with **irredeemables**, which pay no return other than income into perpetuity; or
- Our priority is the short-term cash returns that the investment will generate.

3.1.3 Limitations

This measure, while of some use (particularly in the short-term), has three important drawbacks for the investment markets.

- In addition to the coupon flows, bonds may have returns in the form of the redemption monies. Where the bond has been purchased at a price away from par, this will give rise to potential gains and losses which are excluded from this calculation.
- The calculation completely ignores the timing of any cash flows and the time value of money.
- With some bonds (floating rate notes – FRNs), the return in any one period will vary with interest rates. If the coupon is not constant, then this measure is only of historic value unless the predicted return is used.

These limitations combine to make the flat yield of only marginal use.

3.2 The Japanese gross redemption yield

3.2.1 Calculation

The idea behind the Japanese gross redemption yield (GRY) calculation is to overcome the first of the limitations of the flat yield noted above, specifically that any gains or losses to redemption are ignored. This measure recognises that the total return in any period is a combination of both income and capital components, ie the coupon received plus any gain (minus any loss) for the period.

The Japanese method for calculating the GRY is to take the flat yield and then add the average annual capital gain (or deduct the average annual loss) to redemption, stated as a percentage of the current market price. Thus, we can state the Japanese GRY as:

$$\text{GRY} = \frac{\text{Annual coupon rate}}{\text{Market price}} + \frac{\text{Average annual capital gain to redemption}}{\text{Market price}}$$

or

$$\text{GRY} = \frac{\text{Annual coupon rate}}{\text{Market price}} + \frac{\frac{\text{Redemption price - Market price}}{\text{Years to redemption}}}{\text{Market price}}$$

Example

We hold 10% loan stock (annual coupon) redeemable at par in four years. The current market price is 97.25. Calculate the Japanese GRY.

Solution

The Japanese GRY for the above would be:

$$\text{Japanese GRY} = \frac{10.00}{97.25} + \frac{\frac{100.00 - 97.25}{4}}{97.25}$$

$$= \frac{10.00}{97.25} + \frac{0.6875}{97.25}$$

$$= 0.10283 + 0.00707 = 0.10990 \text{ or } 10.99\%$$

4: FIXED INCOME SECURITIES

3.2.2 Uses

The main use of this method is to provide a quick and easy way of assessing the GRY, which assesses the **total return**, income and gain.

It should be noted that it is not an absolutely accurate measure of return, since it assumes linear capital growth rather than the more realistic compound growth. As a result, it is liable to overstate the effects of any capital gain or loss. Furthermore, this inaccuracy increases the further away a bond is from maturity.

3.2.3 Limitations

While this method does overcome the first limitation of the flat yield, ie its failure to account for any capital gains or losses to redemption, it does not overcome the other noted drawbacks, specifically:

- The calculation completely ignores the timing of any cash flows and the time value of money.
- With some bonds (floating rate notes – FRNs), the return in any one period will vary with interest rates. If the coupon is not constant, then this measure is only of historic value unless the predicted return is used.

The first of these limitations can only be overcome through the use of discounted cash flow techniques as illustrated below. The second is a valid limitation of all yield measures.

3.3 Gross Redemption Yield (GRY)

3.3.1 Calculation

Introduction

The gross redemption yield resolves the issue of the redemption values and the time value of money by using discounted cash flow techniques.

The gross redemption yield is the internal rate of return (IRR) of:

- The dirty price paid to buy the bond.
- The gross coupons received **to redemption**.
- The final redemption proceeds.

Mathematical formulation

This could be expressed mathematically as:

When GRY = r, then:

$$\text{Price} = \sum \frac{C_t}{(1+r)^t} + \frac{R}{(1+r)^n}$$

Alternatively, this may be expressed as:

$$\text{Price} = \frac{C_1}{1+r} + \frac{C_2}{(1+r)^2} + \frac{C_3}{(1+r)^3} + \cdots + \frac{C_n + R}{(1+r)^n}$$

It should be noted that these formulae **cannot** be algebraically solved (except in very rare circumstances) and must be found through trial and error.

3.3.2 Uses

This measure overcomes the major deficiencies highlighted in relation to the flat yield and the Japanese GRY. It considers all cash returns and exactly when they occur.

As a result, the GRY represents a realistic measure of the expected overall future return from a bond at any point in time.

3.3.3 Limitations

As a measure of predicted return, the yield is limited, since it **assumes that interest rates remain constant throughout the period and hence, that any coupon receipts may be reinvested at the same rate as the yield**. If this is the case, then the GRY does represent the return achieved. If rates vary, however, the return achieved will differ from the GRY.

If the bond is not held to redemption, but sold at some earlier date, then the return achieved will be a function of the price of the bond (hence, interest rates) at the disposal date.

Even if the bond is held to redemption, the terminal value will differ, as the reinvested coupons will grow at a different rate, altering the ultimate return achieved.

3.4 The net redemption yield

For tax-paying investors, it is possible to incorporate the effect of taxes in the **net redemption yield (NRY)**. This is calculated in an analogous way to the GRY including only net-of-tax cash flows.

3.5 Relating the yield measures

The flat yield, Japanese GRY and GRY are all pre-tax measures assessing:

- Flat yield – the annual gross income generated.
- GRY – the annual total return (Income + Gain) generated.
- Japanese GRY – an approximation of the annual total return (Income + Gain) generated, which overstates any gain (or loss).

Since the majority of the return from a bond comes in the form of income, we would expect these three measures to be fairly similar, being related as follows.

Bond value	Relationship
Above par (loss to redemption)	Flat yield > GRY > Japanese GRY
At par	Flat yield = GRY = Japanese GRY
Below Par (gain to redemption)	Flat yield < GRY < Japanese GRY

The NRY is a post-tax measure, and as a result would be considerably lower than any of the three pre-tax alternatives for normal straight bonds.

4 YIELD CURVE AND TERM STRUCTURE OF INTEREST RATES

4.1 Introduction

In all of our evaluation exercises so far, we have applied the same interest rate in discounting the cash flows regardless of when they arise. The question is: is this reasonable?

Example

What will be the market values of two zero-coupon bonds which are identical in all respects, except that one matures in one year and the other in five years, if the interest rate is 10%? How will these values change if interest rates fall to 9%?

Solution

Maturity	10%	9%	Change
1 year	$MV = \frac{100}{1.10} = 90.91$	$MV = \frac{100}{1.09} = 91.74$	0.83 or 0.913%
5 years	$MV = \frac{100}{1.10^5} = 62.09$	$MV = \frac{100}{1.09^5} = 64.99$	2.90 or 4.671%

In both absolute and relative terms, the five-year bond shows significantly more price volatility, hence we may conclude that the five-year bond is a more risky investment.

One of the fundamental precepts of investment appraisal is that if an investor faces a higher risk, then he will demand a higher return. On the basis of this, it is unreasonable to be applying the same required return to these two bonds; the required return on a longer dated bond should be at some premium over that of a shorter dated bond to reflect the additional risk.

Thus, there should be a term structure to interest rates and bond yields, which we would normally expect to rise as we consider investment cash flows further and further into the future.

4: FIXED INCOME SECURITIES

4.2 The yield curve

4.2.1 Introduction

The yield curve demonstrates the relationship between bond yields and their maturities.

Normal yield curve

The normal shape of the yield curve is illustrated below.

The normal yield curve

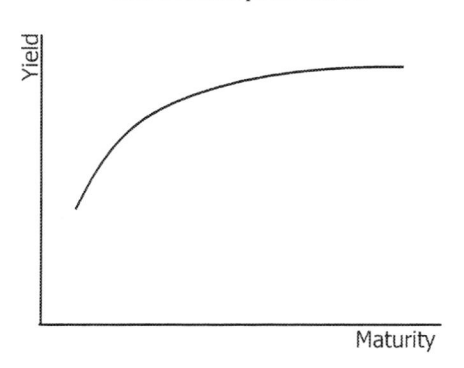

This curve clearly demonstrates the point made above, ie longer maturity results in higher risk which, in turn, results in higher returns or yields.

Problem with these ideas

Unfortunately, the yield curve does not always follow the shape described above, indeed it occasionally becomes inverted with short-term yields exceeding longer-term ones as shown below.

The inverted yield curve

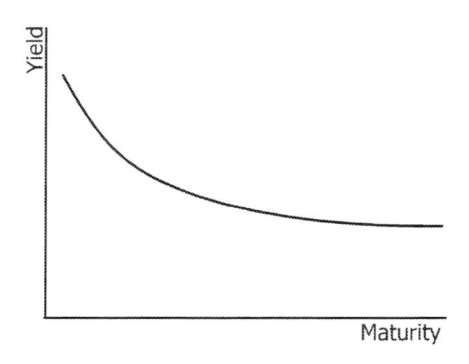

This appears to contradict our fundamental ideas of higher risk means higher return, one of the cornerstones of investment theory and hence we need to consider what factors determine the shape of this curve. There are clearly some other forces at work here in addition to the simple risk return relationship that we have considered so far.

4: FIXED INCOME SECURITIES

4.3 Shape of the yield curve

4.3.1 Introduction

What, then, determines the shape of the yield curve? The risk/return relationship is one factor at work here but, as we noted earlier, there must be other, perhaps more significant factors, otherwise we would never see an inverted yield curve.

A number of theories have been advanced to explain the shape of the yield curve which we outline below.

4.3.2 Liquidity preference

This theory states that if an investor's money is invested in longer term (and therefore riskier) stocks, then they will require a greater return or **risk premia**. Short-term liquid stock carry a lower risk and therefore require a lower return.

This risk premium gives rise to the normal upward sloping yield curve.

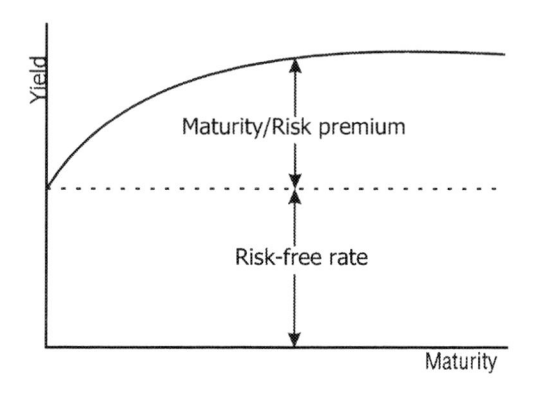

4.3.3 Expectations theory

Expectations theory states that the yield curve is a reflection of the market's expectation of future interest rates. If the market believes that the yield at the long end of the yield curve is high and is likely to fall, then, in order to profit from the increase in prices that this will create, it will buy long-dated stocks. As a result, the demand for these stocks will rise and this demand pressure will force the price to rise. As a consequence, the yield will fall reflecting the expectation of a fall.

On the other hand, if the market believes that rates will have to rise, then the forces will work in the opposite direction and this will lead to a fall in the price and a rise in the yield.

The expectations of the market can clearly be seen in an inverted yield curve.

The inverted yield curve

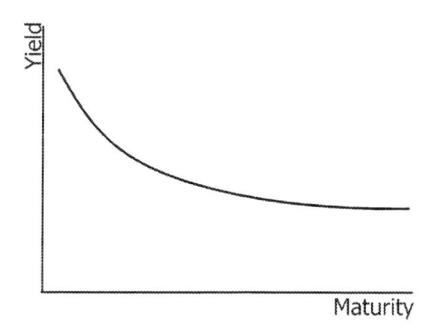

[Graph showing yield decreasing with maturity, with Yield on vertical axis and Maturity on horizontal axis]

Here, the short-term rates are high, but the market anticipates that this cannot last for long and the longer end of the market has anticipated this change by forcing yields down. This can lead to the anomalous situation where the long end of the market, because it has anticipated change, remains constant and the short end (which is technically the least volatile) exhibits all of the movement.

Another key element of the market's expectations will be the **expectation of inflation**. If the market believes that inflation will rise in the future, then the yields on the longer-dated stocks will have to rise in order to compensate investors for the fall in the real value of their money. The expectation of inflation is much more of a problem with the long end rather than the short end.

4.3.4 Preferred habitat and market segmentation – demand effects

This is not a theory to explain the full shape of the yield curve as such. Rather, it should be viewed as an addendum to the above two theories to help explain certain other features observed in the markets, such as humped yield curves in relation to the liquidity preference theory.

Certain maturity ranges are appropriate to particular types of investors. In the UK, the short end of the market is dominated by the financial sector and general insurance companies maintaining a proportion of their assets in liquid investments, whereas the long end is dominated by institutional investors such as pension funds and life assurance companies.

In effect, this gives rise to two markets concentrated at different ends of the yield curve. The impact of this concentrated demand at these two ends is that prices are driven up and hence, yields fall below those that may otherwise have been expected at these points. This may result in a discontinuity or hump in the yield curve.

4: FIXED INCOME SECURITIES

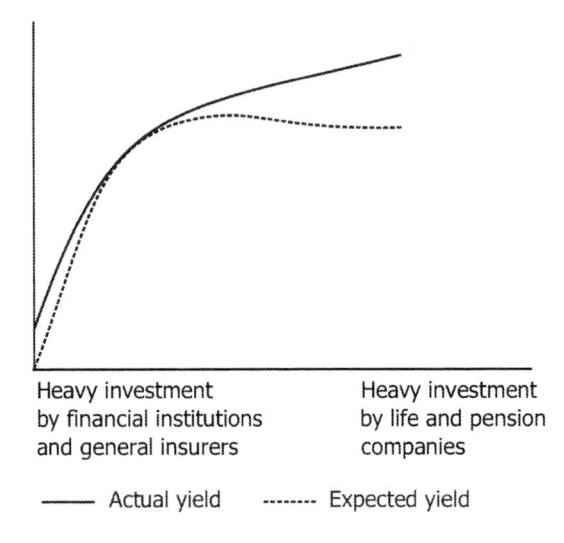

Heavy investment by financial institutions and general insurers

Heavy investment by life and pension companies

—— Actual yield ------ Expected yield

4.3.5 Supply-side factors

The availability of stocks in certain maturity ranges may lead to either an excess or shortage of stock and consequently, an anomalous yield on some stocks. This is more often a problem at the long end of the yield curve where governments may be priced out of the issuance market.

4.4 Spot rates and forward rates

4.4.1 Spot rates

If the cash flows from a one-year bond should be discounted at the yield for one-year bonds, then why should the first year coupon from a five-year bond (received on the same day) be discounted at a different rate (the yield on the five-year bond)? Both represent cash in one year, hence both represent equal risk to an investor.

What we should have are various rates of interest which are appropriate for cash flows at certain dates, regardless of whether they are from a one-year bond or a five-year bond. These are the spot rates.

The spot rate is the rate of interest that the market demands for money from now to a specific future time, ie the rate for one-month money or one-year money or five-year money. If we wished to price a bond, then strictly we should do this using spot rates.

Example

A bond pays an annual coupon of 9% and is redeemable at par in three years. Evaluate this bond if spot rates of interest are:

- 1 year – 7%
- 2 year – 8%
- 3 year – 9%

Solution

Time	Cash flow $	DF (spot rate)	Present value $
1	9.00	$\dfrac{1}{1.07}$	8.41
2	9.00	$\dfrac{1}{1.08^2}$	7.72
3	109.00 (100.00 + 9.00)	$\dfrac{1}{1.09^3}$	84.17
			100.30

4.4.2 Forward rates

Whereas a **spot** rate is a rate of interest that can be agreed today for a deposit or borrowing from today for a fixed period, a **forward** rate is a rate of interest that can be agreed today for a deposit or borrowing from one future date to another.

5 THE RISKS OF HOLDING A BOND

5.1 Introduction

An investor in a fixed income security is exposed to a number of different risks, and any complete assessment of a bond must include consideration of these factors. These risks include the following.

5.1.1 Interest rate risk

This is probably the most important risk because of the powerful relationship between interest rates and bond prices. Duration and modified duration (volatility) are the means of measuring this risk. Convexity is the measure that is used to explain the variation away from the predicted return.

5.1.2 Credit and default risk

Credit and default risk is the risk of the issuer defaulting on its obligations to pay coupons and repay the principal. The ratings by commercial rating companies can be used to help assess this risk.

5.1.3 Inflation risk

Inflation risk is linked to interest rate risk, as interest rates rise to compensate bond holders for inflation.

4: FIXED INCOME SECURITIES

5.1.4 Liquidity and marketability risk

This has to do with the ease with which an issue can be sold in the market. Smaller issues especially are subject to this risk. In certain markets, the volume of trading tends to concentrate into the 'benchmark' stocks, thereby rendering most other issues illiquid. Other bonds become subject to 'seasoning' as the initial liquidity dries up and the bonds are purchased by investors who wish to hold them to maturity.

5.1.5 Issue specific risk

There may be factors specific to the issue, which tend to either increase or decrease the risk, eg issuer options such as the right to call for early redemption or possibly, holder options.

5.1.6 Fiscal risk

Fiscal risk represents risk that withholding taxes will be increased. For foreign bonds, there would also be the risk of the imposition of capital controls locking your money into the market.

5.1.7 Currency risk

For any investor purchasing overseas or international bonds, then there is obviously also the risk of currency movements.

5.2 Interest rate risk

5.2.1 Introduction

The most predictable of these risks is the interest rate risk. Within bond markets, this is sometimes referred to, somewhat confusingly, as the **volatility**. The sensitivity of any bond to movements in the interest rate will be determined by a number of factors.

Sensitivity to maturity

Longer dated bonds will be more sensitive to changes in the interest rate than shorter dated stocks as illustrated by these prices for three 12% bonds of differing maturity subject to differing GRYs.

Coupon %	Maturity (years)	Price for a GRY of 8%	Price for a GRY of 10%	Price for a GRY of 12%
12	4	113.24	106.34	100.00
12	7	120.83	109.74	100.00
12	26	143.23	118.32	100.00

In this example, it is the price of the 26-year bond that exhibits the greatest range as the yield alters (moving from 143.23 to par). The logic behind this is that the longer dated bond is more exposed to the movements of the yield, since it has longer to go to maturity.

Sensitivity to coupon

With regard to the level of coupon, it is the lower coupon stocks that demonstrate the greatest level of sensitivity to the yield.

Coupon %	Maturity (years)	Price for a GRY of 9%	Price for a GRY of 10%	Price for a GRY of 11%
5	15	67.75	61.97	56.85
10	15	108.00	100.00	92.81
15	15	148.30	138.03	128.76

In this example, the price of the 5% bond moves from 61.97 when the GRY is 10%, to 67.75 if GRY drops to 9% (a rise of 9.3%) and to 56.85 if GRY rises to 11% (a fall of 8.2%). The other bonds while exhibiting the same overall relationship are not as responsive to the alteration in the GRY. The 10% bond rises by 8% and falls by 7.2%.

It should be noted that the relationship between the coupon and maturity and the price are not symmetrical (equal for both a rise or a fall in GRY). This is a relationship that we will return to later and is known as **convexity**.

The logic behind this relationship is that the lower coupon bonds have more of their value tied up in the terminal value. The ultimate low-coupon bond is, after all, the zero-coupon bond where the entire value is in the final payment.

The impact of the yield

If yields are particularly high, then the flows in the future are worth relatively little and the sensitivity is diminished. Conversely, if the yield is low, then the present value of flows in the future is enhanced and the bond is more sensitive to the changing GRY.

Summary

Long dated	>	Short dated
Low coupon	>	High coupon
Low yields	>	High yields

While these simple maxims are good indicators of the likely sensitivity to fluctuations in the rate of interest, they do not allow for two bonds to be compared.

For example, which of the following is likely to be the most sensitive to a rise in interest rates – a high-coupon long-dated stock or a low-coupon short-dated stock? It was for this reason that in the 1930s a composite measure of interest rate risk was devised: the **duration**.

5.2.2 Reinvestment risk

An investor in bonds will usually receive coupons over the life of the bond, unless it is a zero-coupon bond. These coupons will often need to be reinvested. If interest rates have fallen since the bond was issued, the interest rate earned on reinvested coupons will be lower than previously expected. This will reduce the investor's return compared to what he expected when buying the bond originally.

4: FIXED INCOME SECURITIES

5.2.3 Macaulay's duration

Introduction

This calculation gives each bond an overall risk weighting, which allows two bonds to be compared. In simple terms, it is a composite measure of the risk expressed in years.

> Duration is the weighted average length of time to the receipt of a bond's benefits (coupon and redemption value), the weights being the present value of the benefits involved.

This concept can be shown diagrammatically as follows:

Duration

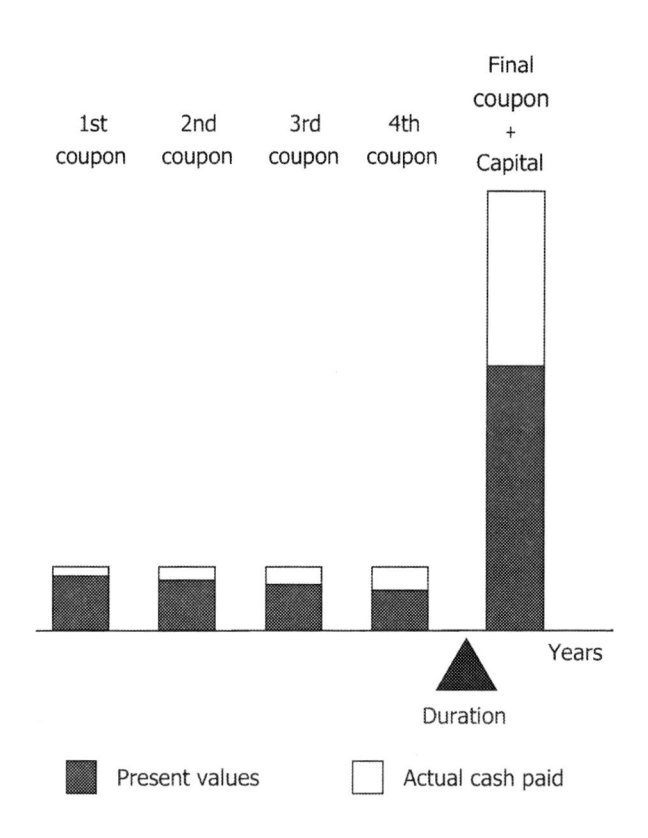

■ Present values   ☐ Actual cash paid

where the fulcrum or point of balance represents the duration of the bond.

Calculation

Mathematically, duration can be expressed using the following formulae.

$$\text{Macaulay's Duration (D)} = \frac{\Sigma (t \times PV_t)}{\text{Price}}$$

or:

$$\text{Macaulay's Duration (D)} = \frac{(1 \times PV_1) + (2 \times PV_2) + (3 \times PV_3) + \cdots + (n \times PV_n)}{\text{Price}}$$

where:

PV_t = present value of cash flow in period t (discounted using the redemption yield)

n = number of periods to maturity

This may look difficult, but can be easily calculated in a normal DCF pricing table which simply adds one column next to the one used for valuation.

Example

A bond pays an annual coupon of 9% and is redeemable at par in three years. Calculate the duration of the bond if interest rates are 8%.

Solution

Time	Cash flow $	DF (8%)	PV $	t × PV $
1	9.00	$\frac{1}{1.08}$	8.33	8.33
2	9.00	$\frac{1}{1.08^2}$	7.72	15.44
3	109.00 (100.00 + 9.00)	$\frac{1}{1.08^3}$	86.53	259.59
			102.58	283.36

Using the above, the duration is:

$$\text{Duration} = \frac{283.36}{102.58} = 2.7623 \text{ years}$$

Macaulay's Duration can also be referred to as the **economic life of a bond**.

4: FIXED INCOME SECURITIES

Use

The uses of duration are:

- As a measure of relative risk for a bond in a similar fashion to the standard deviation or the beta for a share. The higher the duration of a bond, the higher its risk or interest rate sensitivity.

- To calculate modified duration (discussed below).

In the determination of the portfolio holdings it is necessary to establish a bond fund management strategy called immunisation. This strategy is not covered in this chapter but is dealt with in the Investment Management chapter.

Properties of duration

The basic features of sensitivity to interest rate risk are all mirrored in the duration calculation.

- **Longer dated bonds** will have longer durations (Note the duration at an irredeemable = $1 + \frac{1}{yield}$).

- **Lower coupon bonds** will have longer durations. The ultimate low-coupon bond is a zero-coupon bond where the duration will be the maturity.

- **Lower yields** will give higher durations. In this case, the present value of flows in the future will fall if the yield increases, moving the point of balance towards the present day, therefore shortening the duration.

The duration of a bond will shorten as the lifespan of the bond decays. However, the rate of their decay will not be the same. In our example above, a three-year bond has a duration of 2.7623 years. In one year's time, the bond will have a remaining life of two years, and a duration based on the same GRY of 1.9182 years. The lifespan has decayed by a full year, but the duration by only 0.8441 of a year.

5.2.4 Modified duration/volatility

Introduction

At the same time as the Macaulay's Duration was being promoted as a means of expressing the sensitivity of a bond to movements in the interest rate, Hicks was developing a formula to explain the impact of yield changes on price. Not surprisingly, the two measures are linked.

Hick's basic proposition was that the change in yield multiplied by this sensitivity measure would give the resultant percentage change in the bonds price, ie the volatility gives the percentage change in price per unit change in yield.

Calculation

The modified duration formula may be derived through the use of calculus, specifically differentiation of the price equation with respect to interest rates. Fortunately, there is an easier definition, specifically:

4: FIXED INCOME SECURITIES

$$\text{Modified duration/volatility} = -\frac{\text{Macaulay's Duration}}{1 + \text{GRY}}$$

Some texts do not include the minus sign in the calculation of modified duration but insert it on use. We have included it here to emphasise the inverse relationship between prices and yields, ie as yields rise prices fall.

Use

The use of modified duration is to provide a first estimate of the change in the price of a bond that will result from a given change in yields.

Example

Using the example from above:

$$\text{Modified duration} = -\frac{2.7623}{1.08} = -2.5577$$

This is negative, hence we can state that the price will **fall** by 2.5577% or $2.62 (102.58 × 2.5577%) for every one percentage point **increase** in the yield – we must bear in mind the inverse relationship.

Based on this, calculate the change in price and the new resulting price, if yields:

- Fall 0.5%.
- Rise 1.0%.

Solution

Yields fall 0.5%

Alternative 1 – First principles

Bearing in mind the inverse relationship, if yields **fall** 0.5%, then prices will **rise** by $1.31 ($2.62 × 0.5) to $103.89 ($102.58 + $1.31).

Alternative 2 – Mathematical relationship

This relationship may be expressed mathematically as:

$$\text{Proportionate change in price} = \text{MD} \times \Delta Y$$

where

MD = modified duration

ΔY = percentage change in the gross redemption yield (expressed as a decimal)

Applying this relationship gives

Proportionate change in price = MD × ΔY = –2.5577 × (–0.005)
= 0.01279 or 1.279%

This is a positive figure, hence prices will rise by 1.279% or $1.31 ($102.58 × 1.279%) as calculated in Alternative 1 above.

The first principles approach is certainly easier and more intuitive when we are only considering modified duration. The second mathematical relationship approach comes in to its own, however, when we try to incorporate the effects of convexity below.

Yields rise 1.0%

Alternative 1 – First principles

Bearing in mind the inverse relationship, if yields **rise** 1.0%, then prices will **fall** by $2.62 ($2.62 × 1.0) to $99.96 ($102.58 – $2.62).

Alternative 2 – Mathematical relationship

Proportionate change in price = MD × ΔY = –2.5577 × (+0.010) = –0.025577 or –2.5577%

This is a negative figure, hence prices will fall by 2.5577% or $2.62 ($102.58 × 2.5577%) as calculated in Alternative 1 above.

Comments

If a full DCF pricing exercise is carried out, we would find that the prices would become $103.90 if yields fell 0.5% to 7.5%, and $100 if yields rose 1.0% to 9.0%. The modified duration calculation produces a quite accurate result for small changes in yields, however it becomes increasingly inaccurate for larger shifts.

Properties of modified duration

As the modified duration is derived from the Macaulay's Duration, it shares the same properties.

- **Longer dated bonds** will have higher modified durations (Note the modified duration of an irredeemable is = $-\dfrac{1}{\text{yield}}$).
- **Lower coupon bonds** will have higher modified durations.
- **Lower yields** will give higher modified durations.

The higher the modified duration, then the greater the sensitivity of that bond to a change in the yield.

5.2.5 Convexity

Introduction

Modified duration predicts a linear relationship between yields and prices. If the modified duration is two, then if yields rise by 1%, the price will fall by 2%. If the rise in yields had been 3%, then the fall in price would have been 6%.

The price/yield relationship predicted by the modified duration

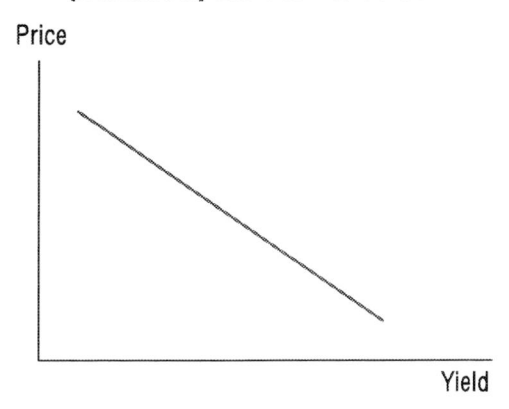

Price vs Yield graph showing a downward sloping line.

The slope of the line is the modified duration.

However, as the yield changes, then so will the duration and consequently, the modified duration. It is this which gives rise to the concept of convexity.

The impact of changing yields on the modified duration

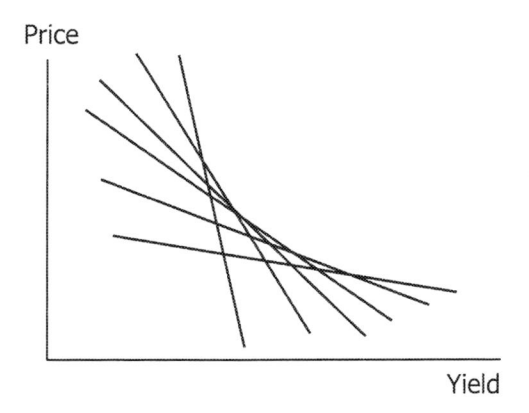

Price vs Yield graph showing multiple downward sloping lines of varying slopes tangent to a convex curve.

As the yield falls, the duration will increase and therefore, so will the modified duration. As modified duration increases, the line will steepen.

The actual relationship between the yield and price is given by the convex function that these individual linear relationships describe. We are after all aware that the relationship between bond prices and interest rates is not linear. The actual relationship between prices and yields is curved, with increases in yields resulting in prices falling, but at a reducing rate, as illustrated by the example at the start of this session.

The actual convex relationship and the linear one predicted by the modified duration formula are illustrated below.

4: FIXED INCOME SECURITIES

Convexity

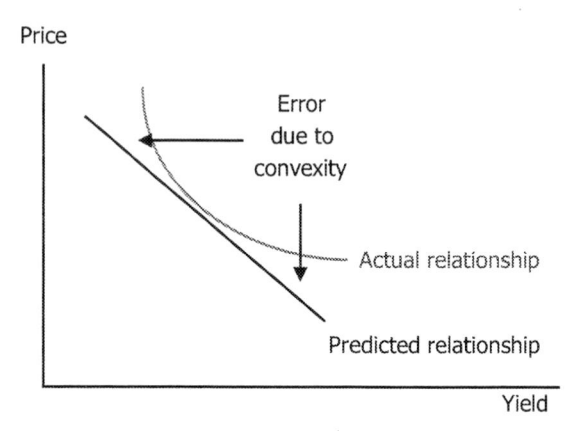

Price

Error due to convexity

Actual relationship

Predicted relationship

Yield

The impact of convexity will be that the modified duration will tend to **overstate the fall in a bonds price and understate the rise**. However, for relatively small movements in the yield, the modified duration will be a good estimate; the problem of convexity only becomes an issue with more substantial fluctuations in the yield.

Definition

Convexity is the change in the modified duration with respect to yields.

Calculation

The convexity formula may be derived once again through calculus, being a function of the second derivative of the price equation with respect to yields.

$$\text{Convexity} = \frac{\Sigma\, t(t+1)\,PV_t}{\text{Price}(1+GRY)^2}$$

NB: Some texts include a ½ in this formula, others include the ½ when it is used within further calculations. How and when this ½ is included is of no relevance to its use as long as all calculations are done consistently.

Once again, this does not look like a very pleasant formula. However, it may easily be dealt with by extending our tabular duration calculation.

Example

Based on the previous duration calculation, calculate convexity (C).

Solution

Time	Cash flow $	Discount factor	PVt $	t × PVt $	t(t + 1)PVt $
1	9.00	$\frac{1}{1.08}$	8.33	8.33	16.66
2	9.00	$\frac{1}{1.08^2}$	7.72	15.44	46.32
3	109.00	$\frac{1}{1.08^3}$	86.53	259.59	1,038.36
			102.58	283.36	1,101.34

Hence:

$$\text{Convexity} = \frac{\Sigma\, t(t+1)PV_t}{\text{Price}(1+\text{GRY})^2}$$

$$\text{Convexity} = \frac{1,101.34}{102.58 \times 1.08^2} = 9.2048$$

Use

The use of convexity is to:

- Give a more accurate assessment of the change in the price of a bond that will result from a given change in yields.
- Indicate the risk of a bond fund immunisation strategy by comparing the convexity of the alternatives. Note, the relative convexity is unaffected by the consistent inclusion or exclusion of the ½ in the calculations. Once again, this is not covered in this section, but dealt with in the Fund Management section later.

Example

Using our ongoing example, calculate the change in the price of the bond, and the new resulting price, if yields:

- Fall 0.5%.
- Rise 1.0%.

Solution

Yields fall 0.5%

Alternative 1 – Using an average modified duration

As we noted above, modified duration changes as yields change, hence using it to forecast price movements will lead to inaccuracies. To overcome this, we could use the

4: FIXED INCOME SECURITIES

convexity information to calculate the average modified duration over the given range of yields and use this to more accurately assess the change in prices as follows.

Modified duration at 8% GRY		−2.5577
Change due to convexity if yields fall 0.5% (−0.005)	9.2048 × (−0.005)	−0.0460
Modified duration at 7.5% GRY		−2.6037
Average modified duration	(−2.5577 − 2.6037) ÷ 2	−2.5807

Giving:

$$\text{Proportionate change in price} = \text{Average MD} \times \Delta Y$$
$$= -2.5807 \times (-0.005)$$
$$= 0.01290 \text{ or } 1.290\%$$

Hence, prices will rise by $1.32 ($102.58 × 1.290%) to $103.90 ($102.58 + $1.32).

Alternative 2 – Mathematical relationship

Note, we could calculate the above average modified duration from the originally calculated modified duration (MD) as:

$$\text{Average MD} = \text{MD} + \tfrac{1}{2}C \times \Delta Y$$
$$= -2.5577 + \tfrac{1}{2} \times 9.2048 \times (-0.005)$$
$$= -2.5807$$

Substituting this into the above price change formula would give:

$$\text{Proportionate change in price} = \text{Average MD} \times \Delta Y$$
$$= (\text{MD} + \tfrac{1}{2}C \times \Delta Y) \times \Delta Y$$
$$= \text{MD} \times \Delta Y + \tfrac{1}{2}C \times \Delta Y^2$$

That is, this whole average modified duration approach may be combined into a single formula to speed the calculation and expressed mathematically as:

$$\text{Proportionate change in price} = \text{MD} \times \Delta Y + \tfrac{1}{2}C \times \Delta Y^2$$

where:

MD = modified duration at the original GRY
C = convexity at the original GRY
ΔY = percentage change in the gross redemption yield (expressed as a decimal)

Applying this relationship gives:

$$\text{Proportionate change in price} = \text{MD} \times \Delta Y + \tfrac{1}{2}C \times \Delta Y^2$$
$$= -2.5577 \times (-0.005) + \tfrac{1}{2} \times 9.2048 \times (-0.005)^2$$
$$= 0.01290 \text{ or } 1.290\%$$

This is a positive figure, hence prices will rise by 1.290% or $1.32 ($102.58 × 1.290%) as calculated above in Alternative 1.

4: FIXED INCOME SECURITIES

Yields rise 1.0%

Applying the formula gives:

Proportionate change in price $= MD \times \Delta Y + \frac{1}{2}C \times \Delta Y^2$

$= -2.5577 \times (+0.010) + \frac{1}{2} \times 9.2048 \times (+0.010)^2$

$= -0.02512$ or -2.512%

This is negative, hence prices will fall by $2.58 ($102.58 × 2.512%) to $100.00, which we know to be correct.

Properties of convexity

Not all bonds have the same degree of convexity. The general rule is that bonds with a higher duration will exhibit the greatest degree of convexity.

For bonds with the same duration, it will be the higher coupon bonds that will be the most convex. The reason for this is that the lower coupon bonds, for example 0% bonds, will have durations that will change little with the alteration in yield. In the most extreme form, the 0% bond will have a duration equal to its maturity and this will not alter as yields move.

Investors may be prepared to pay for convexity. In a volatile market, the convex bonds at any particular maturity interval will outperform the bonds with lesser convexity.

Callable bonds

The nature of callable bonds

Callable bonds enable the issuer to repurchase the bond at a set price prior to its stated maturity. For example, a bond with a 105 call could be bought back by the issuer at a price of $105.

A call option should not be confused with a redemption clause. It is often the case that a bond may be redeemed under predetermined circumstances, so long as the redemption is not being refinanced by a new bond issue. For example, a company may have excess cash balances (possibly due to the sale of assets) available to retire the bond.

The impact of a call provision on the price-yield relationship

The price of a callable bond will change at a different rate to the price of an equivalent straight bond as interest rates change.

You will recall that the relationship between the price and yield of a straight bond is as follows.

4: FIXED INCOME SECURITIES

Price/yield curve for a straight bond

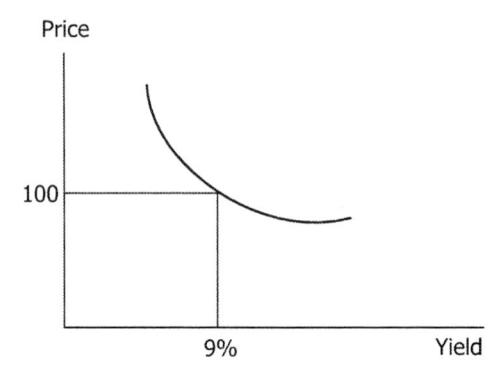

In other words, as interest rates fall, the price of the bond continues to rise.

For a callable bond (assuming that it is callable immediately), the price will not rise as much – for a given fall in interest rates – as a straight bond. For example, take a bond that can be called at 105. As interest rates fall, bond prices rise. The price of a straight bond will continue to rise as interest rates fall and may go above 105. However, the price of the callable bond can never rise above the call price of 105, since the company can buy it back at that price.

Consequently, as interest rates fall, the rate at which the price of the callable bond increases will be slower than the rate at which the straight bond price increases. Once the callable bond price is close to 105, it will hardly change at all, even if interest rates continue to fall.

**Price/yield curve
for a straight versus a callable bond**

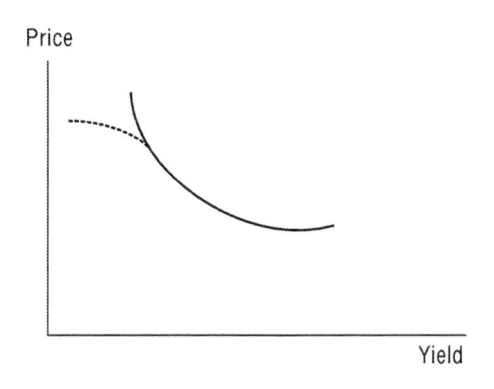

The curve to the right gives the price/yield relationship for both bonds. However, at lower interest rates, the relationships diverge, with the straight bond's price continuing to rise while the price of the callable bond first increases at a declining rate, then stays static.

The fact that price changes decline as interest rates fall is sometimes referred to as **price compression**.

4: FIXED INCOME SECURITIES

Duration for a callable bond

For callable bonds, duration and related measures can be calculated based on the final maturity or on the first call date. The latter assumes that the bond will be called at the first call date. The duration to first call will be lower than the duration to final maturity, since it assumes a shorter effective maturity.

Convexity for a callable bond

The fact that the price of a callable bond hardly changes when interest rates fall to low levels means that the change in price will be **less** than that predicted by modified duration to first call. This is unusual, since it was noted above that modified duration always understated a rise in price and overstated a fall in price. As a result, convexity had to be added to the price change due to modified duration.

For a callable bond at low interest rates, the change due to convexity will be **deducted** from the change due to modified duration rather than added. This is known as **negative convexity**.

Breaking a callable bond into its component parts

A callable bond could be viewed as a straight bond with an embedded option. The company has sold a straight bond to investors but at the same time has bought a call option from the investors, enabling the company to buy back the straight bond at the agreed call price.

As a result, the proceeds on the issue of a callable bond are less than that for an equivalent straight bond. The company effectively receives the proceeds from the straight bond, but then uses part of those proceeds to buy a call option from the bond investors. The net proceeds received are therefore lower.

The bond investor's position is as follows.

Long callable bond = Long straight bond and short call option

The value of this is given by:

> Callable bond value = Straight bond value − Issuers call option value

If the value of the call option increases, then the value of the callable bond will decrease. For example, an increase in the price of the straight bond (caused by a decrease in interest rates) will also result in an increase in the intrinsic value of the call option. Although the straight bond will increase in value, the call option also increases in value, meaning that the callable bond value hardly changes at all.

If interest rates are very high, then the call option will be deeply out-of-the-money, meaning that its value will change by very little for a change in interest rates. Therefore, the price behaviour of the callable bond mimics the behaviour of the straight bond.

An increase in expected volatility of interest rates will increase the value of the option, since it makes the bond price more volatile. This will reduce the value of the callable bond.

4: FIXED INCOME SECURITIES

5.2.6 Simpler measures of sensitivity

Basis point value (BPV)

Basis point value is sometimes referred to as the **price value of a basis point or the dollar value of a basis point**. This is the change in price if the yield changes by one basis point. The more sensitive stocks will have a high BPV.

5.3 Other risk factors

5.3.1 Introduction

At the beginning of this section on risk, we established a number of factors that contribute to bond risks, specifically:

- Interest rate risk
- Credit and default risk
- Inflation risk
- Liquidity risk
- Issue specific factors
- Fiscal risk
- Currency risk

With government gilts, interest and inflation risk represent the greatest dangers to the investor; there is no possibility of default or liquidity problems. Government gilts can therefore be considered a benchmark against which required yields for other bonds can be assessed.

The normal form of evaluation of non-government bonds is to judge them by virtue of such a benchmark government bond establishing the required yield difference between the two stocks and then investigating discrepancies which may be generated by the market.

The required yield	%
Yield on the equivalent benchmark gilt	X
Yield premium for additional credit risk	X
Yield premium on rights given to the issuer (calls)	X
Yield give up on option given to the holder (conversion and put premium rights)	(X)
Yield mark-up for liquidity risk	X
Yield change for tax advantage/(disadvantage)	X
	X

The key reasons for a variance in the yield between a corporate issue and a government bond will be:

- Credit rating
- Name recognition
- Liquidity

In addition, the perceived security of the marketplace is important. In particular, government bond markets will attract money in volatile marketplaces due to the **flight to quality**. The variety of other features that may be added to the bond may create uncertainty and therefore detract from the bond's value rather than add to it.

4: FIXED INCOME SECURITIES

Executive Summary

Definition

- A bond is a negotiable debt instrument for a fixed principal amount issued by a borrower for a specific period of time and typically making a regular payment of interest.

- The interest payment is known as the coupon and it is based on the nominal value of the bond. The nominal value also refers to how much capital shall be paid on maturity.

Issues

- Bonds may be issued by governments, local authorities and companies.

- Rating agencies provide credit ratings on individual bonds based on the credit quality of the bond and its overall risk of default.

- Corporate bonds may be issued with a wide variety of different structures and different levels of security and payment benefits.

Pricing

- Bond pricing is based on the principle of discounted cash flow.

- Redeemable straight bond price $= \dfrac{C_1}{1+r} + \dfrac{C_2}{(1+r)^2} + \dfrac{C_3}{(1+r)^3} + \cdots + \dfrac{C_n + R}{(1+r)^n}$

- Irredeemable straight bond price $= \dfrac{\text{Coupon}}{r}$

- Clean and dirty pricing conventions are designed to ensure:
    - investors pay the correct amount of tax on their income and gains.
    - quoted prices reflect the underlying economic events and market conditions

    Dirty price = Clean price + Period coupon × $\dfrac{\text{Days}}{\text{Days in period}}$

    or

    Price paid = Quoted + Accrued interest from period start

Yields

- The flat yield represents the income return to an investor. The gross redemption yield represents the total return to an investor, on the assumption the investment will be held to maturity.

- Yield curves represent the gross redemption yield on bonds issued by a particular issuer.

Risks

- Macaulay's Duration measures the sensitivity of a bond to changes in interest rates and is measured in **years**.

- Macaulay's Duration $(D) = \dfrac{\Sigma (t \times PV_t)}{Price}$

- Modified duration indicates the percentage change in a bond's price given a 1% change in yields.

- Modified duration/volatility $= - \dfrac{\text{Macaulay's Duration}}{1 + GRY}$

- Convexity measures the curvature in the price/yield relationship.

- Convexity $= \dfrac{\Sigma t(t+1) PV_t}{Price(1+GRY)^2}$

Proportionate change in price $= MD \times \Delta Y + \tfrac{1}{2} C \times \Delta Y^2$

5 Equities

Contents

1 The Nature of Equities 198
2 The Primary Market 200
3 Evaluating Equity 202
Executive Summary 209

5: EQUITIES

1 THE NATURE OF EQUITIES

Equities represent a significant asset class for a fund manager to consider as a result of the very high potential returns that they can generate. The other side of the coin, however, is the risk that the investor may face.

A share means a share of ownership in a company or corporation. In the plural, *stocks* is often used as a synonym for shares especially in the United States, but it is less commonly used that way outside of North America.

We are using the term equities generically as international terminology varies. In North America equities are usually referred to as stocks, whereas they tend to be known as shares elsewhere.

The shareholders (or stockholders) of a company are the owners of the company. Initially, businesses were so small that one individual could finance the whole enterprise. As businesses became larger, it was difficult for an individual to provide sufficient finance for the operation. Companies allow a large number of individuals to pool their capital into one organisation, thereby facilitating the formation of larger companies.

Each original owner (shareholder) provides capital and receives shares. The more the individual contributes, the greater the allotment of shares. As owners, the shareholders take the greatest risks. If the company does badly, they will lose their money. However, they normally have only a **limited liability**, ie limited to the amount that they agreed to contribute.

On the other hand, if the company prospers, then the shareholders will reap the rewards. However, regardless of the company's fortunes, the return to debt will solely be interest and repayment. In contrast, shares do not normally have a fixed return and consequently participate fully in the remaining profits of the business. These profits may be distributed by way of a dividend, or can be retained within the operation in order to increase the potential for future profit.

1.1 Equity shares

Ordinary shares or common stock are often referred to as **equity shares**. Here, the term equity means that they have an equal right to share in profits. For example, if a company has 10,000 ordinary shares, each share is entitled to $1/10,000$ of the profits made during any period.

The rights of ordinary shares are detailed in the company's constitutional documents. However, it is normal for ordinary shares to **possess a vote**. This means that the holder of any ordinary shares may attend and vote at any meetings held by the company. While the day-to-day control of the company is passed into the hands of the directors and managers, the shareholders must have the right to decide upon the most important issues that affect the business, such as:

- Corporate policy
- Mergers and takeovers
- Appointment and removal of directors
- Raising further share capital

1.2 Preference shares/preferred stock

As mentioned above, ordinary shares carry the full risks and rewards of ownership. Another type of share which a company can issue is a **preference share** which takes on **debt-like characteristics** and offers only limited risks and returns.

1.2.1 The normal terms

A preference share is preferred in two basic forms.

- The preference share **dividend must be paid out before any ordinary dividend can be paid**. It is conventional for preference shares to be cumulative and if the dividend is not paid in any one year, the arrears and the current year's dividend must be paid before any ordinary dividend can be paid in the future. The assumption is that preference shares are cumulative unless they are stated not to be so.
- The second form of preferencing is on the order of pay out on a winding-up (liquidation). Preference shares will be paid prior to ordinary shares.

In order to receive these benefits, preference shareholders have to give up a number of rights normally attached to shares. First, the dividend on preference shares is **normally a fixed dividend** expressed as a percentage of the nominal value similar to the coupon on a bond.

In addition, on liquidation the preference shareholders will **only ever receive the nominal value of any shares**. This is not the case for ordinary or equity shares. Equity shares would receive anything that remains.

Finally, it is conventional for preference shares to carry **no voting rights**.

1.2.2 Special features of preference shares

Some preference shares can be specified as **participating shares**. A participating share has a right, when profits reach certain levels, to take a share of those profits as opposed to simply receiving a fixed return. This participation right may also apply to the proceeds on a winding-up (liquidation).

Preference shares may also be issued with **conversion rights**. These rights will allow the preference shares to be converted into ordinary shares at specified rates in the future. As such, the preference share in this instance is more like a convertible bond than a share.

Finally, preference shares may be given specified **redemption dates**. For the most part, shares are not seen to be redeemable, but preference shares frequently carry a redemption date, making them seem, once again, more like debt than shares.

2 THE PRIMARY MARKET

The primary market is the new issuance market. The secondary markets (markets in second-hand securities) exist to enable those investors who purchased investments to realise their investments. It is vital to ensure that the primary market is selective. A poor quality primary market will undermine the liquidity of the secondary market.

2.1 New issues of equities

Any company or corporation that wishes to raise finance through issuing shares to the public must satisfy the legal, regulatory and stock exchange requirements of its country of incorporation, details we do not seek to cover in this book.

2.2 Subsequent issues

2.2.1 Pre-emption rights

There is an obligation in most major markets to ensure that whenever a company issues shares for cash, those shares are first offered to the existing shareholders. This is the right of pre-emption and gives rise to rights issues. It should be noted that pre-emption rights are not internationally universal and do not exist in some pacific rim countries.

2.2.2 Rights issues

Rights issues are simply a way of raising new finance from existing investors. Shares are normally offered at a discount to their price prior to the rights issue being announced. The effect this has is two-fold.

- It will dilute the value of the existing shares in the market place. We will look to calculate this price, known as the theoretical ex-rights price (TERP).

- An investor receiving a rights issue is, in effect, receiving a certificate giving them the right to buy a share in the company. This right is itself tradable on the market. Given that it will be giving the right to buy a share below its current market value, there will probably be a value attributable to the 'nil paid right'. We will look to calculate this nil-paid value.

Theoretical ex-rights prices

It is important to be able to determine the amount the purchaser pays for the rights nil paid.

Example

One for three rights issue at $4.00 when market price is $5.00

	Number	Price $	Value $
Existing holding	3 shares	@ 5.00 =	15.00
Shares issued as a result of the rights issue	1 share	@ 4.00 =	4.00
	4 shares		19.00

5: EQUITIES

As a result of the rights issue, the shareholder has four indistinguishable (fungible) shares with a total value of $19.00.

Therefore, each share now has a value of $\dfrac{\$19.00}{4} = \$4.75$

As a result of the rights issue, the share price will, theoretically, fall from its current market level of $5.00 to $4.75. This price of $4.75 is referred to as the theoretical ex-rights price. This reflects the dilution aspect of issuing one new share at $4.00 when the existing market price of shares is $5.00.

The deeper the discount on the issue of shares, then the less likely is the need for underwriting.

2.2.3 Bonus issues

Bonus issues are also referred to as **scrip issues**, capitalisation issues, cap issues and free issues. Here, the company issues new shares, but does not require a payment for them from the shareholder. The main use of bonus issues is to dilute the price of the share in the marketplace by spreading it over a larger number of securities. This is felt to be important in the UK markets, since shares with too high a value may discourage activity, and therefore liquidity, in a stock.

Example

One for three bonus/scrip issue when market price is $5.00.

	Number	Price $	Value $
Existing holding	3 shares	@ 5.00 =	15.00
Shares issued as a result of the rights issue	1 share	@ free =	0.00
	4 shares		15.00

As a result, each share now has a diluted value of $\dfrac{\$15.00}{4} = \$3.75$.

Many companies in the UK are now offering the shareholders the right to receive their dividend in the form of shares rather than in the form of cash. This is referred to as a **scrip dividend**.

2.2.4 Stock split

Like a scrip issue, a stock split increases the number of shares in issue. There are some slight differences however.

- A 2 for 1 stock split will offer investors two new shares for every one old share held. In other words, the investor will hand back one share and receive two new shares (whereas with a bonus issue investors keep hold of their existing shares).
- As well as reducing the share price, the stock split will reduce the nominal value of shares in issue.

5: EQUITIES

2.2.5 Share buybacks

Instead of using profits to pay a dividend to shareholders, a company can use the cash to buy back its own shares. The implications of doing so are a potential increase in EPS, ROCE and financial gearing, as the equity in the business is reduced.

3 EVALUATING EQUITY

3.1 Introduction

The valuation of a company's shares could never be considered an exact science – there is simply no single right answer. There are, however, a number of possible bases that we could use to try to determine a value of equity. These include:

- Asset-based valuations
- Dividend-based valuations
- Earnings-based valuations

We consider each of these possible bases below.

3.2 Asset-based valuations

3.2.1 Introduction

A business can be seen as a collection of individual assets. As a result, the value of the business could be calculated as the value of those assets, or what those assets would realise if sold off separately.

The value of the company's equity will be the value of the business assets as a whole, less the value of the debt that must be repaid from those assets.

3.2.2 Net realisable value of assets

The minimum selling price for a vendor

The net realisable value of the assets is of relevance to existing shareholders, since it represents the minimum sum for which they should be prepared to sell the shares. There is no point in accepting $1m for a business if the assets could have been sold off separately for $3m.

Establishing realisable values

In calculating realisable values, care needs to be taken in assessing the values of fixed assets and stocks. If the break-up of the company is occurring over a rapid timescale, or as a result of a forced sale, then values will be lower than if the business were run down in an orderly fashion over a period of time.

In addition, we also need to consider any selling costs and tax consequences that may arise as a result of the sale.

3.2.3 Use of asset-based valuations

Asset-based valuations will be appropriate for investment trusts, property companies and capital-based industries, eg manufacturing businesses, where a large amount of the value of the business is tied up in the value of the assets owned. Asset-based valuations will be less useful for service industries, where their value is largely tied-up in the value of the intangibles.

An asset-based valuation is **not** relevant for a minority investor who owns shares in a company which is a going concern, except perhaps for investment trusts and property companies. Since the company is not going to be wound-up, the asset value will never be realised.

3.3 Dividend-based valuations

3.3.1 Introduction

Whereas an asset-based valuation relies on the assumption that the assets can or will be realised, the dividend-based approach assumes that a company is a **going concern** and values the company according to its **dividend flows**. It is of most use to a minority investor who has little influence over a company's affairs and just receives a regular dividend payment.

There are two methods that we could apply to establish the value of equity based on dividend information. These are:

- The dividend valuation model
- Dividend yields

3.3.2 The dividend valuation model

The dividend valuation model states that the market value of a security is equal to the present value of the future expected receipts discounted at the investor's required rate of return. For equity, we can establish formulae to help with these calculations in two circumstances, where we have:

- A **constant dividend**, as in the case of preference shares.
- A **constant growth rate for the dividend** (or constant after a certain time), which may be suitable for ordinary shares.

We can only utilise these formulae for non-redeemable shares. When dealing with redeemable securities, we are likely to need to resort to first principles.

Relevant cash flows

The cash flows involved are:

Time	Inflow/(outflow)
0	Market value ex-div
1 - ∞	(Dividends paid)

5: EQUITIES

Notes

- The outflow at t_0 is the ex-div market value that must be paid to acquire the shares, since we are assuming that the first dividend will be received at t_1.
- If the shares currently in issue are presently cum-div, then we must calculate the ex-div value using the equation:

$$E_{\text{ex-div}} = E_{\text{cum-div}} - d_0$$

where:

$E_{\text{ex-div}}$ = the ex-div market value of the shares
$E_{\text{cum-div}}$ = the cum-div market value of the shares
d_0 = the dividend about to be paid now

3.3.3 Constant dividend

Market value

The investor will be looking for a return to satisfy his required return. If his required rate of return is r_e and the annual perpetuity dividend payment is d, then he will be willing to pay and hence, the ex-div market value (assuming that the first dividend will be paid in one year's time and, therefore, we can correctly apply the perpetuity discount factor) will be:

$$E_{\text{ex-div}} = \frac{d_1}{r_e}$$

That is, the market value is determined by the investor, based on his expectations of future returns and his own required rate of return.

Example

If shareholders require the return on their investment in a certain share to be 10% and they expect the share to yield a dividend of $1.00 per annum in perpetuity, what will be the market value of the shares?

Solution

The ex-div market value of the share will be determined by shareholders to be:

$$E_{\text{ex-div}} = \frac{d_1}{r_e}$$

$$E_{\text{ex-div}} = \frac{\$1.00}{0.10}$$

$$= \$10.00$$

5: EQUITIES

This may appear to be over-simplistic, and you may feel that, in practice, there are many other factors that influence share price. However, the above is an illustration of the dividend valuation model, which provides a good starting point for any analysis.

Required rate of return

This equation can be fairly simply rearranged to give the investor's required rate of return as:

$$r_e = \frac{d_1}{E_{ex\text{-}div}}$$

3.3.4 Constant growth in dividends

Introduction

For ordinary share capital, it is unrealistic to expect a dividend to remain constant. It is more likely that dividends would grow in the future. If we were to assume a constant rate of growth at the rate of g per annum, then:

Gordon's Growth Model

$$E_{ex\text{-}div} = \frac{d_1}{r_e - g}$$

where:

$E_{ex\text{-}div}$ = the ex-div market value of the shares which may need to be calculated using:

$\quad E_{ex\text{-}div}$ = $E_{cum\text{-}div} - d_0$

$\quad E_{cum\,div}$ = the cum-div market value of the shares

$\quad d_0$ = the dividend about to be paid now if we are cum-div

d_1 = the expected dividend in one year's time which may need to be calculated as $d_1 = d_0 \times (1 + g)$

r_e = the investors' required rate of return

g = the expected annual growth rate of the dividends

Investors' required rate of return

This formula can be rearranged to solve for the investors' required rate of return as follows.

$$r_e - g = \frac{d_1}{E_{ex\text{-}div}}$$

$$r_e = \frac{d_1}{E_{ex\text{-}div}} + g$$

5: EQUITIES

Example

A company is about to pay a dividend of $0.10 on its $1.00 ordinary shares. The shares are currently quoted at $2.30. The dividend is expected to grow at the rate of 10% per annum. Calculate the investors' required rate of return.

Solution

Since we are about to pay the dividend, we will assume that the share is currently cum-div. Hence, since we need the ex-div value, we must use the expression:

$$E_{ex\text{-}div} = E_{cum\text{-}div} - d_0$$

to calculate the ex-div price as:

$$E_{ex\text{-}div} = \$2.30 - \$0.10 = \$2.20$$

Then, using the above formula for the required return to equity, we get:

$$r_e = \frac{d_1}{E_{ex\text{-}div}} + g$$

$$r_e = \frac{0.10 \times 1.10}{2.20} + 10\%$$

$$r_e = \frac{0.11}{2.20} + 10\%$$

$$r_e = 5\% + 10\% = 15\% \text{ pa}$$

3.3.5 Calculating the dividend growth rate – 'g'

One problem that we have currently left unanswered is how we establish the investors' expectations regarding the dividend growth rate. There are two approaches we can take to tackling this.

- Look at the past dividend growth rates.
- Consider what causes growth.

Causes of growth – reinvestment

When looking at growth rates it is important to consider what causes growth in dividends, or may cause growth in the future, since it is investors' expectations of the future that we are concerned with.

If a company fully distributes all of its profits this year, then at the end of the year (start of next year) it will be in exactly the same position as it was at the start of this year, ie it will not have grown.

Long-term growth results from retaining a portion of earnings and reinvesting them to generate higher earnings and higher dividends in the future.

5: EQUITIES

This leads to the expression that we could have used to calculate the growth rate directly:

$$g = r \times b$$

where:

r = rate of return on reinvested capital
b = proportion of profits retained and reinvested

3.3.6 Dividend policy

Dividend policy is a strategy developed by a company's directors for the level of dividends they will pay each year. Dividend policy may be expressed in terms of a desired growth rate, eg 5% annual growth in real terms. It may also be expressed as a cover ratio, eg dividends will be covered by a ratio of at least 2× when compared to earnings for the year. Whatever way they do it, the directors will have some target dividend rate.

Reasons for setting a dividend policy

The reason that directors set a dividend policy for their company is that they believe stockholders like to have a stable or steadily growing dividend each year. Typically, they will look at past dividend growth, this year's earnings and expected future earnings levels and from these three factors aim to set an acceptable level of dividend this year which will grow at a roughly constant rate in the future.

3.4 Dividend yield

3.4.1 Basic ratio

The dividend yield of a company is calculated as:

$$\text{Dividend yield} = \frac{d}{E_{\text{ex-div}}}$$

where:

d = the net dividend paid

$E_{\text{ex-div}}$ = the current share price

3.4.2 Comparable company information

The dividend yield for a comparable company can be found from published sources. This can then be used as a surrogate for the required dividend yield for the company in question and inserted into the formula together with our company's own dividend. The required equity valuation will then fall out as the missing figure.

3.4.3 Ensuring consistency of information

It is important to ensure that the dividend yield calculation is being done on the same basis for both the companies.

5: EQUITIES

Typically, published dividend yields are done on a net basis.

In addition, dividend yields may be historic or prospective, ie based on last year's actual dividend or on next year's expected dividend.

3.5 Dividend cover

On the last point of expected growth rates of dividends, one measure that we can look to is the dividend cover.

3.5.1 Basic ratio

Dividend cover is used as an attempt to assess the likelihood of the existing dividend being maintained. The dividend cover is calculated as:

$$\text{Dividend cover} = \frac{\text{Earnings per share}}{\text{Net dividend per share}}$$

3.5.2 Considerations

An unusually high dividend cover implies that the company is retaining the majority of its earnings, presumably with the intention of reinvesting to generate growth.

3.6 Earnings-based valuations

3.6.1 Price to earnings ratio

The typical method of valuing a company based on its earnings levels is to use price to earnings (P/E) ratio, calculated as:

$$P/E = \frac{E_{\text{ex-div}} \text{ per share}}{EPS}$$

where:

EPS = earnings per share

$E_{\text{ex-div}}$ per share = current share price

The P/E ratio expresses the number of years' earnings represented by the current market price.

The P/E ratio for a similar company can be inserted into the formula together with the earnings per share of our company. The required valuation will fall out as the missing figure.

The significance of a P/E ratio can only be judged in relation to the ratios of other companies in the same type of business. If the median P/E ratio for an industry sector was eight, then a ratio of 12 for a particular company would suggest that the shares of that company were in great demand, possibly because a rapid growth of earnings was expected. A low ratio, say four for example, would indicate a company not greatly favoured by investors which probably has poor growth prospects.

Clearly, central to this valuation method is the calculation of the earnings per share.

Executive Summary

- The shareholders of the company are the owners of the company. As the owners they have a right to vote and to dividend payments when they are distributed.

- The majority of shares are 'ordinary' shares with equal rights to share in the profits.

- Preference shares pay a fixed dividend which must be paid before the company can pay out an ordinary dividend. Preference shares also have priority over ordinary shareholders in the event of a company winding-up.

- Bonus issues and stock splits are methods of cosmetically reducing the share price to increase liquidity in the shares.

- The dividend valuation model is one approach to valuing equity. Other methods include asset-based and earnings-based valuations.

6 Property

Contents

1 Characteristics 212
2 Valuation 219
Executive Summary 222

1 CHARACTERISTICS

1.1 Introduction

Property has very many similar characteristics to shares as an investment class. Over the long term the value of property tends to rise and the income an investor could derive from it (rent) also rises, just like the capital value and income from shares.

There are, however, a number of distinguishing characteristics of property that impact on its suitability as an investment vehicle. We need to be aware of these characteristics and be aware of the methods available for making property investments.

For many other types of investment, we have assumed that the markets are perfect, ie that there is perfect competition within those markets. Competition in the property market is far from perfect. Such imperfections include the immobility of the product and the possibility of a low number of buyers and sellers; in extreme circumstances, there may be only one potential purchaser. Invariably, for any property, there will only be one seller, giving him almost monopolistic powers. Even if relatively identical units of property exist, they will not necessarily be offered for sale simultaneously, causing imperfections in this particular market.

To appreciate the risks inherent in these property investments, hence the factors affecting their values, it is essential to appreciate the distinguishing features of property that differentiates it from other types of investments.

1.2 Distinguishing features

1.2.1 Supply features

Heterogeneity

Unlike stock exchange investments, property investments tend to be unique in terms of location, design, condition, size, etc. Although there may be similar substitutes, especially in the case of say, housing, there is frequently a limited amount of supply available. In certain extreme cases, the property may be absolutely unique, for example, it may offer the opportunity to acquire a historical location or location of national interest.

Indivisibility

Property is frequently indivisible, which is also true for single shares in companies, however, the cost of each individual, indivisible unit is significantly higher. As a result, property is often unattainable as an investment medium for the small investor, except through acquiring shares in property companies or through property bonds or other indirect means.

Inelasticity of supply

The physical overall supply of land is virtually fixed and the mix of various land uses is difficult to alter because of planning controls. Due to the time taken to obtain planning permission, arrange finance, construct buildings and arrange disposal, it is very difficult to react quickly to any changes in demand. This inelasticity of supply leaves the property market abnormally vulnerable to economic boom and slump.

1.2.2 Demand features

Costs of transfer

The costs of dealing in property are relatively high, compared to those of other types of investment. Investigation of title, the need for formal contracts and the frequent need to create a mortgage are reasons for employing a solicitor, significantly adding to any costs.

Special problems of management

There are a number of legal and economic problems associated with property management, which may consume a considerable amount of time and money on the part of the investor. For example, where the repairing liabilities fall upon the landlord (the investor), he will need to investigate the repairs that are required, obtain quotes, hire workers and see the work through to completion, which is all very time consuming. This is a dramatic difference compared to gilt-edged stock, where no such management problems are encountered.

Imperfect knowledge

As a result of the relative infrequency of transactions and secrecy concerning details, the information generally available to the market tends to be limited. Although there is an increasing stream of generalised information about transactions from the professional press, this does not remove this market imperfection.

Government intervention

Legal controls

There is great political significance attached to property. After all, countries are defined by the area that they own. It is a government's responsibility to look after the resources of their country as they best see fit, and property is just one of those resources. As a result, government intervention in the property market is rife.

Geographical factors

There are many geographical factors that influence the values of properties. These include: latitude, topography, aspect and local climate conditions, all detailed below.

Latitude

The latitude of an area may be important depending on the use to which the property is to be put. A farm in the south west of England will be suitable for different types of farming to one in the north of Scotland. A hotel on the south coast would expect a longer summer season than one in the north.

Topography

The existence of geographical obstacles, such as hills and rivers, may well determine the catchment area of say, a shopping centre. The dangers of flooding or subsidence may invalidate an area as a potential location for a factory. Topography is all important.

Aspect

The aspect of a property may be important, particularly, in residential and holiday areas.

Local climatic conditions

The local climatic conditions may well determine the demand for certain types of property and knowledge of the local climatic conditions will be important when making any property investment.

Other factors affecting demand

Communications

Clearly, if any property is to be used, it needs to have good communications and be accessible. If the communications and accessibility are poor, this will clearly have an adverse impact on its value. This is especially the case for commercial properties, particularly industrial and warehouse units where it is common to see the proximity of a motorway access point stressed as the most important feature.

Fashion and local demand

Although very difficult to assess, fashion and local demand can have a dramatic impact on the market value of property. It may well be that a property is difficult to market because it has a design or appearance that has become unfashionable.

Individual features of a property

The individual features of a property again will be of great importance in determining its value. Is it a good or bad design, is it functional, is it adaptable, is it well located?

A factory into which it is difficult to install modern equipment because of poor access, or through low load-bearing capacity of the floors, will be relatively unattractive.

State of repair

This will obviously impact upon the current value of the property since, in order to utilise the property, repairs will have to be carried out. This not only costs money, but also time. A property that is in good condition will invariably sell more readily and at a higher price than one which is in a bad condition.

Services

The availability of gas supply, mains electricity, mains water, mains sewers, and telephone connections will undoubtedly be of great importance to a potential purchaser.

The idyllic country cottage will become less attractive when it is discovered that there is only a septic tank at the bottom of the garden.

Potential

A property's potential can greatly affect its attractiveness on the market. It may be in a poor condition, but if improvement is possible then it may readily sell at a good price. This is what has happened to many cottages in certain areas of London.

Time

A price that seems high at the commencement of a development scheme may be just about right by the time the scheme is completed and may seem ridiculously low a year or two later. As a result, time scales should be examined when considering a property investment.

1.2.3 Risk and other considerations

Decentralised market

Unlike a stock exchange, property is not sold on a central market. Property is normally bought and sold through agents in a particular location. Occasionally, major firms operate nationally and even internationally in the purchase of sale of investments for major clients. However, this is not true of the general property market.

Market risk

As a result of this special nature of property, there are a number of general market risks associated with its ownership as an investment. These include:

- The inelasticity of supply and vulnerability to changes in the economic conditions.
- The degree of government intervention, impacting on returns.
- Physical risks, such as fire, earthquakes, flooding, etc.
- Economic risk that a property become obsolete in terms of design or may purpose.

Individual risk

The state of, and trend in, the local economy will be of prime importance in determining the demand for property in that area. An investment in property in a depressed area is highly unlikely to be as attractive as a similar investment in a thriving area, unless the depressed area currently offers investment possibilities at bargain basement prices. Alternatively, inducements such as establishing an area as an enterprise zone may be offered to make the investment worthwhile.

1.3 Types of property

1.3.1 Introduction

Property as a general potential investment may be sub-categorised into a number of different property types, including:

- Shops
- Offices
- Industrial
- Residential
- Agricultural
- Special

We will look at each of these in turn.

1.3.2 Shops

Shops vary substantially in size and type, though the most important factor governing the investment potential of a shop is its position. Also of great importance will be the quality of the property. As a result of this, institutional investment is primarily restricted to modern buildings in prime, urban locations. The majority of such property is now owned by the financial institutions, property companies and other investors.

1.3.3 Offices

The positioning of office properties is less crucial than that of shops, though they should be located in areas served by good transport and other facilities. The exception to this general rule relates to the small, specialised areas such as financial centres, which are traditionally occupied by banking, insurance and shipping agencies, where prestige and a high degree of personal contact are of importance.

Quality of offices tends to be the primary determinant of office values, with location the secondary factor.

1.3.4 Industrial

Accessibility to transport routes, sources of raw material, labour and markets for the products have been the traditional factors governing the location of industrial properties. Such properties have tended to be owner, occupied and, therefore, not available as an investment opportunity. Industrial property has generally been seen as a less attractive investment than shops and offices, largely due to its greater obsolescence and vulnerability to economic recession. However, institutional investment in modern well located factories and warehouses increased substantially over the last few decades, and the majority of such privately-owned premises may now be the subject of a portfolio of investment.

1.3.5 Residential

Residential housing has proved to be unpopular with institutional investors due to its political and social sensitivity, its expense of management and the fact that all but the most valuable property seem liable to remain subject to long-term rent control.

1.3.6 Agricultural

Agricultural property may be sub-divided into farmland and woodland.

Farmland varies in quality from barren hill land to prime arable, and it is mainly this latter class which is the subject of institutional investment (particularly the larger, more efficient units).

An investment in woodland is an investment in land and the growing crop of timber, which may take 60 or more years to mature. The investor will receive no income from his initial cost of establishing and managing a plantation until the first wood stocks are sold, which may be after 20 years or so. An investment in woodlands must therefore be considered long term.

1.3.7 Special properties

Special properties include cinemas, hotels, petrol-filling stations, etc. Such properties often have a quasi-monopolistic element. In the case of cinemas, for example, there may only be one in a particular town. In the case of a petrol-filling station, its position is of such importance that two such properties may be very close together, but one may be less conspicuous from the highway and as such, have a much lower earnings potential. These types of properties therefore present the investor with some difficulties. The valuation of the properties may be dependent on such factors as:

- The business acumen of the tenant.
- The position of the property in relation to surrounding developments.

The investor has no control over these two factors. As a result, the risks of such an investment are high.

1.4 Direct/indirect investment

1.4.1 Direct investment

Freehold

The highest form of property investment or ownership is generally termed, freehold. A freeholder is said to hold the property absolutely and in perpetuity. He may be in possession of the property or he may have forgone the right to possession (occupation) by letting it as an investment. In the latter case, he will be entitled to possession on the expiry of the tenancy and this is described as the landlord's reversion. The ability to gain reversion may be affected by legislation.

Although the freehold is the most powerful direct property investment interest, it is nevertheless subject to some restrictions, such as the use to which the land or buildings may be put and any other local regulations.

Leasehold

A leasehold interest is created out of a freehold interest, and is therefore out of necessity less powerful than a freehold interest. It is of limited duration and is subject to stringent conditions, which may be of a positive or negative nature.

The leaseholder may in turn create a lesser interest or sub-lease, in which event he becomes known as the head lessee paying a head rent. This process may continue down the line and a whole train of interests may be built up.

The lease terms and the quality of the tenant are important in assessing the merits of an investment. In addition, the duration of the lease may also be critical.

A lease contract will normally specify who is liable to pay for repairs, insurances, etc, which may be either the freeholder or the leaseholder. These factors are obviously important from the point of view of making such an investment.

1.4.2 Indirect investment

Property shares

The purchase of shares in property companies offers the small investor who may not have sufficient resources to actually involve himself in property development directly, the chance of an indirect investment in property. Many property companies are large household names and hold a wide spread of properties.

Property open-ended collective investments

At the launch of such a fund, the manager must be confident that he will attract sufficient funds to make adequate property purchases to establish a well spread portfolio.

With open-ended collective investments, the investment will be redeemed at net asset value. However, if many investors choose to sell at one time, the fund may need to invoke its right to postpone encashment of units/shares until property can be sold. This makes property funds potentially illiquid.

Real Estate Investment Trusts (REITs)

Real Estate Investment Trusts (REITs) are 'tax-transparent' property investment vehicles which were first formed in the USA, where the name 'REITs' originated. Other countries, including Japan, the Netherlands the UK and France, now have their own versions of REITs.

A REIT is a company that owns and operates income-producing real estate, which can be commercial or residential. Most of this income is distributed to shareholders and in return the company is exempt from corporation tax.

REITs are designed to securitise the income from rented property assets in a tax-efficient way and to ensure that the return from investing in a property company is more aligned with direct property investment. This is done by removing the requirement for companies to pay corporation tax, thereby taking away "double taxation" at both the corporate and the investor level.

A property company converting to REIT status would benefit from the tax exemption and should be better able to raise funds through the stock market. This is because many property companies currently trade at discount to net asset value, partly as a result of double taxation suppressing the value of the shares. A more tax-efficient vehicle should help to correct this anomaly.

Advantages of pooled property investments

- The investor is 'buying' expert property management.
- The investor can buy into a large, well spread fund. This can be spread according to type, eg office, warehousing, retail and geographically, with reduced risk because of this diversification.
- Although there is some illiquidity in the pooled finds, liquidity is greater than with direct investment.
- A relatively small amount of money can be invested in a pooled fund. A substantial sum would need to be committed to the purchase of even a modest commercial property.

Disadvantages of pooled property investments

- The investor does not have direct control over the properties.
- It may be difficult to realise capital quickly.

2 VALUATION

2.1 Introduction

Together with the application of discounted cash flow techniques, there are five conventional methods of valuation, specifically:

- The comparative method
- The investment method
- The contractor's method
- The residual method
- The profits method

Of these, the comparative and investor's method are considered the most important, though we will consider each in turn.

2.1.1 Comparative method

This is probably the most widely used method, and even if one of the other four methods is used by the valuer, he will still almost inevitably have recourse to comparison as well. The method entails making a valuation by directly comparing the property under consideration with similar properties that have been sold, finding its value from these past transactions.

Ideally, the comparative method should only be used when properties being compared are similar and in the same area, and where good records of recent transactions are available. In practice, it may be necessary to make a valuation when one or more of these conditions is not present; which is when the knowledge of experience of the valuer must be brought to bear.

The method involves few dangers if the market is stable. When it is not, there will clearly be problems in its use, as would also be the case if there were few comparables, or if there were no true comparables.

In using this method, the valuer should always bear in mind the fact that property is heterogeneous and should always ask himself whether any special factors affected the market value of comparables that he is using, or whether any special factors are likely to affect the value of the property which he is considering.

Lastly, when using the comparative method, the valuer should bear in mind that historical comparatives may bear little relevance to current market conditions if, for example, there is a slump in the market. In these situations, past evidence might be of very limited assistance or, in extreme circumstances, it may be positively misleading.

2.1.2 Investment method

This method is used for valuing properties that are normally held as income-producing investments. The value of such an investment is given by:

$$\text{Market value} = \text{Net income} \times \text{Years purchase}$$

where the years purchase is the inverse of the market yield. This can be seen as being the same calculation as used for undated gilts, where a perpetual income is received at a level rate. Freehold properties may be used to produce perpetual income for valuation purposes, hence this approach may be suitable for this or very long leasehold property.

If the income varies in future years, as is the case with ordinary shares, then a currently acceptable yield for these types of investment may be determined from the market.

2.1.3 Contractor's method

This method is used to value the types of properties that seldom change hands and for which there are therefore few comparatives.

The method is to value the property at depreciated, replacement cost, ie value of existing property equals replacement cost of site plus replacement cost of building less depreciation allowance.

The method has the inherent disadvantage of attempting to equate cost to value as well as practical difficulties of assessing the replacement costs involved.

2.1.4 Residual method

The residual method is used to value development sites and properties suitable for redevelopment. In essence, the value of the site to be acquired is established based on the estimated ultimate value of the site following the redevelopment less the costs to be incurred in undertaking the redevelopment.

2.1.5 Profits method

Where comparables are not available, as with certain types of property such as theatres, restaurants and hotels, the valuation may have to be made purely by reference to the profits, which a tenant of reasonable business acumen could make from occupation of the property. The method is inappropriate where it is possible to value by means of comparison, and is generally only used where there is some degree of monopoly attached to the property.

This approach is very similar to the earnings-based valuation method for evaluating shares.

2.1.6 Discounted cash flow

In addition to these methods, valuations can be made using discounted cash flow techniques. The investment method of valuation is a simple form of discounted cash flow, which considers future income flows and multiplies by an appropriate factor (the years purchase).

To utilise discounted cash flow techniques, the future cash flows will be the sums remaining after taking account of anticipated future outgoings, so that only the net income for each future period will be discounted back to its present value. The advantage of a full discounted cash flow valuation over the basic investment method approach is that it can take account of many more variations and assumptions than the latter approach can. It is also possible to build in any unusual variable influences, such as the effects of taxation which may, in some way, be based on the income flows, but will undoubtedly be at least one if not more years later.

In order to utilise this technique, it will be important to know what cash flows will be the income/outgoings of the investor. We, as the investor, need to know whether we are liable to pay the insurance and maintenance costs on the property, assuming it is leasehold.

6: PROPERTY

EXECUTIVE SUMMARY

Distinguishing features

Supply features:

- Hetrogenity
- Indivisibility
- Inelasticity of supply

Demand features:

- Costs of transfer
- Problems of management
- Imperfect knowledge
- Government intervention
- Geographical features
- Others

Property

Types:

- Shops
- Offices
- Industrial
- Residential
- Agricultural
- Special

Property investment

Direct:

- Freehold
- Leasehold
- Life interest

Indirect:

- Property shares
- Property bonds
- Property unit trusts and OEICs
- Property investment trusts
- REITs
- Insurance company property funds
- Offshore property funds

7 Commodities and Alternative Investments

Contents

1 Commodities 224
2 Collectibles 226
Executive Summary 228

7: COMMODITIES AND ALTERNATIVE INVESTMENTS

1 COMMODITIES

1.1 Introduction

Previously we have examined what may be regarded as normal investments. There are, however, two final investment classes for us to consider: commodities and alternative investments, which we consider in this chapter.

Commodities is the generic term for physical resources that are of some value. They are assets (ie they have some value) as a result of their rarity, usefulness and characteristics.

In the main, physical commodities only have a real value to their user, eg the manufacturer who needs the raw material and they frequently deteriorate in value over time (eg foodstuffs). As such, commodities are rarely appropriated as an asset class for most types of fund, though speculators may look to gain from any price changes they exhibit. Most of this speculative trade in commodities is achieved through the use of derivatives which are covered in a separate chapter.

Commodities for investment purposes are essentially raw materials that can be bought and sold easily in large quantities on organised markets. They fall into one of three categories:

- **Energy commodities**: oil, natural gas, coal
- **Hard commodities**: metals (gold, copper, lead, tin, etc) and diamonds
- **Soft commodities**: mostly foodstuffs, such as cocoa, coffee, soya, sugar, etc

The prices of these commodities are, as for all assets, driven by the influences of supply and demand and can, therefore, be significantly affected by factors such as:

- Good/poor harvests
- Exceptionally good/bad weather
- Political unrest in the producing country

As a result, commodities have the following general characteristics:

- They generally produce no income
- Values can change dramatically in response to economic change, natural disasters and other economic shocks
- Commodities may be expensive to store and may be subject to deterioration over time

In relation to the second of these points, natural disasters and other economic shocks often lead to a shortage of supply in essential commodities, leading to significant price rises. Commodities can therefore, be viewed as a hedge against such events.

1.1.1 Cash market

Trade on the cash market is for immediate delivery, known as trading **physicals** or **actuals**, with the price paid being the **spot price**. Payment must be made immediately and charges are made for storage and insurance. There is a standard contract size, 25 tonnes for copper for example, to aid the smooth running of the market.

7: COMMODITIES AND ALTERNATIVE INVESTMENTS

1.1.2 Futures market

Trade on the futures market is for delivery at an agreed future price at an agreed future date. There are rules about how far in advance such futures contracts can be arranged (up to three months for copper for example). The advantages of dealing in futures are the absence of storage costs and the effect of gearing-only, a small margin being required to gain exposure to a large asset value.

1.2 Investment in commodities

1.2.1 Direct investment

Physicals

An investor can buy and sell commodities directly through a commodity broker, or invest in a commodities fund. Dealing in physical commodities is not a practical proposition for most investors because of the minimum quantities that must be traded and the risk of deterioration in quality. The cash market is primarily for users of that raw material/agricultural product, rather than the investor.

For non-deteriorating commodities such as metals, however, it is possible and practical to take a direct holding in the commodity, which will be stored in the exchanges approved warehouse. The investor should consider the storage costs, etc. involved with this option.

Futures

Futures do, however, provide a useful investment vehicle for the purposes of diversifying and hedging as we will discuss in Chapter 8.

Advantages of direct investment

Direct investment offers the following advantages over indirect investment.

- Commodity consumers will want to be able to acquire the commodity possibly in advance of needing it if prices are favourable.
- There will be lower risks (counterparty risk, political risk).

1.2.2 Indirect investment

Shares of commodity companies

One approach to indirect investment would be to acquire shares in a commodity-producing company, eg mines. As commodity prices rise, we could anticipate that the company's revenue, and correspondingly, the share price will rise. The extent of this relationship, however, also depends on how the costs may fluctuate. Although all producers will face the same selling price, they will not all face the same cost pressures and hence, though we may expect share prices to move with the underlying commodity prices, the correlation will not be perfect.

Commodity funds

The choice for most investors is a sterling commodities fund. Authorised unit trusts are not allowed to invest in commodities; hence, if the investor wishes to have a professionally managed fund, he must look offshore. A variety of funds deal in commodities, differing in their areas of specialisation, permitted levels of gearing and ability to go short. Most funds use both the cash and futures markets, hence the fund performance may not exactly correspond to the underlying commodities.

These funds are of interest to an investor who is interested in real assets as a hedge against inflation and is also looking more towards capital growth than income.

In addition to these more normal funds, exposure may be gained to commodities through certain hedge funds, and through Exchange Traded Commodities (ETCs), a variation of ETFs where a number of competing products have been issued.

Like ETFs, ETCs are asset-backed open-ended investments that track the performance of the underlying commodity/index. They are traded and settled like shares and have the support of a market-maker to ensure liquidity and are available on single commodities (eg gold) or on commodity indices (eg energy or precious metals).

Advantages of indirect investment

The advantages of indirect investment are:

- The shares will probably pay a dividend unlike any direct investment
- Lower holding/storage costs
- Lower minimal dealing size

2 COLLECTIBLES

2.1 Introduction

Below are some types of investment that could be called '**collectibles**'.

- Works of art
- Antiques
- Coins
- Stamps
- Vintage cars
- Wine
- Limited edition books
- Diamonds
- Gold items

Collectibles have the following general features:

- They generally produce **no income**.
- They can be **difficult to value**, particularly for unique items.

- **Values can change** with changes in fashion or, for commodities like gold, with inflation.
- Collectibles are **expensive to keep** because they are vulnerable to atmospheric change, burglary and so on. There can be additional costs of custodianship, possibly in a bank, and heavy insurance premiums.
- The **cost of buying and selling** collectibles can be high, with dealers' margins or commissions being substantial.
- Collectibles may have low **marketability**. An item may be difficult to sell in a hurry and the price raised may be a great disappointment.
- **Specialist knowledge** is required in the selection of the item.
- Markets for collectibles are not generally subject to special regulatory regimes, and the less knowledgeable investor may be vulnerable to the unscrupulous expert.

2.2 Collectibles in a portfolio

Investment advisers will not often be called upon to recommend an alternative investment. The client will normally already have an interest in whatever the collectible item may be. The pleasure provided by the activity of collecting items will often be an important aspect.

Collectibles may be of particular use to a higher rate taxpayer who has no intention of disposing of the items during this lifetime. As the artefacts generate no income, the collector will suffer no tax while he holds them. There will be no CGT on death. Inheritance tax will be avoided if the item is given for national purposes or the public good. Collectibles also provide a good hedge against inflation.

7: COMMODITIES AND ALTERNATIVE INVESTMENTS

Executive Summary

- Commodities are essentially raw materials that can be easily bought and sold in large quantities on organised markets.

- Collectibles such as art or antiques can be a part of a portfolio of investments, and this will usually be when the investor has a particular interest in the items collected.

8 Derivative Products

Contents

1. Introduction 230
2. Futures 230
3. Options 249
4. Options Trading Strategies 262
5. Swaps 268
   Executive Summary 271

8: DERIVATIVE PRODUCTS

1 INTRODUCTION

In the minds of the general public, and indeed those of many people involved in the financial services industry, derivative products such as futures and options, warrants and swaps are thought of as very complicated. They are also thought of as having little to do with the real world. Television coverage, showing pictures of young traders in brightly coloured jackets shouting at each other in an apparent frenzy, makes it difficult to imagine that what they are engaged in may be of enormous value to the smooth functioning of the economy.

At the heart of these products is the concept of deferred delivery. The instruments allow you, albeit in slightly different ways, to agree **today** the price at which you will buy or sell an asset at some time in the future. This is unlike normal everyday transactions. When we go to a supermarket, we pay our money and take immediate delivery of our goods. Why would someone wish to agree today a price for delivery at some time in the future? The answer is **certainty**.

Imagine a farmer growing a crop of wheat. To grow such a crop costs money; money for seed, labour, fertiliser and so on. All this expenditure takes place with no certainty that, when the crop is eventually harvested, the price at which the wheat is sold will cover these costs. This is obviously a risky thing to do and many farmers are unwilling to take on this burden. How can this uncertainty be avoided?

By using derivatives, the farmer is able to agree **today** a price at which the crop will ultimately be sold, in maybe four or six months' time. This enables the farmer to achieve a minimum sale price for his crop. He is no longer subject to fluctuations in wheat prices. He knows what price his wheat will bring and can thus plan his business accordingly.

From their origins in the agricultural world, derivative products have become available on a wide range of other assets, from metals and crude oil to bonds and equities. To understand these instruments properly requires some application. There is much terminology to master, and definitions to be understood but, essentially, they are really quite simple. They are products that allow you to fix today the price at which assets may be bought or sold at a future date.

2 FUTURES

2.1 Definition of a future

> A future is an agreement to buy or sell a standard quantity of a specified asset on a fixed future date at a price agreed today.

There are two parties to a futures contract, a buyer and a seller whose obligations are as follows.

- The buyer of a future enters into an **obligation** to buy on a specified date.
- The seller of a future is under an **obligation** to sell on a future date.

These obligations relate to a **standard quantity** of a **specified** asset on a **fixed future date** at a **price agreed today**.

2.1.1 Standard quantity

Exchange-traded futures are traded in standardised parcels known as **contracts**.

For example, the CME T-bond futures contract is for $100,000 nominal, the Eurex Euro-bond futures contract is for £100,000 nominal and the Liffe gilt futures contract is for £100,000 nominal. The purpose of this standardisation is that buyers and sellers are clear about the quantity that will be delivered. If you sold one gilt future, you would know that you were obligated to sell $100,000 nominal of gilts.

Futures are only traded in whole numbers of contracts. So, if you wished to buy £200,000 nominal of gilts, you would buy two gilt futures.

2.1.2 Specified asset

Imagine that you entered into a futures contract on a car. Let us say you buy a car futures contract that gives you the obligation to buy a car at a fixed price of $15,000, with delivery taking place in December.

It is obvious that something very important is missing from the contract – namely any detail about what type of car you are to buy. Most of us would be happy to pay $15,000 for a new Ferrari, but would be rather less happy if all our $15,000 bought was an old Fiat.

All futures contracts are governed by their **contract specifications**. These legal documents set out in great detail the size of each contract, when delivery is to take place, and what exactly is to be delivered.

2.1.3 Fixed futures date

The delivery of futures contracts takes place on a specified date(s) known as **delivery day(s)**. This is when buyers exchange money for goods with sellers. Futures have finite lifespans so that, once the **last trading day** is past, it is impossible to trade the futures for that date.

At any one time, a range of delivery months may be traded (for example most Liffe Eurex, CME and CBOT contracts have **March**, **June**, **September** and **December** delivery months) and as one delivery day passes, a new date is introduced.

In many cases, a physical delivery does not actually occur on the delivery day. Rather, the exchange calculates how much has been lost, or gained, by the parties to a futures contract. It is only this monetary gain or loss that changes hands, not the underlying asset. The **Liffe gilt future** is an example of a **physically settled contract**, whereas equity index future tend to be **cash settled**.

2.1.4 Price agreed today

The final phrase in the definition is the most important of all. The reason why so many people, from farmers to fund managers, like using futures is, as was explained in the introduction to this chapter, that they introduce certainty.

Imagine a farmer growing a crop of wheat. In the absence of a futures market, he has no idea whether he will make a profit or a loss when he plants the seeds in the ground. By the time he harvests his crop, the price of wheat may be so low that he will not be able to cover his costs. However, with a futures contract, he can fix a price for his wheat many months before harvest. If, six months before the harvest, he sells a wheat future,

8: DERIVATIVE PRODUCTS

he enters into an obligation to sell wheat at that price on the stipulated delivery day. In other words, he knows what price his goods will fetch.

You might think that this is all well and good, but what happens if there is a drought or a frost that makes it impossible for the farmer to deliver his wheat?

Futures can be traded, so although the contract obligates the buyer to buy and the seller to sell, these obligations can be **offset** (closed out) by undertaking an equal and opposite trade in the market.

Example

Let us suppose a farmer sold 1 September wheat future at $120 per tonne. If, subsequently, the farmer decides he does not wish to sell his wheat, but would prefer to use the grain to feed his cattle, he simply buys 1 September future at the then prevailing price. His original sold position is now offset by a bought position, leaving him with no outstanding delivery obligations.

This offsetting is common in future markets; very few contracts run through to delivery.

2.2 Futures v forward contracts

The definition of a forward contract is very similar to that of a future in that it is an agreement to buy or sell a specific quantity of a specified asset on a fixed future date at a price agreed today. The differences between futures and forward contracts can best be summarised in the following table.

Attribute	Futures	Forward Contracts
Traded	Exchange traded	OTC
Quality and quantity	Standardised by the exchange for all products	Specified in the contract
Delivery dates	Standard fixed dates	Specified in the contract
Liquidity/ability to close out	Generally good liquidity/easy to close out	May be limited
Counterparty risk	None due to the workings of the clearing and settlement system	Default risk exists
Costs/margin	Relatively low initial costs (margin)	Costs specifically agreed, may be high
Regulation	Significant regulation and investor protection	Less regulated

2.3 Using futures

All sorts of people use futures. Some, like the wheat farmer, may use them to reduce risk, others to seek high returns – and for this, be willing to take high risks. Futures markets are in fact wholesale markets in risk. They are markets in which risks are transferred from the cautious to those with more adventurous (or reckless) spirits. The users of futures fall into one of three categories: the **hedger**, the **speculator** and the **arbitrageur**, whose motivations are as follows.

- **Hedger**: someone seeking to reduce risk.
- **Speculator**: a risk-taker seeking large profits.
- **Arbitrageur**: seeks riskless profits from exploiting market inefficiencies.

In this section, we will look at the first two types of user, starting with the speculator.

2.3.1 The speculator – buying a future

Introduction

A transaction in which a future is purchased to open a position is known as a **long futures position**. Thus, the purchase of the oil future would be described as **going long of the future** or simply **long**.

The purpose of undertaking such a transaction is to open the investor to the risks and rewards of ownership of the underlying asset by an alternative route.

Example

On 1 May, a speculator thinks that the situation in the Middle East is becoming more dangerous and that war is imminent. If war takes place, he would expect oil supplies to become restricted and the price of oil to rise.

The current cash price of oil is $19.00 per barrel, and the futures price is $20.50. The speculator does not have the facilities to store the oil at present.

How can he use the futures market to buy in anticipation of this price rise, and what will his position be if the price rise does occur on 21 May (cash price becoming $35, futures price being $30)?

Solution

Action 1 May: Buy 1 July oil future at $20.50

Since he does not have the facilities to store the oil, he cannot use the cash market, hence the speculator could buy 1 July oil future at $20.50 per barrel. Thus, he is now obliged to buy one contract (here 1,000 barrels) to be delivered on 1 July.

Action 21 May: Sell 1 July oil future at $30

Following the price rise, our speculator can now sell this contract at $30.00 per barrel, realising a profit of $9.50 per barrel or $9,500.

The reason the speculator has made a profit is that the futures market has risen in response to a rise in the cash market price of oil. Generally, futures prices can be expected to move at substantially the same rate and the same extent as cash market prices. This is a far from trivial observation. The cash market and the futures market in this example have both risen: the cash market from $19 to $35 – an increase of $16 per barrel; and the futures market from $20.50 to $30.00 – a rise of $9.50.

8: DERIVATIVE PRODUCTS

The reasons why the price movement should normally be substantially the same in both markets, and why they may differ, are explained in the next chapter.

Summary of position

Risk	Almost unlimited – The maximum loss would occur if the future fell to zero. For our oil speculator, this would be if the July future fell from $20.50 to 0.
Reward	Unlimited – As the futures price could rise to infinity, the profit is potentially unlimited.

2.3.2 The speculator – selling a future

Introduction

A transaction in which a future is sold to open a position is known as a **short futures position**. Thus, the sale of the oil future would be described as **going short of the future** or simply **short**.

The purpose of undertaking such a transaction is to open the investor to the opposite risks and rewards of ownership of the underlying asset.

Example

On 1 July, a speculator feels that the oil market is becoming oversupplied and that oil prices will fall. On that date, the September futures contract is trading at $22.00 per barrel.

How can the speculator use the futures market to profit from this situation and what will be his profit if the price fall does occur on 14 July, when the futures price has fallen to $20.00 per barrel?

Solution

If a speculator thinks that an asset price will fall, he will seek to make a profit by selling the future at the currently high price and subsequently buying it back at a low price. This is not an activity commonly undertaken in the cash markets and therefore needs a little explanation.

There are two ways of making profits.

- Buy at a low price and sell at a high price. For example, we may buy a house at $80,000 and sell it at $100,000 making a $20,000 profit.

- In futures markets, it is equally easy to sell something at a high price and buy it back at a low price. If you thought the property market was going to fall, you could sell a house at $100,000 and buy it back at $80,000 again realising a $20,000 profit.

In the actual property market, it is not easy to go **short** of a house, but in the futures market, in which deliveries are at some future date, it is straightforward.

Action 1 July: Sell 1 September oil future at $22

The speculator is committing himself to delivering an asset he does not own on 1 September.

Action 14 July: Buy 1 September oil future at $20.00

By 14 July, the future price has fallen and the speculator **buys back** his short futures position, thus extinguishing any delivery obligations. The profit can be calculated again as $2.00 per barrel or $2,000 in total.

Summary of position

Risk	Unlimited.
Reward	Limited, but large. The future can only fall to zero.

2.3.3 The hedger – Protecting against a fall

Speculators use futures to take on risks in the hope of large profits. Hedgers use futures to reduce the risk of existing cash market positions. They are motivated by a need for certainty and security.

Let us think about the position of an oil producer. The producer's profitability will be determined largely by the price of crude oil. When times are good, and the demand for oil is high, he will make good profits. However, if oil prices fall, he may find that the market price for oil is so low that the price does not cover the costs of extracting the oil from the ground. It is in helping people such as this that futures have their most important application.

The following graph shows the oil producer's exposure to the price of oil.

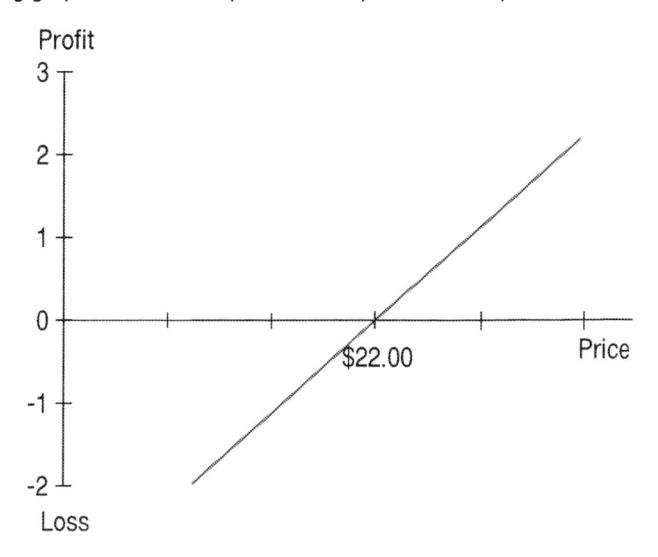

8: DERIVATIVE PRODUCTS

This shows that if prices go up, so do profits; if the price falls below a certain level, losses will emerge. This position is described as a **long position**.

How can the risk from a fall in price be reduced?

This can be done by selling futures and thereby entering into a contract that will obligate the futures seller to deliver oil at some time in the future at a price agreed today.

Through this mechanism, the oil producer can establish a sale price for his, say, July production of oil some time in advance, without having to wait until July when the price may be much lower. When futures are sold to hedge a long cash market position, it is known as a **short hedge**.

The theory of futures hedging is based on the future's position, producing profits or losses to offset the losses or profits in the cash market.

Example

An oil producer will have 100,000 barrels of crude oil available for delivery in July. He is nervous about the price of oil and expects it to fall sharply. On 1 May, the cash market price of oil is $22 a barrel, and the July future is trading at $23.

How can he use the futures market to hedge his position and minimise the risk of owning the asset (note, one contract is 1,000 barrels), and what will his position be if by 15 June the price has fallen to $18 in the cash market and $19 in the futures market?

Solution

Action 1 May: Sell 100 July oil futures at $23

(100 because each contract represents 1,000 barrels, and the producer is hedging 100,000 barrels.)

The oil producer is now long in the physical market (that is, he has 100,000 barrels for July delivery). He is also short 100,000 barrels in the futures market.

Action 15 June: Buy 100 July oil futures at $19

The profit from the futures trade should, if we have constructed the hedge properly, compensate the producer for the fall in oil prices. Let us see if this is true by first calculating the futures profit and then calculating the oil market loss.

Futures profit

   Profit per barrel = $4.00 per barrel ($23.00 – $19.00)

   Total profit = $400,000 ($4.00 × 100,000 barrels)

Cash market loss

   Loss per barrel = $4.00 per barrel ($18.00 – $22.00)

   Total loss = $400,000 ($4.00 × 100,000 barrels)

As can be seen, the profit and loss net each other out, demonstrating that the fall in oil prices did not hurt the producer.

It can be shown on a graph as follows.

8: DERIVATIVE PRODUCTS

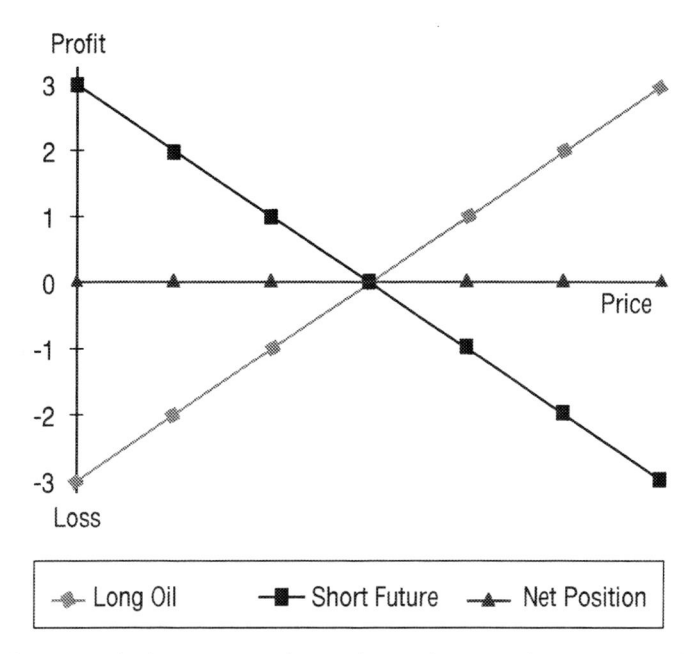

Profit/Loss chart with Long Oil, Short Future, and Net Position lines.

Whether the price of oil goes up or down, the producer need not worry as he has, by selling futures, **locked-in** a sale price for his oil.

The numbers in this example are slightly unrealistic, as there is a perfect offset between cash and futures markets. In the real world, futures do not always move precisely in line with the cash market. This point will be examined in more detail later on.

In the example above, we have seen how futures can be used to protect the oil producer against a price fall with a short hedge.

Short hedge: protects against price fall.

2.3.4 The hedger – protecting against a rise

The scenario that we are considering here is that an investor wishes to acquire an asset at some time in the future when cash is available, but is concerned that the current price may rise making the asset unaffordable. He therefore wishes to protect against this price rise.

Example

A chemical company, whose principal raw material is crude oil, is becoming nervous about a rise in oil prices.

The current cash price of crude oil is $18.00, and the November future trades at $18.50 per barrel.

How can the company use the futures market to hedge against any price rise and what will their position be if the cash price rises to $24.00 and the futures price to $24.50 on 10 October?

8: DERIVATIVE PRODUCTS

Solution

To protect itself against the possibility of a rise, the company could agree today the price it will pay for oil to be delivered in November. To guarantee the purchase price, all the company need do is buy or go long in the futures contract.

Action 20 September: Buy 10 November oil futures at $18.50

(To hedge its requirement for 10,000 barrels.)

Action 10 October: Sell 10 November oil futures at $24.50

Has the hedge worked?

Cash market loss

To find out, let us see how the price rise would have affected the cost of purchasing the physical oil.

	$
Cash price on 10 October	24.00
Cash price on 20 September	18.00
Cost increase per barrel	6.00

For the quantity required by the chemical manufacturer (10,000 barrels), this movement would have increased its costs by $60,000 ($6 × 10,000).

This increased cost should, in whole or in part, be offset by the futures profit.

Futures profit

	$
Futures price on 10 October	24.50
Futures price on 20 September	18.50
Futures profit per barrel	6.00

Hence, the total profit on the futures contract is $60,000, which covers the price increase.

Thus, while the physical oil will now cost more to acquire, the extra cost of purchase will in fact be covered by the futures profit.

	$
Cash price of 10,000 barrels of oil at 10 October	240,000
Less futures profit	(60,000)
Net cost	180,000

This equates to $18 per barrel, the cash price on 20 September.

This is an example of a long hedge, which protects against a rise.

Long hedge: protects against a rise.

8: DERIVATIVE PRODUCTS

2.3.5 Summary

In short hedges, you sell futures to protect an existing holding.

In long hedges, you buy futures to protect an anticipated holding.

2.3.6 Cross-hedging

Unfortunately, it may be the case that there is no futures contract based on the underlying cash instrument to be hedged, and a contract based on a similar underlying must be used. This is known as cross-hedging.

In such a situation, the hedged asset and the futures contract may not move together precisely. As a result, the investor will end up with some residual risk. This risk will depend on such factors as:

- Risk levels of the two instruments.
- Dividend/coupon levels.
- Maturity dates.
- Time span covered by the hedged underlying instrument and the instrument delivered under the future.

2.4 Some specific contracts and their uses

2.4.1 Introduction

In order to understand the use of futures to a fund manager we need to be familiar with contracts he may wish to use, how he may use them and why. We consider three categories of contract, in particular:

- Equity index futures
- Interest rate futures
- Bond futures

We will illustrate the use of these futures with the aid of the FTSE-100 Index Future, the Three-Month Sterling Future and the UK Gilt Future respectively. The principles, once understood, can then easily be applied to other futures so long as care is taken regarding the contract specification, in particular the contract size, tick size and tick value.

One bit of terminology we will introduce here is the **tick**. There are two aspects to this.

- The **tick size** is the smallest permitted quote movement on one contract.
- The **tick value** is the change in the value of one contract if there is a one-tick change in the quote.

These two factors enable us to calculate our futures dealing profit or loss by using:

Profit = Quote change in ticks × Tick value × Number of contracts

When we look at interest rate futures contract in particular, it will be most convenient to calculate the profit this way.

8: DERIVATIVE PRODUCTS

2.4.2 Equity index future

Purpose and characteristics

An equity index future allows the investor to gain or hedge exposure to equities. The FTSE-100 Index future that we are using for illustration fixes the price at which the underlying index may be bought or sold at a specific future date.

The general characteristics of this contract are as follows.

Unit of trade

Unit of trade = Index value × £10

That is, a contract can be valued by multiplying the index value by £10. If, for example, the index stood at 6,000, then one contract would have a value of 6,000 × £10 = £60,000.

What this means is that:

- A speculator may gain £60,000 of exposure to the market by buying a contract.
- A hedger who already holds shares could use the contract to hedge his exposure to £60,000 of those shares.

Delivery

This contract is **cash settled**. That is, rather than the two parties exchanging the underlying asset and the pre-agreed price at the delivery date, they simply settle up by the payment from one to the other of the difference in value.

Quotation

The quote given is in index points.

Tick

The tick size, the smallest permitted quote movement, is 0.5 index points, which corresponds to a tick value of £5.00 (0.5 × £10).

Uses

As we indicated above, we may use this contract to gain exposure to, or hedge exposure against, the index, ie the stock market in general.

Example

We are managing a £20m pension fund portfolio and we believe that the market is about to fall. The index and the future currently stand at 6,000.

The alternatives that we have are as follows.

- Sell the portfolio and move into cash/bonds – this will avoid the market fall, but will clearly incur massive dealing costs.
- Set-up a short hedge using the futures contract.

8: DERIVATIVE PRODUCTS

Short hedge

The future is quoted at 6,000, hence each contract will hedge £60,000 (6,000 × £10) of our exposure. To hedge the full portfolio, we will therefore need 333$^{1}/_{3}$ contracts (£20m ÷ £60,000). However, we can only deal in whole contracts, therefore we will sell 333 contracts (the closest whole number).

Let us now consider what our position is if the market (and the futures contract) fall 200 points.

Cash position

		£
Old portfolio value		20,000,000
New portfolio value = £20m × $\frac{5,800}{6,000}$		19,333,333
Loss		(666,667)

Futures position

	Points	
Sold index at	6,000	
Bought index to close position at	5,800	
Gain	200	= 400 ticks

Hence, the total profit on our 333 contracts will be:

Profit = Ticks × Tick value × Number of contracts
      = 400 × £5.00 × 333 = £666,000

As we can see, our futures profit almost exactly cancels the loss on the portfolio and hence represents a good hedging strategy.

Hedge ratio

One assumption we have made here is that our portfolio is as volatile as the index, ie it has $\beta = 1$. If this is not the case, then we may need to sell more or less contracts to achieve the hedge. The important determinant is the relative volatility.

By definition, the futures contract has a $\beta = 1$. If the portfolio has a $\beta = 1.2$, then a 1% change in the index will cause a 1% change in the value of a future but a 1.2% change in the portfolio value. We will therefore need 1.2 times as many futures contracts to provide sufficient profit to cancel any losses suffered in the portfolio. When we hedge with futures, we should use:

$$\text{Number of contracts} = \frac{\text{Portfolio value}}{\text{Futures value}} \times h$$

where h is the hedge ratio, which reflects the relative volatilities of the portfolio and the hedging instrument. For the FTSE contract:

$$h = \frac{\text{Volatility of portfolio}}{\text{Volatility of futures}} = \frac{-\beta_p}{\beta_f} = -\beta_{pf} \text{ since } \beta 1$$

The negative sign indicates that we are going short the future when we are long the stock.

Risk in a hedged portfolio

In theory, a correctly hedged portfolio, ie one with the correct hedge ratio, should exhibit no risk whatsoever, assuming the portfolio is fully diversified and exhibits no unsystematic risk. In practice, however, risk in a hedged portfolio may arise due to:

- Using the incorrect hedge ratio as a result of incorrectly assessing the beta of the portfolio.

- Unsystematic risk within the portfolio that the hedge cannot eliminate (hedging with an index future can only eliminate systematic risk, since the index moves with the market, ie moves with systematic factors only). Unsystematic risk can only be eliminated by further diversification within the portfolio.

To establish the level of risk remaining in any hedged portfolio we can use the Capital Asset Pricing Model (CAPM) relationships:

$$\sigma_i^2 = \sigma_s^2 + \sigma_u^2$$

and:

$$\sigma_s = \beta \sigma_m$$

Hence:

$$\sigma_s^2 = \beta^2 \sigma_m^2$$

from which it follows that:

$$\sigma_i^2 = \beta^2 \sigma_m^2 + \sigma_u^2$$

Given what was said above, a short futures hedge can only eliminate the systematic risk by reducing the net beta of the position. If h is the hedge ratio, again negative if we have a short position, then the net beta of the hedged position will be $\beta + h$, giving the risk of the hedged position as:

$$\sigma_h^2 = (\beta + h)^2 \sigma_m^2 + \sigma_u^2$$

The advantage of this second approach is that it clearly demonstrates the sources of any residual risk, systematic or unsystematic.

Example

$\sigma_i = 18\%$

$\sigma_m = 20\%$

$Cor_{im} = 0.8$

Now:

$$\sigma_s = \sigma_i Cor_{im} = 18 \times 0.8 = 14.4\%$$

and:

$$\beta = \frac{\sigma_s}{\sigma_m} = \frac{14.4}{20} = 0.72$$

Using:

$\sigma_i^2 = \sigma_s^2 + \sigma_u^2$ for the portfolio, we get:

$$18^2 = 14.4^2 + \sigma_u^2$$

giving:

$$\sigma_u^2 = 324 - 207.36 = 116.64$$

That is, $\sigma_u = 10.8\%$

Based on the above, calculate the risk of the hedged portfolio, if:

- A simple reverse hedge is applied, ie a hedge ratio h = −1.
- A hedge ratio of h = −0.72 is used, corresponding to the β of the portfolio.

Solution

Simple reverse hedge

$$\sigma_h^2 = (\beta + h)^2 \sigma_m^2 + \sigma_u^2$$

Now h = −1, hence:

$$\begin{aligned}
\sigma_h^2 &= [0.72 + (-1)]^2 \times 20^2 + 10.8^2 \\
&= (-0.28)^2 \times 20^2 + 116.64 \\
&= 31.36 + 116.64 = 148
\end{aligned}$$

σ_h = 12.166% − that is the unsystematic risk plus the residual unhedged systematic risk.

Hedge ratio of −0.72

$$\sigma_h^2 = (\beta + h)^2 \sigma_m^2 + \sigma_u^2$$

Now h = −0.72, hence:

$$\begin{aligned}
\sigma_h^2 &= [0.72 + (-0.72)]^2 \times 20^2 + 10.8^2 \\
&= (0.0)^2 \times 20^2 + 116.64 \\
&= 116.64
\end{aligned}$$

σ_h = 10.8% − just the unsystematic risk, all the systematic risk having been hedged.

8: DERIVATIVE PRODUCTS

2.4.3 Interest rate future

Purpose and characteristics

The purpose of an interest rate contract is to provide a means to gain or hedge interest rate exposure for a given period from a given future date. The contract we are using for illustration here is the three-month sterling futures contract that can hedge UK interest rates for a three-month period.

The general characteristics of the three-month sterling futures contract are as follows.

Unit of trade

The unit of trade = £500,000, ie the contract measures the effects on the total interest costs of interest rate changes on a notional borrowing of £500,000 for three months.

NB: the £500,000 does not change hands, just the interest effect.

Delivery

This contract is **cash settled**, that is the two parties simply settle up by the payment from one to the other of the difference in value between the interest bill for three months at the rate agreed when the contract was traded and the actual rate that arises.

Quotation

$$\text{Quotation} = 100 - \text{Rate of interest}$$

where the rate of interest is the **forward rate** for the three months from the delivery date. Hence, if three-month forward rates from the delivery date are 8%, the contract will be quoted at 92 (100 – 8).

Tick

The tick size, the smallest permitted quote movement, is 0.01, ie one basis point, which corresponds to a tick value of £12.50 (£500,000 × 0.01% × $^3/_{12}$).

Uses

As we indicated above, we may use this contract to gain exposure to, or hedge exposure against, interest rate movements.

Example

If a speculator believes interest rates will, say, rise, then he will know that this contract will fall in value. He could then open his position by selling now at a high price and buying to close his position later, realising a profit if his view turns out to be correct.

Three-month forward rates from June are currently quoted as 8.26%. The speculator sells 107 contracts now (January) and closes out his position in May when the three-month forward rates from June have moved to 9.14%. What gain does he make?

Solution

	Forward rate	Quote
Sell in January	8.26%	91.74
Buy in May	9.14%	90.86
		0.88 = 88 ticks

Hence, the total profit on the 107 contracts will be:

Profit = Ticks × Tick value × Number of contracts
= 88 × £12.50 × 107 = £117,700

Example

An investor wants to borrow £5m for three months from June, but is worried that interest rates will rise from their current levels. The forward rate for three months from June is currently quoted as 7.23%.

What action should the borrower take now?
If the rate has risen to 8.8% by June, what position will he be in?

Solution

Action now

If the borrower is correct that interest rates are rising, then he will suffer a higher interest burden than at present. He therefore needs a futures position that will yield profits when interest rates rise to offset this loss. Hence, as for our speculator above, he should sell futures contracts, and in particular sell ten contracts, since each one will hedge £500,000 of the loan.

Final position

Cash position

	£
Interest actually paid on loan £5m × 8.80% × $^3/_{12}$	110,000
Interest due at original rate £5m × 7.23% × $^3/_{12}$	90,375
Extra interest suffered	19,625

Futures position

	Forward rate	Quote
Sell in January	7.23%	92.77
Buy in June	8.80%	91.20
		1.57 = 157 ticks

Hence, the total profit on the 10 contracts will be:

Profit = Ticks × Tick value × Number of contracts

= 157 × £12.50 × 10 = £19,625

and will exactly offset the extra interest suffered.

2.4.4 Bond future

Purpose and characteristics

The purpose of a bond futures contract is to provide a means to gain or hedge exposure to bond markets. It can be considered as similar to the equity index futures in that it can be used in the management of bond funds to hedge or gain exposure. It effectively represents a bond index contract.

The general characteristics of the UK gilt futures contract that we are using for illustration are as follows.

Unit of trade

The unit of trade = £100,000 nominal of a notional 6% gilt, ie gilts with a nominal value of £100,000.

Delivery

This contract is **physically settled**, that is the seller of the future must deliver gilts and the buyer must pay the pre-agreed price. Clearly, however, there is a problem here with the contract being based on a notional gilt (as is the case with all bond futures). To overcome this difficulty the exchange specifies a range of eligible deliverable gilts for each delivery date that the seller may choose to satisfy delivery, and the seller decides which gilts he delivers. The decision is always to deliver whichever is cheapest at the delivery date, referred to as the cheapest to deliver (CTD).

These eligible deliverable gilts all have differing maturities and coupons, hence differing prices and differing interest rate sensitivities. To try to cater for these price and sensitivity differentials, the exchange calculates a **price factor or conversion factor** for each deliverable gilt before trading starts in the contract, ie a scaling factor that will be applied to the futures price in order to determine the price actually paid for the delivered gilt. The relationship between the price of the CTD and that of the future being:

CTD gilt price = Futures price × Price factor

The seller of the future also has the choice as to which date to make delivery. The contract is due for delivery on any day in the delivery month. The seller will therefore decide whether he would prefer to receive the accrued interest from holding the gilt for the month, or hold cash on deposit earning interest.

If interest rates are low compared to the coupon rate, then he will hold the gilt as long as possible, making delivery on the last day. If, however, interest rates are high compared to coupon rates, then he will deliver on the earliest date and hold cash.

8: DERIVATIVE PRODUCTS

Quotation

The quotation is similar to gilts quotes, ie price per $100 of nominal value.

Tick

The tick size, the smallest permitted quote movement, is £0.01 per £100 nominal value, which corresponds to a tick value of £10 (£100,000 × 0.01 × $^1/_{100}$).

Uses

As we indicated above, we may use this contract to gain exposure to, or hedge exposure against, movements in bond markets. Its use is similar to the FTSE Index above.

Hedge ratio

As we noted with the FTSE contract, in order to achieve a hedge with a future, we must apply the following relationship.

$$\text{Number of contracts} = \frac{\text{Portfolio value}}{\text{Futures value}} \times h$$

Here, h represents the relative volatility of the share portfolio compared to the future (= market). With bonds, the appropriate measure of relative volatility would be relative duration, giving:

$$h = \frac{\text{Volatility of portfolio}}{\text{Volatility of futures}} = -\frac{\text{Portfolio duration}}{\text{Futures duration}}$$

Once again, the negative sign indicates that we are going short the future when we are long the stock. The duration of a bond portfolio is calculated as the weighted average of the durations of the bonds within the portfolio. However, what is the duration of the futures contract? Imagine that we knew that the cheapest-to-deliver bond (CTD) on a one-year futures contract was an 8% 12-year annual coupon bond with a price factor of 1. Calculate:

- The current bond price when interest rates are either 8% or 9%, and the corresponding one-year futures prices.
- The bond price and futures price at the maturity of the futures contract in one year at those same rates.

8: DERIVATIVE PRODUCTS

Current bond and futures prices

Time	Cash (£)	DF (8%)	PV (£)	DF (9%)	PV (£)
1–12	8.00	$\frac{11}{0.08}\left(1 - \frac{1}{1.08^{12}}\right)$	60.29	$\frac{11}{0.09}\left(1 - \frac{1}{1.09^{12}}\right)$	57.29
12	100.00	$\frac{1}{1.08^{12}}$	39.71	$\frac{1}{1.09^{12}}$	35.55
Bond price			100.00		92.84
Cost of carry		Interest	8.00	(£92.84 × 9%)	8.36
		Coupons	(8.00)		(8.00)
Futures price			100.00		93.20

Bond and futures price at maturity of the futures contract one year later

Time	Cash (£)	DF (8%)	PV (£)	DF (9%)	PV (£)
1–11	8.00	$\frac{11}{0.08}\left(1 - \frac{1}{1.08^{11}}\right)$	57.11	$\frac{11}{0.09}\left(1 - \frac{1}{1.09^{11}}\right)$	54.44
11	100.00	$\frac{1}{1.08^{11}}$	42.89	$\frac{1}{1.09^{11}}$	38.76
Bond and futures price			100.00		93.20

We can see from the above that the price of the futures contract today is the same as that of the CTD at the maturity of the futures contract under each of the interest rate scenarios. Hence, the sensitivity of the futures contract to interest rate changes (its duration) is the same as that of the CTD **as at the maturity date of the futures contract**.

This is all very well in theory, however, in practice, we will never know which bond will be the CTD until the maturity date of the futures contract. Having said that, we will always be aware of which deliverable bond will be the CTD assuming interest rates, etc remain constant to maturity. Hence, we will be able to assess the position now, though this hedge may not be static and may need modifying as economic factors (and the CTD) vary.

Static versus dynamic hedges

Ignoring the issue of identifying the CTD, there is another practical factor to consider. Even if the CTD does not vary, the hedge may not be static, since the duration of the bond portfolio will decrease across the period, whereas the duration of the futures contract will not. As a result, we may need to vary the hedge ratio continuously as the portfolio duration varies over the hedge period, though this depends on the scenario.

If we wish to hedge against a movement in interest rates and will be terminating the hedge as soon as this movement has occurred, we will need to hedge dynamically. That is, we will continually adjust the hedge ratio as the portfolio's duration alters to ensure that the sensitivity of the futures contracts and the portfolio are always identical. We will initially base the hedge ratio on the portfolio's duration at the start date, though by the time that the hedge is released it will be based on a different duration, the portfolio's duration at the termination date.

If, however, we intend to set up a hedge to a given future date, then we can set-up a static hedge. Since we know the date that the hedge will be released, we will know the potential portfolio values and interest rate sensitivity as at that date. It will be of no relevance to us exactly when, say, interest rates changed. We will simply be interested in the impact on our portfolio at the end of the hedge period. We therefore need to base the hedge throughout the period on this sensitivity, ie the duration, of the bond portfolio at the termination date of the hedge.

As a result, when we release the hedge, we should find that the hedge ratio is based on the portfolio's duration at that termination date whether we have hedged statically or dynamically.

3 OPTIONS

3.1 Definition

> An **option** is a contract that confers the right, but not the obligation, to buy or sell an asset at a given price on or before a given date.

All the comments relating to standard quantities, specified assets, fixed future dates and price agreed today, that we noted above for futures, still apply.

3.2 Using options

3.2.1 The speculator – buying an option

Conventionally, a speculator anticipating a rise in the price of shares would simply buy the shares for immediate delivery and then hold them, hoping to sell them for a profit once the price rose. If we imagine that the price of a share is $6.00 and that the speculator buys just one share, the expenditure would be $6.00.

Another way of representing the hope of a rise in share prices would be to buy an option on a share – specifically, an option that would give the right, but not the obligation, to buy a share at a price of $6.00 for a period of three months. The purchase of this option would cost, say, $0.50.

Remember that an option is a contract for a future delivery, so it would not be necessary to pay $6.00 in the first instance; the only money to be invested at this point is the $0.50.

One advantage is immediately apparent. Options are cheaper than purchasing the underlying asset.

8: DERIVATIVE PRODUCTS

Example

If three months later, as expected, the price of the share has risen from $6.00 to $7.00, what will be the position of

- The speculator who bought the physical share?
- The speculator who bought the option on the share?

Solution

Physical share

		$
Sale price		7.00
Purchase price		(6.00)
Profit		1.00

On an investment of $6.00, the investor has made a profit of $1.00 in just three months.

Option on share

Now let us look at the profit for the options buyer. Three months ago, he entered into a contract that gave him the right, but not the obligation, to buy a share at $6.00. When purchased, that right cost just $0.50 per share. With the share now trading at $7.00, the right to buy at $6.00 must be worth at least $1.00 – the difference between the current price and the stated price in the contract.

This right to buy at $6.00 was purchased for $0.50. With the market price at $7.00 at the end of the option's life, the option will now be worth $1.00, hence:

		$
Sale price		1.00
Purchase price		(0.50)
Profit		0.50

On an investment of $0.50, a $0.50 profit has been achieved. In percentage terms, this profit is spectacularly greater than on the conventional purchase and sale of the physical share.

One important thing to note is that options can be traded. It is not necessary for the underlying asset to be bought or sold. What more commonly occurs is that **options** are bought and sold. Thus, an option bought at $0.50 could be sold to the market at $1.00, realising a 100% profit with the investor never having an intention of buying the underlying asset.

At this stage, it is necessary to introduce some of the vocabulary used in the options market.

3.3 Terminology

In the definition of an option given earlier, an option was described as being the right, but not the obligation, to buy or sell. The right to buy and the right to sell are given different names.

- The right to buy is known as a **call option**.
- The right to sell is known as a **put option**.

The rights to buy (call) or sell (put) are held by the person buying the option who is known as the **holder**.

The person selling an option is known as a **writer** and is obliged to make (call) or take (put) delivery on or before the date on which an option comes to the end of its life. This date is known as its **expiry date**.

Options can also be differentiated by their exercise style. Most options are known as **American style**, which means that the holders can exercise at any time until the expiry date. A less common type of exercise is the **European style** exercise. In these types of options, the holder can only exercise on the expiry date. The exchange stipulates the type of exercise style in its contract specifications. Most option contracts traded on Liffe are American style.

The following diagram shows the relationship between holders and writers.

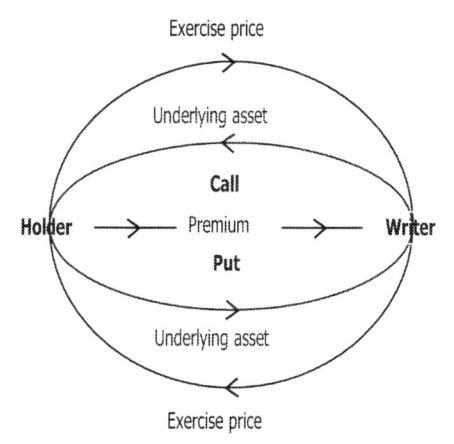

```
                    Exercise price
                         →
              ┌─────────────────────┐
              │   Underlying asset  │
              │         ←           │
              │        Call         │
    Holder  → │      Premium      → │  Writer
              │        Put          │
              │         →           │
              │   Underlying asset  │
              └─────────────────────┘
                         ←
                    Exercise price
```

The first thing to understand is the flow of **premium**. Premium is the cost of an option. In our share example, the premium was $0.50 and this is paid by the holder and received by the writer.

In return for receiving premium, the writer agrees to fulfil the terms of the contract, which of course are different for calls and puts.

3.3.1 Call options

Call writers agree to deliver the asset underlying the contract if **called** upon to do so. When options holders wish to take up their rights under the contract, they are said to **exercise** the contract. For a call, this means that the writer must deliver the underlying asset for which he will receive the fixed amount of cash stipulated in the original contract.

8: DERIVATIVE PRODUCTS

Thus, for a share call option that gives the holder the right, but not the obligation, to buy at $6.00, this would mean that the writer would be required to deliver the share to the holder at $6.00. The option holder will only want to buy at $6.00 when it would be advantageous for him to do so, ie only when the real or market price is somewhat higher than $6.00. If the market price were less than $6.00, there would be no sense in paying more than the market price for the asset.

Call options writers run very considerable risks. In return for receiving the option's premium, they are committed to delivering the underlying asset at a fixed price. As the price of the asset could, in theory, rise infinitely, they could be forced to buy the underlying asset at a high price and to deliver it to the option holder at a much lower value. The price at which an options contract gives the right to buy (call) or sell (put) is known as the **exercise price** or **strike price**.

3.3.2 Put options

The dangers for put options writers are also substantial. The writer of a put is obligated to pay the exercise price for assets that are delivered to him. Put options are only exercised when it is advantageous for the holders to do so. This will be when they can use the option to sell their assets at a higher price than would be otherwise available in the market.

3.3.3 Summary

To summarise, options writers, in return for receiving a premium, run very large risks. This is similar to the role undertaken by insurance companies. For a relatively modest premium, they are willing to insure your house against fire, but if your house burns down, they will be faced with a claim for many thousands of pounds. The reasons why insurers and options writers enter into such contracts are that houses do not often burn down, and markets do not often rise or fall substantially.

If writers price options properly, they hope to make money in most instances. Options writing is not for the faint hearted, nor for those without substantial resources. That said, many conservative users do write options as part of strategies involving the holding of the underlying asset. Such strategies are **covered** (as opposed to **naked**) and much less risky. We discuss these later.

When investors buy or hold options, the risk is limited to the option's premium. If the market moves against them, they can simply decide not to exercise their options and sacrifice the premium. Remember, options holders have the right, **but not the obligation** to buy (call) or sell (put). If it does not make sense to buy or sell at the exercise price, the holder can decide to **abandon** the option.

3.4 Describing options

Another way in which options are described relates to their maturity. Options are instruments with limited life spans. The date on which an option comes to the end of its life is known as its **expiry date**. The expiry date is the last day on which the option may be exercised or traded. After this date, the option disappears and cannot be traded or exercised.

Below are quoted the prices for **call options** based on the shares of a fictitious company, XYZ plc. The options give an entitlement to buy (call) the company's shares. The **underlying price is 76**.

XYZ calls

Exercise price	Expiry date		
	Jan premium	April premium	July premium
60	23	28	33
70	12	18	23
80	5	8	12

You will notice that there are a range of exercise prices and expiry dates available. Normally, you would expect there to be exercise prices available both below and above the underlying price.

There is also a range of expiry dates available – this allows investors a choice as to the maturity of their options. As one expiry date passes, a new expiry date is introduced, thus maintaining the choice of dates.

A similar range of exercise prices and expiry dates would be available in XYZ puts. The premiums quoted for calls and puts would, however, be different.

3.5 How much would you pay?

In our table, the premium that is quoted for the April 60 call is 28. To find out how much this would be, we must know two things: first, how the product is quoted and second, the contract size.

Options are traded on a wide variety of assets from currencies, bonds and shares to metals, oils and commodities. Each market has different conventions. For example, share option prices for UK companies are quoted in pence per share.

Governing the operation of options contracts are contract specifications that set out, amongst other things, rules specifying how they are quoted, expiry dates and when exercise prices are introduced. These documents are important because they enable everyone to understand the details of the contract. Exchange-traded options, such as futures contracts, are **standardised**, with the method of quotation and contract size being fixed. The only variable is the option's premium.

So what does a quote of 28 for the April 60 call mean? The premium for shares is quoted in pence, hence '28' means 28 pence per XYZ share.

To determine how much the option costs, we must consult the contract specification again to find out the contract size. If we are dealing with a NYSE Liffe equity contract this would be **1,000 shares per contract**.

All options, like futures, are traded in standardised lots or contracts. It is only possible to trade in whole numbers of contracts. You could not, for example, buy 1½ April 60 calls.

We know that the quote for XYZ options is in pence per share and that the contract size is 1,000 shares. Therefore, one XYZ April 60 call would cost $280 ($0.28 × 1,000 shares).

3.6 The simple uses of options

3.6.1 Buying a call

Introduction

This strategy is motivated by a view that an asset's price will rise.

Risk – The investor's risks are limited to the premium he pays for the options. So, if the 80 call could be bought for a premium of 5, this 5 is all he risks. The premium of the call option will only be a fraction of the cost of the underlying asset, so the option can be considered less risky than buying the asset itself.

While this is true, remember that the whole premium is at risk and it is easy to lose 100% of your investment, albeit a relatively small amount of money.

Reward – The rewards from buying a call are unlimited. As the contract gives the holder the right to buy at a fixed price, this right will become increasingly valuable as the asset price rises above the exercise price.

Imagine an investor who buys one XYZ call option which gives him the right, but not the obligation, to buy the XYZ asset at a fixed price of 80 between now and the option's expiry date in January. The cost of this option is 5.

If the asset price rises to 120, the right to buy at 80, ie the premium of the 80 call, must be worth at least 40. The net profit for the call would be 35 (40 – 5). Of course, if the price of XYZ falls below 80 at the option's expiry date, the 80 call will be worthless and 100% of the initial 5 invested will be lost. This loss occurs because no sensible person would want the right to buy at 80 if they could buy the asset more cheaply elsewhere.

Graphically

By using graphs, we can show how much an option will be worth at expiry.

On the vertical axis of the graph is profit/loss and on the horizontal axis is the asset price.

8: DERIVATIVE PRODUCTS

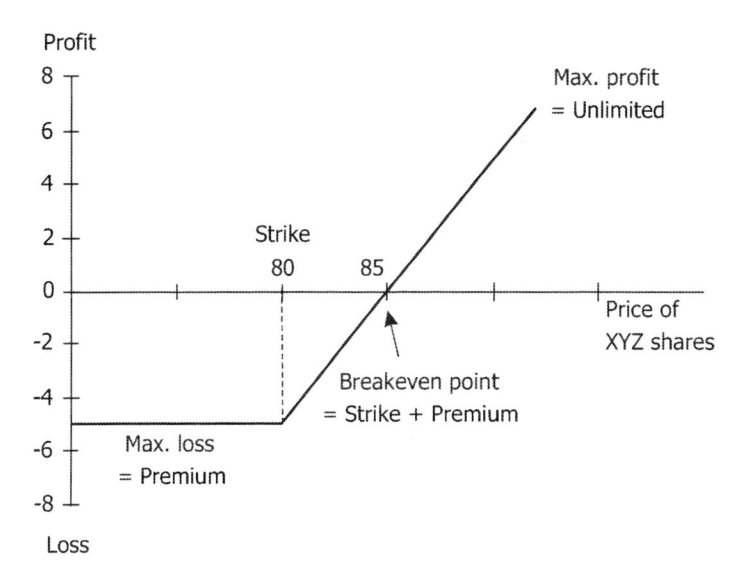

Holder of 1 XYZ January 80 Call Premium 5

```
Profit
 8 ┬                              Max. profit
                                  = Unlimited
 6 ┼
 4 ┼
 2 ┼      Strike
          80        85
 0 ┼──────┼─────────┼──────────┼──── Price of
                                      XYZ shares
-2 ┼
              Breakeven point
-4 ┼          = Strike + Premium
-6 ┼   Max. loss
       = Premium
-8 ┴
Loss
```

What the graph shows is that losses of 5 are made anywhere below 80, while profits emerge above 85. 85 represents the **breakeven** point. This is the point at which the original investment is recouped and it is calculated by simply adding the premium to the exercise price, eg 80 + 5 = 85. The buying of a call to open a position is known as a 'long call'.

3.6.2 Selling a call

Introduction

Risk – The selling or writing of a call without, at the same time, being in possession of the underlying asset, is extremely risky. The risk is unlimited because the writer has a duty to deliver the asset at a fixed price regardless of the prevailing asset price. As the share price could, in theory, rise to infinity, the call writer assumes an unlimited risk. This strategy is sometimes called naked call writing and as it suggests, can leave you feeling very exposed.

Reward – You might ask why someone would assume such an unlimited risk. The answer, of course, is the hope of a profit. The maximum profit the writer can make is the premium he receives. Let us look again at an 80 call with a premium of 5. The seller of this call will receive the 5 premium, and providing the asset price at expiry is less than 80, no-one will rationally want to exercise the right to buy. The graph for selling a call is set out below. You will see that it is the equal and opposite of buying a call.

8: DERIVATIVE PRODUCTS

Graphically

Writer of 1 XYZ January 80 Call Premium 5

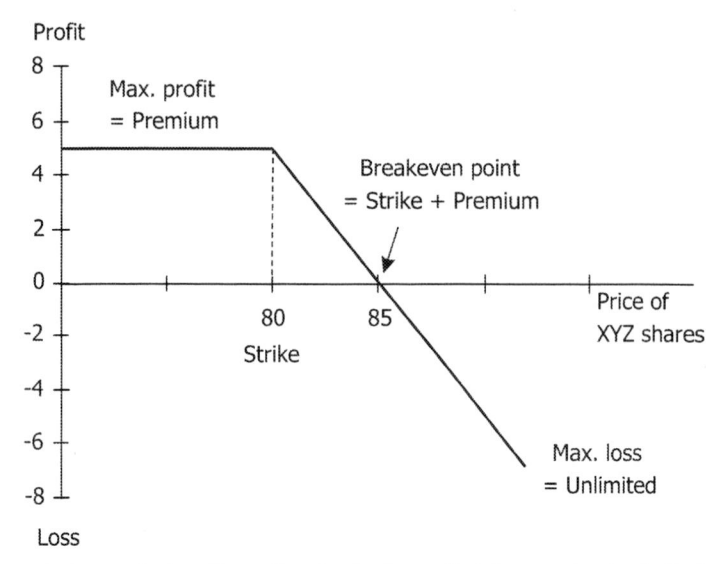

```
Profit
8
              Max. profit
6             = Premium
                              Breakeven point
4                             = Strike + Premium
2
0 ─────────────────────────────────────────── Price of
              80        85                     XYZ shares
-2           Strike
-4
-6                                 Max. loss
-8                                 = Unlimited
Loss
```

As the graph demonstrates, the call writer believes that the asset price is likely either to stay the same or fall. If this happens, the writer simply pockets the premium received and will not have to deliver the asset. The selling of a call to open a position is known as a 'short call'.

3.6.3 Buying a put

Introduction

Risk – As when buying a call, the risk is limited to the premium paid. The motivation behind buying a put will be to profit from a fall in the asset's price. The holder of a put obtains the right, but not the obligation, to sell at a fixed price. The value of this right will become increasingly valuable as the asset price falls.

Reward – The greatest profit that will arise from buying a put will be achieved if the asset price falls to zero.

Graphically

Holder of 1 XYZ July 80 Put Premium 8

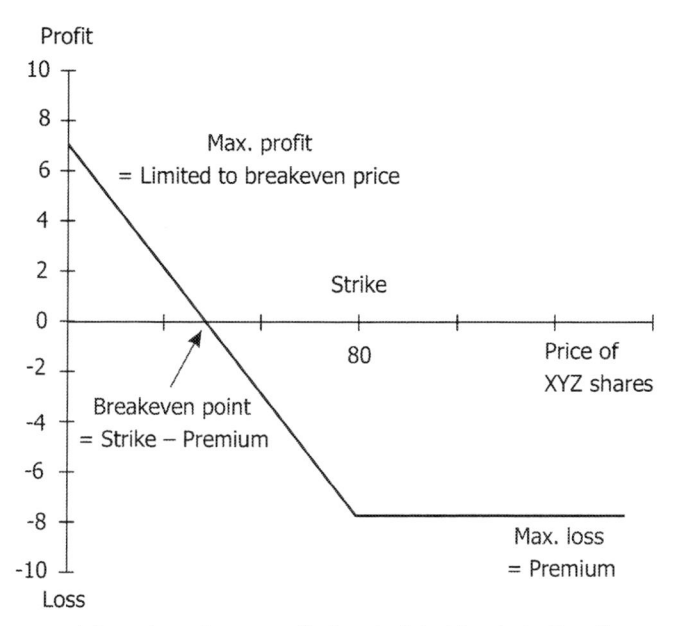

```
Profit
 10 ┬
  8 ┤
  6 ┤      Max. profit
        = Limited to breakeven price
  4 ┤
  2 ┤
                        Strike
  0 ┼────┼────┼────┼────┼────┼────┼
                         80          Price of
 -2 ┤                                XYZ shares
        Breakeven point
 -4 ┤   = Strike – Premium
 -6 ┤
 -8 ┤
                              Max. loss
-10 ┴                         = Premium
  Loss
```

The breakeven point, and maximum profit, is calculated by deducting the premium from the exercise price, eg 80 – 8 = 72. Like the purchase of a call, the premium needs to be recovered before profits are made. The buying of a put to open a position is known as a 'long put'.

3.6.4 Selling a put

Introduction

Risk – The selling of a put is dangerous, as the writer enters into an obligation to purchase an asset at a fixed price. If the market price of that asset falls, the put writer will end up paying a large amount of money for what could be a valueless asset. The worst case will arise when the asset price falls to zero. If this happens, the loss will be the exercise price less the premium received.

Reward – What the put option writer hopes for is that the put will not be exercised. This will occur if the asset has a price above the exercise price at expiry. The maximum reward is the premium received. The selling of a put to open a position is known as a 'short put'.

Graphically

Writer of 1 XYZ July 80 Put Premium 8

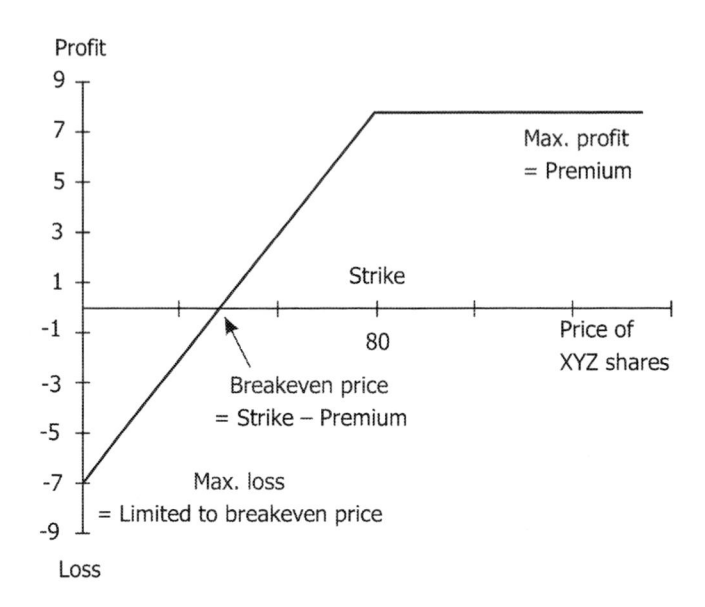

```
Profit
 9
 7                                    Max. profit
 5                                    = Premium
 3
 1              Strike
-1        ↓                           Price of
-3        80                          XYZ shares
          Breakeven price
-5        = Strike – Premium
-7    Max. loss
-9    = Limited to breakeven price
Loss
```

The four basic strategies outlined above form the building blocks of the more complicated option techniques. You should ensure that you are clear about three things.

- What is the motivation behind each trade?
- What are the risks associated with them?
- What are the rewards?

3.7 Options on futures

The options discussed so far have been options which, upon exercise, result in the purchase or sale of a tangible underlying security, such as a share.

More common than those discussed above are options on futures. This apparently complex term merely describes particular options, the exercise of which results in a long or short futures position.

Thus, the exercise of a **long call** results in the holder establishing a **long futures** position in the same delivery month.

The exercise of a **long put** results in the holder establishing a **short futures** position in the same delivery month.

Clearly, the attributes of futures products and tangible assets are quite different. Two characteristics are worth highlighting – gearing and risk.

3.8 Option pricing

Why are some options more expensive than others? Below the prices for **call options** on a particular asset are provided. The **underlying price is 98**.

8: DERIVATIVE PRODUCTS

Exercise Price	Expiry date		
	Jan premium	April premium	July premium
70	29	31	32
80	19	21	22
90	10	12	13
100	3	4	5
110	1	2	2.5
120	0	0.5	1

Two influences on options prices are readily apparent: (a) **the underlying security price** and (b) **time until expiry**.

3.8.1 Underlying security price

Compare the value of the January 70 call and the January 90 call from the table. The 70 call is priced at 29 while the 90 call is priced at 10. Why?

Remember that we are looking at call options, ie the right to buy. The value of the 70 call is greater than the 90 call because the right to buy at a low price (70) must be more attractive than the right to buy at a high price (90).

It is also worth noting that the **call premium** will be **higher**, the **higher the price** of the **underlying asset** becomes, when compared against the exercise price, as again the call option would be more attractive.

Why is the 70 call priced at 29?

We can readily explain at least part of the premium. If we bear in mind that the underlying stock is trading at 98, the right to buy at 70 must be worth at least 28. If the 70 call was worth less than 28, it would be possible to buy the call, exercise it to acquire stock and immediately sell the stock at the market price of 98 and thereby realise a risk-free profit. Markets do not give away money. The 70 call, with an underlying stock at 98 must be worth 28. This value of 28 is known as the option's **intrinsic value**.

The option is not just valued at 28, its price is 29, so where does the 1 come from?

This part of the premium is known as **time value**. The amount of time value in an option is a function of probability of the chance of further movements in the underlying asset.

The premium of the 70 call is made up of two things – intrinsic value and time value.

Intrinsic value + Time value = Premium
28 + 1 = 29

Not all options have intrinsic value. If you look at the table, you will see the premium of the January 110 call is 1.

The 110 call has no intrinsic value because it gives the right to buy at a level above the current price of 98. It is, therefore, not immediately valuable. However, because things may change between now and expiry, the option has a time value of 1. The **longer** the

8: DERIVATIVE PRODUCTS

option's **time until expiry**, the **greater the time value** and hence the **greater the premium** for **both call and put options**.

Options that have intrinsic value are described as being **in-the-money**.

Options that have only time value are described as being **out-of-the-money**.

Practitioners sometimes describe options as being **at-the-money**. This term has nothing to do with intrinsic value, it merely describes the option exercise price that is nearest to the current underlying price. Thus, the 100 call from our table, as the exercise price nearest the underlying (98), would be the 'at-the-money' option.

3.9 Volatility

Aside from time and underlying security price, the most important other factor is **volatility**.

Volatility is a measure of how much an underlying price varies. If an underlying asset varies a great deal, the risk for the options writer becomes larger and the premiums he demands rise accordingly. If, however, an option is sold on an unvolatile asset, the premiums will be lower. At times of crisis or change, such as wars or elections, people become uncertain about the future. This uncertainty brings with it higher options premiums.

The impact of changes in volatility is quite straightforward.

> If volatility rises, call and put premiums increase.

> If volatility falls, call and put premiums decrease.

3.10 Interest rates

A less important influence on option prices is interest rates. The basic relationship is

> Interest rate rises − call premiums rise
> − put premiums fall

The reasons for these changes are related to the cost of hedging the option's position, but need not detain us here. However, it is important to recognise that interest rate changes are of only minor importance. Volatility changes are much more influential.

3.11 Sensitivity of option values

It has already been noted that there are five factors that influence the fair value of all options. They are:

- Value of the underlying asset
- Exercise price
- Time to expiry
- Volatility
- Interest rates

8: DERIVATIVE PRODUCTS

NB: Dividend payments will also influence the fair value of options on dividend-paying stock.

A change in any one of these factors will impact on the price of an option. A holder of an option will want to know what the exact impact is likely to be, ie they will wish to know how sensitive their options are to changes in these factors.

Sensitivities are named after Greek letters, as follows.

Sensitivity to	Known as
Underlying asset	Delta
Changes in delta	Gamma
Time decay	Theta
Volatility	Vega
Interest rates	Rho

3.11.1 Delta

Delta can be defined in a number of ways.

First, delta is the **rate of change of an option's premium with respect to the underlying security**. For example, an option with a delta of 0.25 can theoretically be expected to move at one-quarter of the rate of the underlying. If the underlying goes up or down by 4, the option could be expected to go up or down by 1 – all other factors remaining constant.

Second, delta can be thought of as being the **probability** that an **option will expire in-the-money**. Thus, a delta of 0.25 or 25% means that there is only a small chance of being in-the-money; a delta of 0.9 or 90% gives an obviously higher chance.

Third, delta can be thought of as the **theoretical number of futures or underlying units** of which the holder of the call option is long, or of which the holder of a put option is short. For example, if the delta of a call (put) is 0.25, the holder of a call (put) is theoretically long (short) a quarter of a futures contract. In this example, the call holder's position at this instant is equivalent to a long position in a quarter of a future, ie the holder will make or lose money at a quarter of the rate of a futures contract.

3.11.2 Positive and negative deltas

If you are long of a call, you have a positive delta, ie if the underlying asset goes up, so does the call option premium, a move to the benefit of the holder.

If, conversely, you are short of a call and the market moves up, such a move is to your disadvantage, as the option becomes more expensive – you have a negative delta.

Put holders benefit from downwards moves, but are hurt by upwards moves. They are negatively correlated with the underlying.

Finally, short puts are helped by upmoves, but hurt by downmoves; they have positive deltas.

Long calls / Short puts	Positive delta
Long puts / Short calls	Negative delta

It should be noted that the delta of the underlying asset or futures contract is **always 1. If you are long of a future you have a positive delta, if short, a negative delta of 1. Similarly, the delta of a holding of the underlying is also 1.**

3.11.3 Gamma

The **sensitivity of delta** to a change in the value of the underlying asset is known as gamma.

3.11.4 Theta

This is the measure of the change in the theoretical value of a call or put option as **time to expiry increases**.

3.11.5 Vega

This is the measure of the effect on the theoretical value a change **in volatility** will have.

3.11.6 Rho

Rho is the measure of the sensitivity of an option's theoretical value to a change in **interest rates**.

4 OPTIONS TRADING STRATEGIES

4.1 Motivation

Before embarking on a detailed discussion of the attributes of the various options trades, let us first think about the reasons why they are undertaken.

The first and most obvious reason for speculating in the markets is that investors have a view on their future direction, be it up or down. These are **directional** trades and may be either **bullish** (the investor feels the market is likely to go up) or **bearish** (the investor feels the market is likely to go down). Investors may also feel the market is likely to go up or down very markedly, or only slightly. There are option trades to accommodate all views.

People also trade because they feel the market is likely to be highly volatile or remain broadly static. These investors do not know in which direction the market may move, but have opinions as to its likely variability. These types of trades are known as **volatility** trades and options are unique in allowing investors to trade in this way.

Others use options not to speculate, but for more conservative ends. These may be to reduce portfolio risks or to enhance returns. A number of the more important trades are reviewed in the pages that follow. Although the language may appear bizarre and the

8: DERIVATIVE PRODUCTS

graphs complicated, it should be remembered that they are all built up from the four simple trades examined earlier.

STRATEGY 1	**Long Straddle**
MOTIVATION	Volatility – undertaken to exploit increasing variability.
CONSTRUCTION	Purchase of call and put with same exercise price and expiry.
COMMENTS	Straddles are bought when investors feel that the market may move considerably either up or down. They are also bought when the investor feels that option premiums do not fully reflect likely volatility. Consequently, if the perception of volatility rises, so will the premiums of the purchased options, thereby giving an opportunity to sell the purchased options at higher prices.
EXAMPLE	BUY 100 CALL @ 0.98, BUY 100 PUT @ 1.91
GRAPH	

8: DERIVATIVE PRODUCTS

STRATEGY 2	**Short Straddle**
MOTIVATION	Volatility – undertaken to exploit decreasing variability.
CONSTRUCTION	Sale of call and put with same exercise price and expiry.
COMMENTS	This trade is undertaken by investors who believe that the market will trade within a narrow range. It is also undertaken by investors who believe options premiums to be expensive and likely to fall. As can be seen from the graph below, the risks from this trade are potentially unlimited.
EXAMPLE	SELL 100 CALL @ 0.98, SELL 100 PUT @ 1.91
GRAPH	*Profit/Loss graph showing an inverted V peaking at price 100 with profit of 3, crossing zero on both sides.*

STRATEGY 3	**Long Strangle**
MOTIVATION	Volatility – expect large increase in market variability.
CONSTRUCTION	Purchase of call and put with same expiry but different strike.
COMMENTS	Generally a lower cost alternative to a long straddle, but which requires greater movement for profitability.
EXAMPLE	BUY 101 CALL @ 0.62, BUY 99 PUT @ 1.40
GRAPH	*Profit/Loss graph showing a V-shape with a flat bottom around price 100 at loss of -2, rising on both sides.*

8: DERIVATIVE PRODUCTS

STRATEGY 4	**Short Strangle**
MOTIVATION	Volatility – expect large reduction in market variability.
CONSTRUCTION	Sale of call and put with same expiry, but different strike.
COMMENTS	Alternative to short straddle, generally breakevens are more widely displaced and thus position is less quickly loss-making.
EXAMPLE	SELL 101 CALL @ 1.47, SELL 99 PUT @ 2.55
GRAPH	*Profit/Loss graph centred at 100, with flat top at profit of 2 between the strikes, sloping down on both sides.*

STRATEGY 5	**Short Butterfly**
MOTIVATION	Volatility – undertaken to exploit increasing variability.
CONSTRUCTION	Sale of low-strike call/put. Purchase of two mid-strike calls/puts. Sale of high-strike call/put.
COMMENTS	Alternative to long straddle/strangle. May be expensive to execute because of commissions. Note also its limited profit.
EXAMPLE	SELL 103 PUT @ 0.62, BUY 2 104 PUTS @ 1.04, SELL 1 105 PUT @ 1.63
GRAPH	*Profit/Loss graph with a V-shaped loss centred at 104, bottoming at −1, flattening to a small profit of about 0.2 on either side.*

8: DERIVATIVE PRODUCTS

STRATEGY 6	**Long Butterfly**
MOTIVATION	Volatility – undertaken to exploit reducing variability.
CONSTRUCTION	Purchase of low-strike call/put. Sale of two mid-strike calls/puts. Purchase of high-strike call/put.
COMMENTS	Patently less risky than short straddle/strangle. But beware high commission and execution costs.
EXAMPLE	BUY 103 CALL @ 1.52, SELL 2 104 CALLS @ 0.94, BUY 1 105 CALL @ 0.53
GRAPH	*(Profit/Loss graph peaking at 104)*

STRATEGY 7	**Covered Call**
MOTIVATION	Normally neutral subject to strike.
CONSTRUCTION	Long position in stock and sale of call. If call sold is out-of-the-money, the trade is bullish; if at-the-money, call is sold, trade is neutral; if in-the money, call is sold, trade is bearish.
COMMENTS	Very familiar investment strategy that can enhance returns in static markets, while also providing limited protection against falls. (Protection Call premium). The trade is commonly used by fund managers who already hold a stock, but are neutral about the share's prospects in the short term. To enhance the returns over any dividend flows, they sell the call and thereby receive premium. In doing this, they effectively give up the opportunity to profit if the share unexpectedly rises above the exercise price.
EXAMPLE	BUY ABC STOCK @ 99.07, SELL 100 CALL @ 0.98
GRAPH	*(Profit/Loss graph, capped above 100)*

8: DERIVATIVE PRODUCTS

4.2 Summary

Bullish	Bearish	Volatile	Stable
Long Call	**Short Call**	**Long Straddle**	**Short Straddle**
Short Put	**Long Put**	**Long Strangle**	**Short Strangle**
		Short Butterfly	**Long Butterfly**
			Covered Call

267

5 SWAPS

5.1 Interest rate swaps

5.1.1 Definition

Alongside the exponential growth of exchange-traded derivatives over the past decade, there has been a similar, if less visible, growth in **over-the-counter (OTC)** products, especially swaps. While exchange-traded structures, by virtue of their standardisation, liquidity and visibility, have provided the investment community with much needed risk management tools, some attributes of these markets are particularly irksome. The limited availability of products, fixed delivery dates, standardised contract sizes, limited exercise prices and expiry dates and the strictures of exchange margining rules have all conspired to make the bespoke OTC markets particularly attractive. One significant disadvantage of over-the-counter products is their lack of a clearing house. With exchange-traded derivatives, the existence of the clearing house virtually eliminates counterparty risk. In the over-the-counter market, very considerable counterparty risks exist between buyers and sellers. In this section the most important OTC product – the interest rate swap – is examined.

> An interest rate swap is a contract which commits two counterparties to exchange, over an agreed period, two streams of interest payments, each calculated using a different interest rate index, but applied to a common notional principal amount.

5.1.2 Key points

Only interest is exchanged in the swap; there is **no exchange of principal**. Swaps do not, therefore, impact on the balance sheet, only on the profit and loss account. They are, therefore, classed as 'off balance sheet instruments'.

Cash movements that take place at intervals during the swap's life are normally netted. For example, in a swap in which one side is paying a fixed rate and the other a floating rate, such as six-month LIBOR, only the cash difference is exchanged. This reduces credit risks.

An interest rate swap

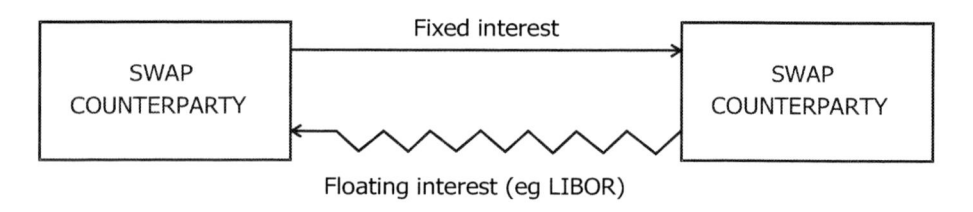

```
                    Fixed interest
    ┌─────────────┐ ──────────────→ ┌─────────────┐
    │    SWAP     │                 │    SWAP     │
    │ COUNTERPARTY│                 │ COUNTERPARTY│
    └─────────────┘ ←~~~~~~~~~~~~~~ └─────────────┘
              Floating interest (eg LIBOR)
```

The above is an example of the most common type of interest rate swap in which a fixed rate of interest is exchanged for a floating rate of interest and is known as a coupon swap. The floating rate is normally measured by an index such as LIBOR.

5.1.3 How swaps are traded and quoted

The market in interest rate swaps is an OTC market. Trading is conducted over the telephone and price information is disseminated through quote vendor systems such as Reuters and Telerate.

In interest rate swaps, the floating rate in a coupon swap (the most common) is assumed to be six-month LIBOR. Negotiation, therefore, concentrates on the fixed rate, sometimes called the swap rate.

5.1.4 Why use interest rate swaps?

As with futures and options, there are three basic motivations – speculation, hedging and arbitrage.

5.2 Currency swaps

5.2.1 Definition

A short-term currency swap is a contract which commits two parties to exchange pre-agreed foreign currency amounts now and re-exchange them back at a given future date (the maturity date). The flows include both capital payment and interest.

5.2.2 Primary and secondary currencies

Primary currency

One currency is defined as the primary currency and most deals are structured such that the nominal value of the primary currency exchanged on the two dates is equal.

Secondary currency

The other currency is the secondary currency and the nominal value of this exchanged on the two dates is a function of the spot rate and the swap market forward rate.

5.2.3 Buyer and seller

Terms

The terms buyer and seller are a little awkward in relation to currency dealing since each party is giving (selling) one currency and receiving (buying) the other.

The terms buyer and seller relate to these swap arrangements from the point of view of the primary currency cash flows at inception. The **buyer** is the person who, at inception, purchases the primary currency (selling the secondary currency), the **seller** is the individual who, at inception, sells the primary currency (buying the secondary currency).

8: DERIVATIVE PRODUCTS

Cash flows

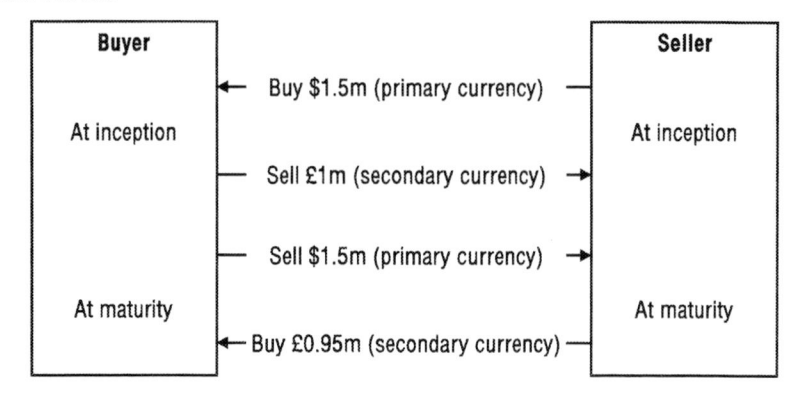

Buyer		Seller
At inception	← Buy $1.5m (primary currency) —	At inception
	— Sell £1m (secondary currency) →	
	— Sell $1.5m (primary currency) →	
At maturity	← Buy £0.95m (secondary currency) —	At maturity

5.2.4 Dealing

The market in short-term currency swaps, as for interest rate swaps, is an OTC market. Trading is conducted over the telephone and price information is disseminated through quote vendor systems.

5.3 Equity swaps

5.3.1 Definition

Equity swaps are similar in concept to interest rate swaps. The buyer pays the return on a money market deposit (eg LIBOR) and in exchange receives the total return on an equity investment (capital gains plus dividends). The two payments are usually netted and are generally exchanged between two and four times annually. As with interest rate swaps, **no exchange of principal** is involved.

Example

A fund manager enters into a one-year FTSE 100 index swap with a notional principal amount (NPA) of $20m and quarterly reset dates.

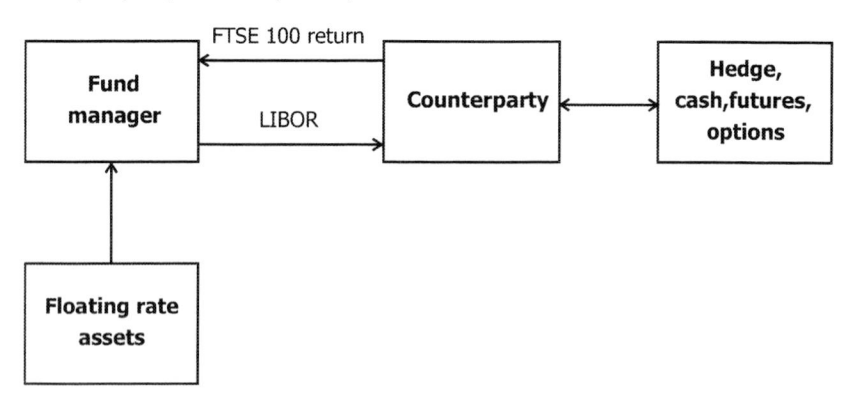

```
                    FTSE 100 return
         Fund    ←─────────────────   Counterparty   ←──→   Hedge,
         manager  ─────────────────→                        cash, futures,
                         LIBOR                              options
           ↑
           │
    Floating rate
       assets
```

5.3.2 Uses of equity swaps

Indexation

As a route to indexation, the equity swap may hold certain advantages over either a physically constructed fund or one synthesised using futures.

Speculating and hedging

Counterparties can use swaps to either gain or hedge their own exposure to physical equities.

The opportunities for swap counterparties to run a matched book in equity swaps are limited, as while the index funds are naturally receivers of index returns, there are fewer people who would wish to pay equity returns other than over a short period of time (as they would for short futures).

There is therefore a fundamental disequilibrium that may limit further growth.

Arbitrage

There are opportunities for arbitrage profits where offsetting equity swaps and futures positions are taken and futures trade away from their fair value.

5.4 Inflation swaps

Investors who have traditionally wanted a return tied-in with movements in inflation have targeted investments such as index-linked gilts. There is an increasing market for inflation-linked solutions. Inflation swaps offer investors the opportunity to generate a return linked in to a particular inflation rate. In return for receiving the rate on an index such as the consumer price index, the investor will agree to pay a fixed amount in return.

8: DERIVATIVE PRODUCTS

Executive Summary

- A derivative is an investment whose value is derived from the value of something else.
- A future is an agreement to buy or sell a standard quantity of a specified asset on a fixed future date at a price agreed today.
- An option is a contract that confers the right but not the obligation to buy or sell an asset at a given price on or before a given date.
- A call option is a right to buy and a put option is a right to sell.
- Option and future positions can be combined together to form trading strategies.
- Swaps are a form of over-the-counter derivative (OTC). There are many different types of swaps including interest rate, currency and equity swaps.

9 Foreign Exchange

Contents

1. The Benefits of Overseas Investment 274
2. The Risks of Overseas Investment 274
3. Currency Rates 279
4. Exchange Rate Forecasting 282
5. Hedging of Foreign Currency Risk 285
6. Overseas Investment 288
   Executive Summary 294

9: FOREIGN EXCHANGE

1 THE BENEFITS OF OVERSEAS INVESTMENT

1.1 Introduction

As companies have expanded overseas, world equity markets have developed and foreign exchange controls have been lifted by many countries. Consequently, the importance of understanding, analysing and managing foreign currency exposure has increased.

Investors now have the opportunity to fully diversify their portfolios through overseas investment from around the world. In addition, investors may use a foreign currency as an asset of itself if they believe that it is appreciating relative to their base currency.

Foreign exchange, and the potential for exchange rate fluctuations, adds an extra dimension to the risk/return profile for an overseas investment.

The theoretical benefits of global investing are derived from modern portfolio theory. This argues that all investors invest in an efficient portfolio. An efficient portfolio is one that is not dominated by any other portfolio in terms of risk and return. If we ignore the possibility of a risk-free asset, all efficient portfolios lie on the efficient frontier.

The domestic efficient frontier, obtained when an investor invests only in his own domestic market, is dominated by an efficient frontier that includes global asset portfolios. Overseas diversification benefits include the following.

Markets	■ Diversification away from reliance on a single economy. ■ Diversification of portfolio to take in overseas markets.
Industrial sectors	■ Investment in sectors not available in the UK, such as mining.
Currencies	■ Less exposure to one currency. ■ Exposure to currency risk where the investor feels that this is of benefit.
Correlations	■ International assets are not perfectly positively correlated to domestic assets.

In addition, overseas diversification offers the potential for extremely **high returns in emerging markets**. The availability of investment trusts investing overseas provides a practical means of achieving a relatively diversified overseas investment at a low level of investment.

2 THE RISKS OF OVERSEAS INVESTMENT

Although overseas investment has many advantages, there are also a number of risks ie problems arising through such exposure.

9: FOREIGN EXCHANGE

Inherent risk	■ High risk in emerging markets due to the unsophisticated domestic investor base and overheating economies.
	■ Political risk in certain volatile countries.
	■ Legal rights of the investor is likely to differ from those in the UK.
	■ Ability of foreign investors to participate/invest.
Liquidity risk/ Hedging	■ Ability to realise investment, especially in adverse market conditions.
	■ Lack of developed derivatives for hedging purposes leads to less efficient portfolio management.
Currency risk/ Hedging	■ Exposure to adverse currency movements.
	■ Exchange control regulations in certain countries.
	■ Unavailability of suitable currency hedging products.
Lack of regulation	■ Lack of market regulation in emerging markets.
	■ Inadequate financial regulation/reporting standards.
Information/ Communications	■ Inadequate/problematic, eg may require foreign language expertise.
	■ Costly to gather.
	■ Unreliability.
Taxation	■ Potential double taxation problems.
	■ Additional local taxes.

We examine the more significant of these below.

2.1 Foreign exchange risk – The effect of exchange rate movements

The risks an investor may face with respect to foreign currency fluctuations (foreign exchange risk) may be categorised under one of three headings.

- Transaction risk
- Translation risk
- Operating or economic risk

2.1.1 Transaction risk

Definition

Transaction risk is the risk that the sterling value of any foreign currency receipts or payments may vary as a result of exchange rate fluctuations, resulting in a change in the anticipated investment cash flows.

9: FOREIGN EXCHANGE

Example

A company holds $5m in US$ bonds to be redeemed in three months' time. The current (spot) exchange rate is $1.60:£1. How much will be received in three months' time if the exchange rate at that date is:

- $1.60:£1?
- $1.50:£1?
- $1.70:£1?

Solution

$1.60:£1

At this rate, the sterling amount receivable would be $\dfrac{\$5,000,000}{1.60}$ = £3,125,000

$1.50:£1

At this rate, the sterling amount receivable would be $\dfrac{\$5,000,000}{1.50}$ = £3,333,333

$1.70:£1

At this rate, the sterling amount receivable would be $\dfrac{\$5,000,000}{1.70}$ = £2,941,176

Conclusion

We can see that as a result of a relatively minor fluctuation in exchange rates, the sterling amount receivable has moved dramatically. Clearly, this variability may well affect the decision as to whether the investment should be undertaken.

2.1.2 Translation risk

Definition

Translation risk is the risk that the sterling value of any foreign denominated assets or liabilities, or foreign denominated income or expenses, will vary from one year to the next as a result of changes in exchange rates, which will impact on the investment performance.

NB: This type of risk has no direct cash flow implications. Rather, what we have is variability of reported assets and profits in sterling, which may be caused purely by exchange rate fluctuations, with the assets and profits in local currency terms being fairly stable. As a result, apparent performance may be distorted.

Example

A UK investor holds £100m of US bonds. Interest rates in the US are static, hence bond prices in dollars are stable.

What will be the sterling value of this investment if the exchange rate is:

- $2:£1?
- $1:£1?

Solution

	$2:£1		$1:£1	
	$m	£m	$m	£m
Investments	100	50	100	100

What we appear to have is a return of 100%, with the portfolio rising from £50m to £100m. In truth, the true performance of the asset has been zero, it being worth $100m at both the start and end of the year. This apparent spectacular performance in sterling terms completely results from the foreign currency movement across the year. This factor is clearly outside of the control of the investor, and may go the other way just as rapidly.

2.1.3 Operating or economic risk

Definition

Operating or economic risk will not be suffered directly by the investor, though the risks of some of his investments may incorporate this as a function.

Operating or economic risk arises as a result of a company's competitive position. It is the risk that the sterling value of a company's cash flow may vary as a result of foreign exchange fluctuations, regardless of whether:

- There is no overseas trade/transactions/assets and liabilities.
- All overseas trade/transactions are fully hedged.

Example 1

A UK tour operator specialises in providing guided tours to overseas visitors. Since operations are conducted in the UK, he bills all of his customers in sterling. His revenue will, therefore, depend on two things

- The sterling charge per tour sold.
- The number of tours sold.

If sterling were to strengthen, then the tours would appear significantly more expensive to the foreign visitors and hence, the number of tours sold (and consequently, revenue) would fall.

In this example, there is no exporting or importing involved, but the revenues and profits of the company will be impacted upon by exchange rate fluctuations.

Example 2

Jaguar Cars export to the US, where it competes primarily against Mercedes and BMW. As a result, the relative demand for its products depend on its relative cost in dollars which, in turn, depends on the strength of the dollar against sterling and euro, respectively.

Jaguar's US performance is therefore influenced by any relative movement between sterling and euro, even though none of these transactions are being denominated in euro.

2.2 Additional transaction costs

2.2.1 Foreign currency transactions

Dealing in overseas markets will probably have to be done in overseas currencies, incurring dealing costs.

2.2.2 Information gathering

The investor will have less knowledge about overseas markets than his domestic UK market. This represents a risk that inappropriate investment decisions will be made. In order to avoid this problem, substantial costs will need to be incurred to understand and analyse the overseas companies and markets in which the investor is interested.

2.3 Taxation

2.3.1 Local taxes

Additional tax costs can be incurred when receiving dividends from overseas companies. Initially, the company may suffer high rates of corporate taxation on its profits, reducing its level of post-tax income significantly. Second, when dividends are paid, withholding taxes may be deducted, further reducing the final return to investors.

2.3.2 Double taxation treaties

The cost of overseas taxation will be mitigated by double taxation treaties. These mean that, where overseas tax has already been suffered on income, additional local tax may not be payable.

2.4 Political risk

Unexpected changes overseas can lead to major catastrophes. Nationalisation of industries without compensation, changes in government, reversals of policy and changes in tax rates will all significantly affect the returns available to investors.

3 CURRENCY RATES

In order to be able to analyse foreign currency risk in more detail, it is important to be able to perform basic foreign currency calculations.

3.1 Spot rates

The spot market is the market for **immediate currency trades**. Delivery will take place **two business days (T + 2)** after the deal is made. The market has no formal marketplace and trading takes place via telephones with prices being quoted on screen services.

3.1.1 Quotation of spot rates

The spot market quotes bid/offer prices (spot rates) in the form of a spread, normally based against the US$. The main exceptions to this is £:$ (known as cable) and €:$, where the $ is quoted against the £/€.

Whichever currencies are involved, exchange rates are quoted as the number of units of one currency per single unit of another. For convenience, we will refer to these as the **secondary** and **primary** currencies, respectively. You may also hear them referred to as variable and fixed, or quoted and base – you should view these terms as inter changeable.

As we have just noted, most currencies are quoted against the US$, and any quote where the $ is the secondary or variable currency would be referred to as a **direct quote** (eg $s per £1). An **indirect quote** is where the exchange rate is stated with the US$ as the primary currency (eg £s per $1).

3.1.2 The spread

Using cable as an example:

$1.4275–$1.4385

The $ buyers' rate	The $ sellers' rate
£1.00 will get $1.4275	$1.4385 will get £1.00

To assist in remembering which rate to use, remember that the bank **always gives you the worst rate**. For example, if you want to buy dollars with £1.00, the bank will give you the least dollars it can, ie $1.4275 rather than $1.4385 in return. Alternatively, if you have dollars and want to buy £1.00, then the bank will charge you the most it can, ie $1.4385 rather than $1.4275.

3.2 Forward rates

> The forward market is a market in currencies for delivery at an agreed date in the future. The exchange rate at which delivery takes place is agreed now.

9: FOREIGN EXCHANGE

3.2.1 Quotation of forward rates

Forward rates are quoted as **premiums (pm)** or **discounts (dis)** to the spot rate. It is possible for rates to be quoted at par where the spot and forward are the same.

Example

Spot	$1.4275–$1.4385
One-month forward	0.37–0.35c pm
Three-month forward	1.00–0.97c pm

Calculate the three-month forward rate.

Solution

It is important to remember that these rates are quoted in cents, whereas the spot rate is quoted in dollars.

A premium implies that the currency is becoming more expensive (strengthening against sterling), ie £1.00 will buy fewer dollars. Hence, to obtain the forward rate the premium is **subtracted** from the spot rate. Similarly, the discount is **added**. This will be the rule regardless of the nature of the quote, **direct or indirect**, premiums are subtracted and discounts are added.

Based on the above figures, the three-month forward rate is:

Spot rate	$1.4275–$1.4385
Less premium	($0.0100–$0.0097)
	$1.4175–$1.4288

3.2.2 Calculation of forward rates

One important factor to remember about this market is that it does not reflect an expectation of what the spot rate will be in three, six or nine months' time. It is simply a mathematical result of the difference in interest rates in the two countries.

Example

In the example below, three-month sterling interest rates were 10%, meaning the interest rate for the three-month period is 2.5% (10% × 3/12). Three-month dollar rates were 6%, meaning the interest rate for the three-month period is 1.5% (6% × 3/12).

Now spot rate				Three months' time forward rate
£1,000	→	@ 3-month £ rates at 2.5%	→	£1,025
↓				↓
@ $1.4275				Therefore @ $1.4135
↓				↑
$1,427.50	→	@ 3-month $ rates at 1.5%	→	$1,448.91

The forward rate is simply calculated on the basis that the money is invested at the current rate of interest in the two countries. At the end of the period, the relationship between the value of the two deposits gives the forward rate.

$$\frac{\$1,448.91}{£1,025} = \$1.4135$$

If this relationship were not the case, then it would be possible to make an arbitrage profit by borrowing in one currency, converting it at today's spot rate into the other currency and placing this on deposit for, say, three months. At the same time, a forward contract could be taken out to reverse the original spot transaction, locking-in a profit.

3.2.3 Interest rate parity formula

The link between exchange rates and interest rates can be worked through using first principles as above. Alternatively, the link can be summarised by the **interest rate parity** formula, which says that:

$$\text{Forward rate} = \frac{1+r_\$}{1+r_£} \times \text{Spot rate}$$

where:

$r_\$$ = dollar (variable currency) interest rate for the relevant period.

$r_£$ = sterling (fixed currency) interest rate for the relevant period.

Example (continued)

$$\text{Forward rate} = \frac{1.015}{1.025} \times \$1.4275 = \$1.4135$$

It is worth noting the specific way in which $r_\$$ and $r_£$ are calculated. They should be based on the number of days in the period. For example, if dollar interest rates for a three-month (91-day) period are 8%, the relevant value for $r_\$$ is (8% × 91/360) 2.02%. If sterling interest rates for a three-month (91-day) period are 10%, then the relevant value for $r_£$ is (10% × 91/365) 2.49%.

The use of a **360-day year for dollar** interest rates and a **365-day year for sterling** is market convention. When banks work out the yield they wish to pay or receive, they take this into account in their quote.

3.3 Cross rates

Details of exchange rates are included in the *Financial Times* every day for sterling.

9: FOREIGN EXCHANGE

It is possible to use these rates to estimate the exchange rate between other currencies, eg the yen and the euro, by using the exchange rates for each against sterling or the dollar. The rates established are called cross-rates.

Example

From the currency data in the illustration below, the closing rates for sterling euro are 1.6356–1.6368, that is £1 buys €1.6356 and £1 costs €1.6368. The exchange rate for sterling yen are 187.737–187.856, that is £1 buys ¥187.737 and £1 costs ¥187.865. What is the euro yen exchange rate?

Solution

The approach is to imagine that in order to buy yen, a German investor uses euro to buy sterling and then, sterling to buy yen.

£1.00 costs €1.6368. That £1.00 will then buy ¥187.737. This gives an exchange rate of €1.6368 to ¥187.737 or ¥114.698 to the euro when selling euro to buy yen.

In order to calculate the other side of the exchange rate, assume that an investor buys sterling with yen and then uses that sterling to buy euro.

£1.00 costs ¥187.865. That £1.00 will then buy €1.6356. This gives an exchange rate of €1.6356 to ¥187.865 or ¥114.860 to the euro when selling yen to buy euro.

The predicted exchange rate is therefore   114.698–114.860

It is inevitable that these rates will be very similar to the actual rates, otherwise there would be opportunities for arbitrage profits by buying and selling across the three currencies.

4 EXCHANGE RATE FORECASTING

4.1 Introduction

In order to be able to make informed decisions on currency exposure and overseas investment, it is important to be able to appreciate the factors affecting exchange rates and the likely future direction of exchange rate movements.

Analysis of exchange rates focuses on key economic factors which affect currencies. It considers the performance and interaction of a number of key economic variables, such as growth, inflation and exchange rates. This may be done by constructing a model of the world economy with certain defined relationships and interactions between key variables. Assumptions are made about the key variables and forecasts of exchange rates are produced.

The problem with this approach, known as econometric modelling, is that it is fairly rigid and formal. It is difficult to alter relationships between variables to reflect changing circumstances and the impact of national and international crises.

A more flexible approach is to adopt subjective values, where the forecaster identifies key variables for a period of time and then makes assumptions about these and their relationship to each other over the period.

4.1.1 Shorter-term factors affecting exchange rates

Interest rates

In the short term, exchange rates will be influenced by supply and demand for a currency. If, for example, two economies have had stable exchange rates and one decides to increase interest rates, then this change will attract 'hot money' from around the world seeking higher returns, the effect being that the currency will suddenly rise. This exchange rate will however be artificially high – the currencies were previously stable. We would, therefore, expect that the currency would weaken to its original rate over time. As a result, a good estimator of the short-term future exchange rate would be the interest rate parity relationship introduced above, which incorporates the effect of this depreciation over time, ie:

$$\text{Future exchange rate} = \frac{1+r_s}{1+r_p} \times \text{Spot rate}$$

where:

r_s = interest rate for the secondary currency for the relevant period
r_p = interest rate for the primary currency for the relevant period

Balance of payments

If the economy has a balance of payments surplus, then it is exporting goods with a higher value than it is importing. In order to pay for these goods, overseas customers will need to purchase the currency. Demand for it will increase, meaning that the currency will strengthen. Alternatively, if the economy has a balance of payments deficit, then companies will need to sell the local currency to buy overseas currencies to fund their purchases. This will cause the local currency to weaken.

Economic growth

Economic growth will stimulate demand for a currency both through capital flows into the country, due to attractive investment opportunities, and current account flows, due to increased supply and demand for the country's traded goods and services. Alternatively, a credit boom which causes demand for overseas goods and services will cause the currency to weaken.

Fiscal and monetary policies

Taxation and public spending policies have a direct impact on economic growth. Government borrowing plans will impact on interest rates, as will monetary policy, which aims to reduce or increase money supply through changes in interest rates.

Natural resources

The discovery or existence of valuable natural resources, such as oil, can cause a currency to strengthen dramatically.

Currency block membership

Some currencies are pegged to the US dollar, such as certain Middle Eastern currencies. Such formal or informal relationships should be noted, since they will have a key impact on the exchange rate.

Political events

Central bank intervention can affect exchange rates, although experience has shown that it is sometimes the speculators who win the day rather than the central authorities. On top of this, events such as elections, public opinion polls, government ministers' statements and press releases can all affect the exchange rate.

4.1.2 Longer term factors – Inflation and purchasing power parity

Introduction

In the shorter term, the exchange rate is determined by supply and demand factors and, to a greater or lesser extent, market sentiment. Longer term exchange rates are determined by purchasing power parity, which is a relationship between economies and the levels of inflation they suffer. Purchasing power parity (PPP) is best explained by way of a small example.

If a basket of goods costs £100 in London and the same basket of goods costs €160 in Frankfurt, this suggests the exchange rate between the two countries will be £1 = €1.60. However, if the two economies suffer differing rates of inflation, then over time, the exchange rate will alter.

If, after a number of years, the basket of goods now costs £125 in London, due to the impact of inflation on UK prices, and yet it remains at €160 in Frankfurt, this would suggest that the exchange rate between the two currencies is now £1 = €1.28, a decline in the value of sterling.

Short-term supply and demand features may well mask this overall trend, but purchasing power parity gives an underlying theme to the foreign exchange markets. If one economy consistently has an inflation rate in excess of its competitors, then its currency will deteriorate against its trading partners.

The International Fisher Effect

We have seen above that longer term exchange rates are theoretically determined by purchasing power parity and the inflation differential between two currencies. We have also seen above that short-term future exchange rates are determined by reference to interest rate differentials. These two concepts are brought together by the Fisher effect, which links together interest rates, inflation and the foreign exchange markets.

Fisher states that the nominal rate of return (r), ie the interest rate charged or monetary return, is equal to the real rate of return (R) adjusted to compensate for the effect of inflation (i) as follows.

$$(1 + r) = (1 + R)(1 + i)$$

If we now go back to the relationship that we established earlier for short-term exchange rates, we had:

$$\text{Future exchange rate} = \frac{1+r_s}{1+r_p} \times \text{Spot rate}$$

Now, the Fisher relationship must apply in all economies, hence

$$\frac{1+r_s}{1+r_p} = \frac{(1+R_s)(1+i_s)}{(1+R_p)(1+i_p)}$$

The assumption of PPP is that the real rate of return, R, should equate between countries in the long term. If this were not the case and one country always offered a superior return, then investors would only invest in that country, resulting in prices rising and returns falling until an equilibrium was reached.

As a result, in the long term, we will have:

$$(1 + R_s) = (1 + R_n)$$

These two terms then cancel out in the previous equation as follows.

$$\frac{1+r_s}{1+r_p} = \frac{\cancel{(1+R_s)}(1+i_s)}{\cancel{(1+R_p)}(1+i_p)} = \frac{1+i_s}{1+i_p}$$

This is the International Fisher Effect, that interest rate differentials in the long term equate to inflation rate differentials over the same period.

Making this substitution in our future exchange rate formula above gives us that in the long term, the difference in exchange rates is generated by the differential in inflation rates, ie:

$$\text{Future exchange rate} = \frac{1+i_s}{1+i_p} \times \text{Spot rate}$$

where $(1 + i_s)$, $(1 + i_p)$ reflect the compound effect of inflation over the relevant period.

That is, exchange rate differentials in the long term are driven by inflation rate differentials between the two economies concerned.

5 HEDGING OF FOREIGN CURRENCY RISK

The risk referred to above that movements in exchange rates will cause variability in returns, either in the form of cash flows or asset values, can be reduced or eliminated by use of various foreign currency hedging techniques.

9: FOREIGN EXCHANGE

5.1 Forward contracts

5.1.1 Trading

When an importer is buying goods from overseas in foreign currency, he has the risk that when the time comes to pay for the goods, the exchange rate will have moved against him. This risk can be removed by taking out a forward contract for the date he intends to pay for the goods at the date he purchases them. The forward contract fixes the rate today for delivery of the currency at a future date. The relevant rate is the forward rate.

5.1.2 Investment

The same principle can be used by an investor. In our transaction risk example earlier, the returns from the US$ bond were variable, depending on movements in exchange rates.

If we can estimate the expected US$ return in advance, however, then we can take out a forward contract for that amount when we originally purchase the investment, or at some later date.

Example

We hold $5m nominal of US$ corporate bonds when the exchange rate is $1.60:£1, meaning that the sterling value of the bonds is £3.125m. We expect that we will receive a coupon of 8% ($0.4m) and can sell the bonds for $5.06m in a year's time, ie we expect a total return of $5.46m in one year. In addition, the forward rate at the beginning of the year for delivery dates one year, hence is 1.56:1. What return can we achieve avoiding currency risk?

Solution

If we take out a forward contract to sell $5.46m for sterling at a rate of $1.56:£1 in one year's time, we will receive £3.50m. This gives a return of:

$$R_£ = \frac{3.500 - 3.125}{3.125} = 12\%$$

5.1.3 Problems with forward contracts

The advantage of the forward contract is that it locks into a certain rate of exchange in the future. There are however a number of problems.

- Since the forward rate is locked-in at the outset, the investor cannot take advantage of any favourable exchange rate movements. In our case, for example, if spot rates had been 1.50:1 at the end of the year, then we would in hindsight have done better by not taking out a forward contract at 1.56:1 and instead selling the dollars on the spot market at the rate of 1.50:1.

9: FOREIGN EXCHANGE

- The forward contract is for a fixed amount. If the amount of dollars that we receive is different to the amount of the forward contract we have taken out, then the difference will represent an outstanding exposure.

- For example, assume that the worst happens and a US$ corporate bond issuer becomes insolvent and pays no capital or interest. As a result of the forward contract we have entered into, we are now obliged at the end of the year to sell $5.46m for sterling at a rate of 1.56:1. This means that we will have to buy $5.46m on the spot market to complete the transaction and will either make a profit or loss on the transaction, depending on the spot rate.

- It is necessary to estimate the expected proceeds from the investment, which is not easy for risky investments such as equities.

- A series of dividend flows would each require a separate forward contract, increasing costs and administration.

- As the maturity of the investment becomes more distant, it becomes more difficult to obtain competitively priced forward contracts. The reason for this is that the forward market is most active in the three- to six-month period. Very long maturities are harder for the banks to cover and hence are more expensive and illiquid.

5.2 Borrowing and depositing

An alternative means of hedging an expected receipt in another currency would be through borrowing and depositing. That is to borrow now in that other currency, convert the money received into sterling at today's spot rate and place this sterling on deposit, then to use the expected receipt in the other currency to repay the borrowing on maturity.

Example

In our case above, we are expecting to receive $5.46m in one year's time. We can borrow US dollars at an annual rate of 7% and sterling deposits are paying 9.75%. How can we hedge our position?

Solution

We borrow sufficient dollars so that the capital plus interest at 7% comes to $5.46m in one year's time. This will entail borrowing (5.46m/1.07) $5.103m.

This can be converted into sterling immediately using today's spot rate of 1.6:1, giving £3.189m immediately, thus removing exchange rate risk. In one year's time, the borrowing of $5.103m is repaid together with 7% interest of $0.357m, the repayment being funded by the receipt of $5.460m from coupon and sale of the US$ bonds.

The £3.189m sterling now held can be placed on deposit for the year, growing to £3.500m. This is the same total receipt in one year as it would be, had we taken out a forward contract instead (above). This will always be the case. If there are two ways of achieving the same end result, then they must have the same value as, if they do not, any difference will be arbitraged away.

The key problem with borrowing is that, as with the forward contract, it creates an exposure to foreign currency which will still be there if the expected receipts from the investment do not flow through. In our case, even if we receive no cash from the US$ investment, we are still obliged to repay the dollar borrowing in one year's time and will have to purchase dollars to do so.

5.3 Options

The currency option avoids many of the problems noted above for borrowing and use of forward contracts. The currency option gives the buyer of the option the right, but not the obligation, to buy or sell foreign currency at a specified rate and a specified date or range of dates in the future. The right to buy currency is a call option, the right to sell currency is a put option. The cost of buying the option is the premium.

The key benefit of the option is that it enables the company to benefit from favourable exchange rate movements but protects it from adverse movements. The option need only be exercised if it favours the buyer to do so. This means that an investor could buy an option for the higher range of expected receipts from an investment.

For example, if we were expecting receipts of up to $130, we could buy options to sell the full $130. If the amount received is less than $130, then we only exercise an appropriate amount, and have a choice as to what to do with the remainder. If the dollar has weakened, we can buy dollars at the low price and then sell them, as this option entitles us to, at the higher price. If the dollar has strengthened, then we just let the option expire worthless. Hence, the excess amount covered by the options is not an exposure, as it will never result in a loss.

The problem with an option is that a premium needs to be paid. The larger the amount to which the option relates, the higher the premium. Likewise, the greater the chance that the option can be exercised profitably, the higher the premium.

6 OVERSEAS INVESTMENT

6.1 Overseas investment returns

Any foreign currency fluctuation is liable to impact on the returns on overseas investment. If a currency appreciates by 5% against sterling, then an investment in simply the bank notes of that currency (a 0% return in that currency) would produce a 5% sterling return. If an investment is made in securities that offer a return in the local currency, then the sterling return needs to be amplified by the effects of the exchange gain. This relationship is a compounding one, ie

$$(1 + r_£) = 1 + r_$)(1 + r_{FX})$$

Where:

$r_£$ = sterling return achieved
$r_$$ = overseas investment return in local currency
r_{FX} = return due to exchange rate fluctuations

This can be demonstrated with a simple example that approaches the problem in two alternative ways.

9: FOREIGN EXCHANGE

- First principles.
- The above compounding formula.

Example

A UK investor invests in US bonds that produce a return in dollars of 10% over the period. The exchange rate at the start of the period is $1.56:£1 and at the end is $1.50:£1. Calculate the return achieved by the UK investor.

Solution

First principles

Consider what would have happened to an investment of £100 made at the start as follows.

Start value		$ Return		End value		£ Return
£	$			$	£	%
100.00 →	156.00	→		171.60 →	114.40	14.4
@1.56		+10%		@1.50		

Compounding formula

Clearly, the dollar has appreciated against sterling, moving from 1.56 to 1.50 across the period. The resultant currency return = $\frac{1.56}{1.50}$ = 1.04, ie the dollar has appreciated by 4% against sterling. The sterling return can now be calculated using:

$(1 + r_£) = (1 + r_\$)(1 + r_{FX})$
$= 1.10 \times 1.04 = 1.144$

Hence: $r_£ = 0.144$ or 14.4%

6.1.1 Currency returns

It may appear strange that the currency return has been calculated above as:

$$(1 + r_{FX}) = \frac{\text{Opening exchange rate}}{\text{Closing exchange rate}}$$

when we would normally calculate a gain using

$$(1 + r) = \frac{\text{End value}}{\text{Start value}}$$

9: FOREIGN EXCHANGE

This is due to the way that the rates are quoted above, ie as the number of dollars per pound. As a result:

- The value of $1 at the start of the year was $\dfrac{£1}{1.56}$ = 64.103p.

- The value of $1 at the year end was $\dfrac{£1}{1.50}$ = 66.667p.

Hence, the gain was:

$$(1 + r) = \dfrac{\text{End value of \$1}}{\text{Start value of \$1}} = \dfrac{66.667}{64.103} = 1.04$$

Algebraically, this is:

$$(1 + r) = \dfrac{\text{End value}}{\text{Start value}} = \dfrac{£1}{1.50} \div \dfrac{£1}{1.56} = \dfrac{£1}{1.50} \times \dfrac{1.56}{£1} = \dfrac{1.56}{1.50} \text{ as we used above.}$$

If, however, the exchange rates had been quoted against the dollar, ie as £0.64103:$1 at the start and £0.66667:$1 at the end, then the currency gain would need to have been calculated as:

$$(1 + r_{FX}) = \dfrac{\text{Opening exchange rate}}{\text{Closing exchange rate}} = \dfrac{66.667}{64.103} = 1.04$$

What we can see is that the currency gain is calculated by dividing one of the opening exchange rate and the closing exchange rate by the other, but which depends on the way that the exchange rates are quoted.

The best approach may be to determine whether there has been a currency gain or loss and divide the opening and closing rates appropriately.

6.2 Overseas investment risks

As foreign exchange fluctuations augment the returns achieved by a sterling investor, they also augment the risks of overseas investment.

The method we apply here to calculate the total risk (including the foreign exchange effect) represents an approximation, since it assumes an additive rather than a compounding relationship. However, it is reasonably accurate unless risks from either the security or the currency are very large.

The method is based upon the portfolio theory risk combination model:

$$\sigma_{a+b}^2 = p_a^2\sigma_a^2 + p_b^2\sigma_b^2 + 2p_a p_b \sigma_a \sigma_b \text{Cor}_{ab}$$

taking a as the overseas security and b as the exchange rate, say.

Now normally, when we use this formula, we are splitting our funds between two investments and only part is exposed to one risk and the rest to the other. Here, all of our funds are exposed to both types of risks, hence in this situation:

- $p_a = 1$ since all of our money is exposed to the investments risk.
- $p_b = 1$ since all of our money is also exposed to the currency risk.

9: FOREIGN EXCHANGE

Hence, the formula becomes:

$$\sigma_£^2 = \sigma_\$^2 + \sigma_{FX}^2 + 2\sigma_\$\sigma_{FX}\text{Cor}_{\$FX}$$

where:

$\sigma_£$ = risk to the sterling investor
$\sigma_\$$ = risk of the overseas investment in local currency terms
σ_{FX} = foreign exchange risk
$\text{Cor}_{\$FX}$ = correlation between investment and currency returns

Example

A UK investor invests in US bonds whose risk in dollars is 5%. The exchange rate risk for the same period is assessed at 5%. Calculate the risk to the UK investor if the correlation between currency and security returns are:

- 0.4
- −1

Solution

Cor = 0.4

$$\sigma_£^2 = \sigma_\$^2 + \sigma_{FX}^2 + 2\sigma_\$\sigma_{FX}\text{Cor}_{\$FX}$$
$$\sigma_£^2 = 5^2 + 5^2 + 2 \times 5 \times 5 \times 0.4 = 70$$
$$\sigma_£ = 8.3666\%$$

Cor = −1

$$\sigma_£^2 = \sigma_\$^2 + \sigma_{FX}^2 + 2\sigma_\$\sigma_{FX}\text{Cor}_{\$FX}$$
$$\sigma_£^2 = 5^2 + 5^2 + 2 \times 5 \times 5 \times (-1) = 0$$
$$\sigma_£ = 0\%$$

As ever, if the returns are perfectly negatively correlated, they may produce a perfect hedge as demonstrated here.

6.3 Impact of foreign exchange on overseas investments

6.3.1 Fixed interest

The International Fisher Effect referred to above suggests that, in the long run, countries with high nominal rates of interest, and correspondingly high bond yields, will see their currencies depreciate. This means that exchange rate variations and returns from securities may be negatively correlated. This is especially the case for fixed interest securities where yields, interest rates and inflation levels are clearly linked. It is less obvious for equities where factors other than interest and inflation also affect the nominal returns.

Example

The current exchange rate is $1.50:£1. Interest rates and bond yields in the UK and the US are 8% and 6%, respectively. Estimate the exchange rate in one year and calculate the expected return to a sterling investor from investing in either the UK bond or the US bond.

Solution

Future exchange rate

$$\text{Future exchange rate} = \text{Spot rate} \times \frac{1+r_s}{1+r_p}$$

$$\text{Future exchange rate} = 1.50 \times \frac{1.06}{1.08} = 1.47222$$

Expected returns

UK investor

$$r_£ = 8\%$$

US investor

$$1 + r_£ = (1 + r_\$)(1 + r_{FX})$$

$$= 1.06 \times \frac{1.50}{1.47222} = 1.08$$

Giving:

$$r_£ = 0.08 \text{ or } 8\%$$

Hence, in deciding whether to invest in overseas bonds or UK bonds, the investor needs to take a view on exchange rate movements. If he believes that the foreign currency will end the year stronger than is implied by interest rate (and bond yield) differentials, then the overseas bond would be expected to produce the superior sterling return. If, however, he expects the currency to be weaker than implied, then the UK bond would be preferable.

By not hedging against foreign exchange risk, an investor can theoretically reduce variability in his real sterling rate of return, since a high nominal rate of interest for an overseas country implies a high inflation rate and a depreciating currency. Alternatively, by hedging against the foreign exchange risk, an investor can fix a certain nominal return in sterling terms.

6.3.2 Equity markets

In the case of equities, the correlation (negative) between changes in exchange rates and security returns is not so strong. In these circumstances, international diversification can be used to maintain levels of return and reduce risk. Falls in value of one overseas currency can theoretically be set-off against rises in value of other currencies compared to sterling.

6.4 Methods of investing

6.4.1 Direct investment

This has a number of disadvantages and few of the advantages of overseas investment, unless the individual has significant resources, time and knowledge of the local markets in question.

6.4.2 Purchasing shares on the London Stock Exchange

This is cheaper and easier, and the type of overseas company listed in the UK is likely to be reliable and to give out trustworthy and periodic information. It may be difficult to achieve a wide spread of investments however, unless the individual has significant personal resources.

In addition to purchasing shares in overseas companies in London, it is also possible to purchase shares in UK companies that have significant overseas exposure. For example, a company with a number of Japanese motor dealerships could be seen as a play on the Japanese market.

6.4.3 Indirect investment

Investment via unit trusts and investment trusts is probably the easiest and best route for the individual wishing to gain overseas exposure. They give all the above benefits and compensate for most of the problems, such as lack of expertise.

9: FOREIGN EXCHANGE

EXECUTIVE SUMMARY

- The spot market is the market for immediate currency trades.
- A forward currency transaction is an agreement to buy or to sell a currency at a future date at a price agreed today.
- Forward rates are quoted at a premium or discount to the spot rate.
- Forward rates are computed on the basis of interest rate parity.
- Longer-term exchange rates are determined by purchasing power parity which is the relationship between economies and the level of inflation they suffer.

10 Performance Measurement and Appraisal

Contents

1. Introduction 296
2. Measurement of Returns 296
3. Appraisal of Performance 304
4. Risk-Adjusted Performance Attribution 315
   Executive Summary 320

1 INTRODUCTION

An investor who has been paying someone to actively manage their portfolio will clearly wish to monitor how well the fund manager is doing his job. Such information can then be used to:

- Alter or update the portfolio investment constraints in order to achieve a particular objective.
- Communicate investment objectives to the fund manager, which should affect how the fund is managed.
- Identify strengths and weaknesses of particular fund managers.

When measuring a fund's performance we have three objectives to establish.

- What was the performance achieved? We need to be able to **measure performance**.
- Was the fund performance relatively good or bad? We need to be able to **appraise performance**.
- Did this situation arise due to skill (or lack thereof) or just fortune? We need to be able to **attribute performance**.

2 MEASUREMENT OF RETURNS

2.1 Introduction

In order to reflect all the actions of our fund managers, any performance measures must include both dividends and capital growth. As such, we must always be looking at the market values of any securities held in the fund, as opposed to their historical costs.

2.2 Holding period return

2.2.1 Introduction

Each investment is characterised by a cost and a pattern of cash flows. We could describe a fund's performance by stating the dividends plus capital growth (final market value less initial value) as a percentage of the initial amount invested.

Example 1

Suppose Investment A costs $100 and at the end of six months, returns $10, before being sold for $110. How can it be compared with Investment B, bought at $50, held for one year and then sold for $70 with no income paid out? Obviously, the different costs must be taken into account, as well as the different returns and time periods involved.

2.2.2 Basic calculation

Calculating the percentage holding period return for each investment avoids the problem of comparing different size investments. This return is simply the gain during the period held (money received less cost) divided by the initial cost, ie:

$$r_p = \frac{(D_1 + V_1) - V_0}{V_0}$$

where:

- r_p = holding period return
- D_1 = any returns paid out from the investment/fund at the end of the period
- V_0 = is the initial cost at the start of the holding period
- V_1 = the value of the investment at the end of the holding period

Solution 1a

Using this equation, the holding period returns for Investments A and B can be calculated as:

Investment A

$$r_a = \frac{(D_1 + V_1) - V_0}{V_0} \times 100$$

$$r_a = \frac{(10 + 110) - 100}{100} \times 100 = 20\% \text{ in six months}$$

Investment B

$$r_b = \frac{(D_1 + V_1) - V_0}{V_0} \times 100$$

$$r_b = \frac{(0 + 70) - 50}{50} \times 100 = 40\% \text{ in a year}$$

2.2.3 Using the results – annualising

The holding period returns of A and B are not directly comparable, since B was invested for twice as long as A. When A was sold, the proceeds could have been reinvested for another six months, but we do not know what return would have been available to the investor at that time. To compare the returns, they must be for a standard period. This is achieved by using the equivalent period interest rate formula to annualise the returns as follows.

10: PERFORMANCE MEASUREMENT AND APPRAISAL

Solution 1b

Investment A

r_a = 20% in six months

Hence, annualising this return, we get:

$1 + r = (1 + R)^n$

$1 + r = 1.2^2 = 1.44$

$r = 0.44$ or 44% pa

Investment B

r_b = 40% pa

We have now got a standardised measure of return, the annualised holding period return.

However, the problem that arises with this measure is what happens if there have been significant cash inflows to/outflows from the fund during the period, other than the period end dividend? These could significantly distort the results.

Example 2

A fund has a start value of $10m. Halfway through the period, it has the same value and a further $10m is deposited. At the end of the period, it is worth $20m, no dividends having been paid.

What is the fund's performance?

Solution 2a

Using our equation above, we have:

$$r_p = \frac{D_1 + V_1 - V_0}{V_s} \times 100$$

$$r_p = \frac{0 + 20m - 10m}{10m} \times 100 = +100\%$$

But has the fund really generated a 100% return? In truth, it has generated no return whatsoever. Its terminal value is simply the sum of what was initially held plus the funds added. No return or growth has been generated.

This simple approach is therefore inadequate. We must in some way account for the deposits and withdrawals that occur during the period over which we are determining the performance.

2.3 Money-weighted returns

A money-weighted return (MWR) is the internal rate of return (IRR) of the fund opening and closing values along with any deposits into/withdrawals from the fund.

If r is the money-weighted return then, using present value ideas, the current fund market value must be equal to the future fund cash payouts discounted at this rate, ie

$$V_s = \frac{CF_1}{(1+r)^{t1}} + \frac{CF_2}{(1+r)^{t2}} + \cdots + \frac{CF_n}{(1+r)^{tn}} + \frac{V_n}{(1+r)^{tn}}$$

where:

V_s	=	current fund value
CF_n	=	cash inflow/outflow from the fund at time t_n during the period, including dividends paid out by the fund
V_n	=	fund value at the end of the period
r	=	**money-weighted return**

This has the advantage over our simple holding period return calculation above of considering all the relevant cash flows **and** their timings.

Note that this formula cannot be solved; the money-weighted return (or IRR) must be found through trial and error/interpolation in a normal DCF tabular calculation. Furthermore, in applying this approach, we must assume we buy the fund at the start and sell it at the end.

Solution 2b

Applying this to Example 2 above, we get:

Time	Comment	Cash flow $m	Discount Factor	Present value $m
0	'Buy' the fund	(10)	1	(10)
½	Further investment	(10)	$\frac{1}{1.00^{½}}$	(10)
1	'Sell' the fund	20	$\frac{1}{1.00^{1}}$	20
				0

Giving a money-weighted return of 0%, the solution we wanted.

Unfortunately, this method does not always give the expected results.

10: PERFORMANCE MEASUREMENT AND APPRAISAL

Example 3

Our fund starts the year with a value of $20m. It falls to $10m by the middle of the year when a further $10m is invested bringing the fund back up to $20m in total. It then rises to $40m at the year-end. Calculate the money-weighted return.

Solution 3a

Before we calculate the money-weighted return, let us consider what we expect. Each $1 we held at the start of the period fell in value to 50p by the middle of the period but rose back to $1 by the end. Once more our overall performance has been zero.

Time	Comment	Cash flow $m	Discount factor	Present value $m
0	'Buy' the fund	(20)	1	(20.00)
½	Further investment	(10)	$\frac{1}{1.40693^{½}}$	(8.43)
1	'Sell' the fund	40	$\frac{1}{1.40693^{1}}$	28.43
				0.00

The money-weighted return is 40.693%, clearly not what we expected.

2.3.1 Results

The performance appears good because there was more money invested in the second half of the period when the fund was performing well. The performance has been **money-weighted**, biasing this measure towards the performance during the period when money invested was at its peak.

What is needed is a measure that is unaffected by cash inflows to and outflows from the fund (deposits and withdrawals) over which the fund manager has no control.

2.4 Time-weighted returns

The time-weighted return achieves this objective. The method is to calculate the returns between any cash flow dates, using our original holding period formula, and then combine them in a similar fashion to compound interest to establish the return for the full period.

When calculating the returns between each cash flow (deposits, withdrawals, dividends), we will take:

V_s = fund value immediately **after** the cash flow that marked the **start** of the sub-period (or start of the period if it is the first sub-period).

V_e = fund value immediately **before** the cash flow that marked the **end** of the sub-period (or end of the period if it is the last sub-period).

10: PERFORMANCE MEASUREMENT AND APPRAISAL

For the purposes of clarity of calculations, it is always useful to draw a graphical representation of how the value of the fund has changed over time.

Solution 2c

In relation to Example 2 above, we had a mid-period deposit and hence we need to evaluate two sub-periods, the sub-period before that date and the subsequent one.

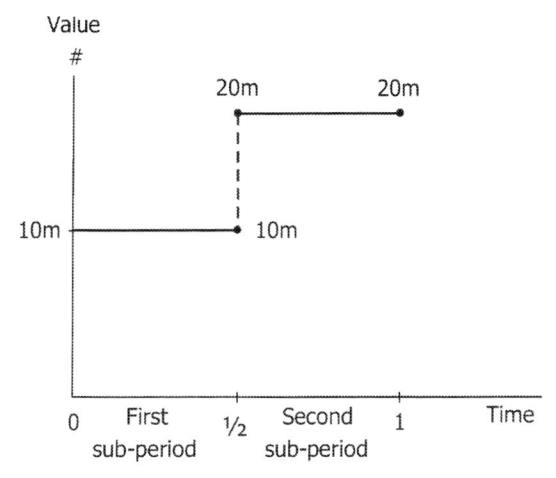

The idea here is that the fund manager controls the change in the fund value over time (ie the solid horizontal lines above). He does not control the timing and scale of any cash inflows or outflows (the vertical dotted line). The fund manager should only be assessed on the factors he controls, which is the aim of the time-weighted return.

First sub-period

Using:

$$r_1 = \frac{(D + V_e) - V_s}{V_s} \times 100$$

We get

$$r_1 = \frac{(0 + 10m) - 10m}{10m} \times 100 = 0\%$$

Second sub-period

V_s is now $20m following the $10m deposit marking the start of this sub-period, hence:

$$r_2 = \frac{(D + V_e) - V_s}{V_s} \times 100$$

Gives

$$r_2 = \frac{(0 + 20m) - 20m}{20m} \times 100 = 0\%$$

Combining

Clearly, if there is no return during either sub-period the combined periods return is zero. Demonstrating this formally to give the full period return r_p:

$$1 + r_p = (1 + r_1) \times (1 + r_2)$$

$$1 + r_p = (1 + 0) \times (1 + 0) = 1$$

$$r_p = 0$$

Solution 3b

In relation to Example 3 above, again we have two sub-periods to evaluate.

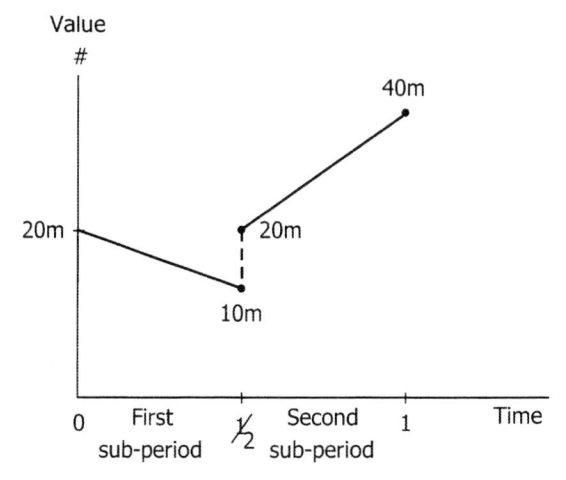

Once again, the fund manager controls the change in value over time (ie the solid diagonals), and it is this change in value over this time that he should be appraised on.

First sub-period

The fund starts with a value of $20m which falls to $10m, hence:

$$r_1 = \frac{(D + V_e) - V_s}{V_s} \times 100$$

Gives

$$r_1 = \frac{(0 + 10m) - 20m}{20m} \times 100 = -50\%$$

Second sub-period

Following the deposit of a further $10m the fund value starts this sub-period with a value of $20m which rises to $40m, hence:

$$r_2 = \frac{(D + V_e) - V_s}{V_s} \times 100$$

10: PERFORMANCE MEASUREMENT AND APPRAISAL

Gives:

$$r_2 = \frac{(0 + 40m) - 20m}{20m} \times 100 = +100\%$$

Combining

Combining these two sub-periods to give a full period return r_p using:

$$1 + r_p = (1 + r_1) \times (1 + r_2)$$

Gives:

$$1 + r_p = (1 - 0.5) \times (1 + 1) = 1$$

$$1 + r_p = 0.5 \times 2 = 1$$

$$r_p = 0$$

Hence, the overall periodic return is reported as zero as we felt it should be.

By combining the returns as effectively compound interest in each sub-period we are **time-weighting** the returns.

2.4.1 Results

The time-weighted return is unaffected by either the timing of cash inflows/outflows or the value of funds invested in the period. It therefore represents a good measure of the manager's performance.

Example 4

A fund starts the year with a value of $100m. The value of the fund at the end of each quarter and the cash inflows/(outflows) following those valuations are:

	Q1	Q2	Q3	Q4
Value	105	107	116	117
In/(out)	(2)	3	(4)	(2)

Calculate the time-weighted return for the year.

10: PERFORMANCE MEASUREMENT AND APPRAISAL

Solution 4

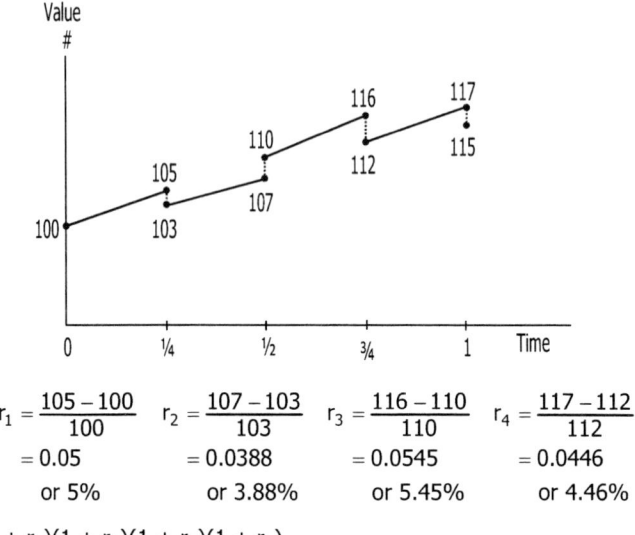

[Graph showing values over time: starting at 100, jumping to 105 then falling to 103 at ¼; rising to 110 then falling to 107 at ½; rising to 116 then falling to 112 at ¾; rising to 117 then falling to 115 at 1]

$$r_1 = \frac{105-100}{100} \qquad r_2 = \frac{107-103}{103} \qquad r_3 = \frac{116-110}{110} \qquad r_4 = \frac{117-112}{112}$$

$$= 0.05 \qquad\qquad = 0.0388 \qquad\qquad = 0.0545 \qquad\qquad = 0.0446$$

$$\text{or } 5\% \qquad\qquad \text{or } 3.88\% \qquad\qquad \text{or } 5.45\% \qquad\qquad \text{or } 4.46\%$$

$1 + r_{yr} = (1 + r_1)(1 + r_2)(1 + r_3)(1 + r_4)$

$\qquad\qquad = 1.05 \times 1.0388 \times 1.0545 \times 1.0446 = 1.2015$

$r_{yr} \qquad = 0.2015 \text{ or } 20.15\%$

2.5 Conclusion

In general, the **money-weighted method** of measuring returns for the purposes of evaluation is considered **inappropriate**, since this measure is strongly influenced by the size and timing of cash flows outside the control of the fund manager.

The **time-weighted** return does not suffer this problem and must be considered **more appropriate**.

3 APPRAISAL OF PERFORMANCE

3.1 Introduction

We have now established a way of assessing the return achieved, but how can we tell whether this is good or bad, eg is a return of 5% good? Clearly, we cannot answer this question unless we have a yardstick to measure against, eg interest rates and general market performance.

Given that the basis of most finance theory is that investors are rational and risk-averse, it is appropriate to determine whether they are being adequately compensated by way of absolute return for that absolute risk. Methods that we can utilise for this purpose include:

- Comparison of total returns to a benchmark index.
- Comparison of total returns to the capital market line or the securities market line.
- Excess return per unit risk measures, determining how well the excess absolute return over the risk-free rate compensates for the total risk.

3.2 Comparison to a benchmark index

3.2.1 Introduction

In order to assess how well a fund manager is performing, we need a yardstick for comparison. One such suitable yardstick may be a benchmark index. Once we have determined an appropriate benchmark, we can then compare whether the fund manager outperformed, matched, or underperformed.

The appropriate benchmark is one that is consistent with the preferences of the fund's trustees and the fund's tax status. For example, a different benchmark is appropriate if the fund is a gross fund and does not pay taxes (eg a pension fund), than if it is a net fund and does pay taxes (eg a general insurance fund).

Similarly, a general market index will not be appropriate as a benchmark if the trustee has a preference for high-income securities or an aversion to certain securities, eg rival companies. The FTSE All Share Index would not be an appropriate benchmark if half the securities were held overseas.

There will therefore be different benchmarks for different funds and different fund managers. The benchmark is likely to be an index of one kind or another, hence it is important to understand the structure of the relevant index. The structure of indices has been discussed in an earlier chapter.

As discussed previously, the characteristics that are required to render an index suitable as a benchmark are that it is:

- Specified and unambiguous.
- Appropriate to the preferences of the fund (eg a UK blue chip fund may utilise the FTSE-100 Index).
- Appropriate to the currency of the fund.
- Investable, ie composed of investments that could conceivably be held in the fund.
- Measurable, ie the return can be calculated on a frequent basis as required.
- Representative of achievable performance, ie it has an arithmetic weighted composition (remember that the return of a portfolio is an arithmetic weighted average of the individual stock returns).
- Measures the relevant component of performance, ie total return indices for total return performance and capital value indices for capital growth.

10: PERFORMANCE MEASUREMENT AND APPRAISAL

3.2.2 Performance appraisal

Once we have established a suitable benchmark we can appraise the fund manager's performance by reference to it. The benchmark performance can be quite simply calculated as the weighted average of the holding period returns on the relevant benchmark indices.

Example

A pension fund manager has a portfolio with an initial value of $100m. The company for whom the fund is run is internationally based with 80% of its employees in the UK and 20% in the US. As such, it requires a corresponding international investment strategy concentrating on a diversified spread of shares.

The company feels that the fund manager should be able to at least match the following two indices on the relevant portions of the fund.

- FTSE-100 Index on the UK portion.
- S&P 500 Index on the US portion.

The values on these indices at the start and end of the year were:

	FTSE 100	S&P 500
End of year	4520	1000
Start of year	4000	920

The fund had a capital value of £113m at the end of the year, there having been no cash inflows and outflows during the year. What return has the fund manager achieved, what return has the benchmark portfolio achieved and has the fund manager achieved his target of at least matching the benchmark?

Solution

Fund performance

Since there have been no cash inflows/outflows during the year, we can use the simple holding period return formula to assess the fund performance, giving:

$$r = \frac{(D + V_e) - V_s}{V_s} \times 100$$

Gives

$$r = \frac{(0 + 113m) - 100m}{100m} \times 100 = +13\%$$

Benchmark performance

FTSE-100 Index:

$$r = \frac{4520 - 4000}{4000} = 0.13 \text{ or } 13\%$$

S&P 500 Index:

$$r = \frac{1000 - 920}{920} = 0.087 \text{ or } 8.7\%$$

Weighted average:

$$r = (80\% \times 13\%) + (20\% \times 8.7\%)$$
$$r = (0.8 \times 13\%) + (0.2 \times 8.7\%) = 12.14\%$$

Appraisal

Actual performance	+13.00%		
Original benchmark	+12.14%	+0.86%	**Outperformance**

The fund manager has achieved a return of 13% against the benchmark portfolio return of 12.14%. Hence, the fund manager has achieved his target of outperforming the benchmark.

Note, however, that this conclusion is only valid so long as the total return achieved was at no higher a level of risk than that of the underlying index. If this actual return has been achieved at a significantly elevated level of risk, this conclusion would be invalid.

In addition, no account has been taken of currency effects in this example.

3.2.3 Performance attribution/decomposition

The above performance appraisal assumed that the fund manager made no decisions regarding asset allocation, rather he simply took the 80:20 split proposed by the company and concentrated on selecting stocks within those sectors. Thus, we have established in the above example that the fund manager is good at stock selection.

The fund manager may however be free to determine his own asset allocation. If this is the case, then we may wish to appraise his performance in the two-key investment management areas of:

- Asset allocation
- Stock selection

To achieve this, we need to consider the actual performance and the performance of the following two benchmark portfolios.

- A portfolio with the asset allocation determined by the fund manager – a **revised benchmark**.
- A portfolio with the asset allocation as proposed by the client – the **original benchmark**.

10: PERFORMANCE MEASUREMENT AND APPRAISAL

Example

Based on the above data, but now assuming that the fund manager has decided on a different asset allocation, investing 85% in UK equities and 15% in the US, establish how the fund manager has performed.

Solution

Fund performance

As before, the fund performance is +13%.

Revised benchmark

The performance of the revised benchmark can be calculated in exactly the same way as for the original benchmark.

FTSE-100 Index:

$$r = \frac{4520 - 4000}{4000} = 0.13 \text{ or } 13\%$$

S&P 500 Index:

$$r = \frac{1000 - 920}{920} = 0.087 \text{ or } 8.7\%$$

Weighted average:

$$r = (85\% \times 13\%) + (15\% \times 8.7\%)$$
$$r = (0.85 \times 13\%) + (0.15 \times 8.7\%) = 12.35\%$$

Original benchmark

The original benchmark performance is unaltered at +12.14%.

Appraisal

Actual performance	+13.00%	+0.65%	**Stock selection gain**
Revised benchmark	+12.35%		
Original benchmark	+12.14%	+0.21%	**Asset allocation gain**

The actual performance has exceeded both benchmarks but what does this tell us?

The actual fund and revised benchmark have the same asset allocation (85% UK, 15% US), hence any difference in performance must be attributable to stock selection. As a result, we can say that the fund manager has boosted fund performance by 0.65% (13.00% – 12.35%) as a result of superior stock selection, or $650,000 based on our original fund size of £100m (£100m × 0.65%).

The revised benchmark and original benchmark are based on the same indices (same stocks), hence any difference between them must be due to asset allocation. As a result, we can say that the fund manager has boosted fund performance by 0.21% (12.35% – 12.14%) as a result of superior asset allocation, or £210,000 based on our original fund size of $100m ($100m × 0.21%).

3.2.4 Dealing with foreign currency

Introduction

When undertaking international investment, the fund manager has two decisions to make.

- Which broad markets/geographic areas should he invest in (eg Europe, Far East, America, etc)?
- Which specific countries should he invest in within those areas?

This is very similar to the asset allocation/stock selection decision above, which considered:

- Which asset classes should he invest in (eg shares, bonds, property, etc)?
- Which specific securities within those classes should he invest in?

The approach adopted is, therefore, very similar.

Approach

The approach to international investment appraisal is to isolate out asset performance and currency influences and deal with each separately using the above ideas.

Example

An international portfolio is being assessed against a benchmark with a 60:40 allocation between Latin America and the Far East. The actual allocation adopted by the fund manager is 70:30. The performances of the fund and benchmark have been decomposed into asset and currency components as follows.

	Actual Asset %	Actual Currency %	Benchmark Asset %	Benchmark Currency %
Latin America	10.0	6.0	10.0	5.0
Far East	12.0	3.0	11.0	4.0

Decompose the returns into asset allocation, stock selection and currency components.

10: PERFORMANCE MEASUREMENT AND APPRAISAL

Solution

	Actual Asset %	Actual Currency %	Benchmark Asset %	Benchmark Currency %
Latin America	10.0	6.0	10.0	5.0
Far East	12.0	3.0	11.0	4.0
70:30 Portfolio	10.6	5.1	10.3	4.7
60:40 Portfolio			10.4	4.6

Asset performance

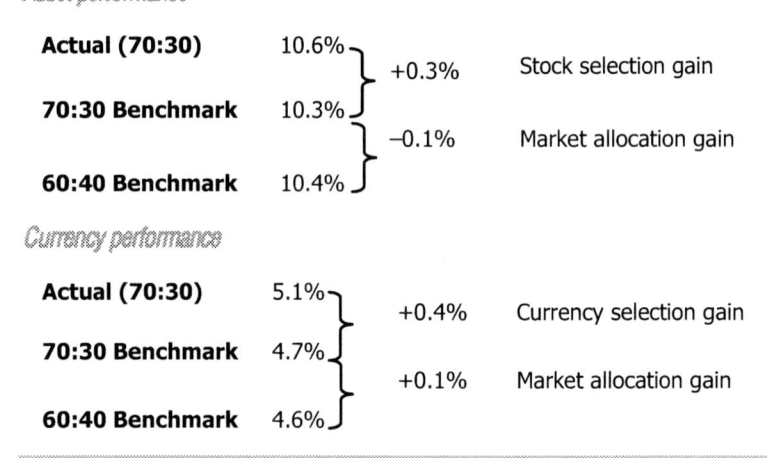

Actual (70:30)	10.6%	
		+0.3% Stock selection gain
70:30 Benchmark	10.3%	
		−0.1% Market allocation gain
60:40 Benchmark	10.4%	

Currency performance

Actual (70:30)	5.1%	
		+0.4% Currency selection gain
70:30 Benchmark	4.7%	
		+0.1% Market allocation gain
60:40 Benchmark	4.6%	

3.3 Jensen measure/comparison to SML

3.3.1 Introduction

We have now established a way of measuring and appraising the return, though measuring return in isolation with no consideration of the risk involved is inappropriate for investment decisions. We must somehow take account of the risk inherent in the portfolio that has generated this return.

The appropriate measure of risk to use depends on whether the beneficiary of the fund's investments has other well-diversified investments or whether this is his only set of investments. In the first case, the market risk or β of the fund is the best measure of risk, in the second case, the total risk or standard deviation of the fund σ_i would be the best measure.

If, on the other hand, the portfolio is a bond fund, then the appropriate measure of market risk is of relative duration.

Hence, as an alternative to simple comparison to a benchmark index with no consideration of risk, we could use the expected returns of the securities based on the capital market line (for total risk) or the securities market line (for systematic risk).

We will illustrate this with the following example.

Example

Two fund managers are employed to manage portions of a large pension fund. They both have the same objectives, etc. Details about their portfolios are given below.

Fund	Return %	Beta factor β_p
A	19%	1.05
B	22%	1.20

Over the same period the risk-free rate was 8% and the stock market generated a return of 18%.

3.3.2 The Jensen measure

If the risk measure is systematic risk, the relevant alpha value is defined with respect to the security market line:

$$\bar{r}_p = r_f + \beta(\bar{r}_m - r_f)$$

The corresponding alpha value is again:

$$\alpha_p = r_p - \bar{r}_p$$

This is known as the Jensen differential performance index.

$$\bar{r}_p = r_f + \beta(\bar{r}_m - r_f)$$

Gives:

$$\bar{r}_a = 8\% + 1.05(18\% - 8\%) = 18.5\%$$

$$\bar{r}_b = 8\% + 1.20(18\% - 8\%) = 20.0\%$$

The Jensen measure:

$$\alpha_p = r_p - \bar{r}_p$$

Gives:

$$\alpha_a = r_a - \bar{r}_a = 19.0\% - 18.5\% = 0.5\%$$

$$\alpha_b = r_b - \bar{r}_b = 22.0\% - 20.0\% = 2.0\%$$

Hence, we can say that on this risk-adjusted basis (systematic risk) fund manager B has outperformed fund manager A.

10: PERFORMANCE MEASUREMENT AND APPRAISAL

3.4 Excess return per unit risk

There are four performance measures that we need to be aware of, each distinguished by the risk measure used. Three of these are relevant to general share portfolios, one is specific to bond portfolios. These are:

Share portfolio measures

- The Sharpe measure
- The Treynor measure
- The Information ratio

Bond portfolio measure

- The excess return to relative duration measure.

We will illustrate these with the following example.

Example

Two fund managers are employed to manage portions of a large pension fund. They both have the same objectives, etc. Details about their portfolios are given below.

Fund	Return %	Beta Factor β_p	Total Risk σ_p
A	19%	1.05	20
B	22%	1.20	30

Over the same period the risk-free rate was 8% and the stock market generated a return of 18% at a risk of 19%.

3.4.1 Sharpe measure

The Sharpe measure uses as its gauge of risk, the total portfolio risk or standard deviation.

The Sharpe measure is calculated as:

$$\text{Sharpe measure} = \frac{r_p - r_f}{\sigma_p}$$

where:

r_p = portfolio return
r_f = risk-free return over the same interval
σ_p = portfolio risk (standard deviation of the portfolio returns)

As noted above, this measure is appropriate where this portfolio represents the full set of investments of the client (**an undiversified investor**). The higher the measure, the better the performance, which can be achieved by either **better stock selection** or **greater diversification**.

10: PERFORMANCE MEASUREMENT AND APPRAISAL

Solution

$$\text{Sharpe measure} = \frac{r_p - r_f}{\sigma_p}$$

Gives:

$$\text{Fund A} = \frac{19\% - 8\%}{20} = 0.55$$

$$\text{Fund B} = \frac{22\% - 8\%}{30} = 0.47$$

Hence, we can say that on a risk-adjusted basis (total risk) fund manager A has out performed fund manager B.

3.4.2 Treynor measure

The Treynor measure uses as its index of risk, the systematic risk or β of the portfolio. The Treynor measure can be calculated as:

$$\text{Treynor measure} = \frac{r_p - r_f}{\beta_p}$$

where:

r_p = portfolio return
r_f = risk-free return over the same period
β_p = portfolio beta

The Treynor measure is appropriate where this fund represents just one of many investments held by the client who is well diversified. The higher the measure, the better the performance of the fund when we take account of risk. This measure cannot be improved through diversification, since only systematic risk remains in the portfolio, and can only be improved through **better stock selection**.

Solution

$$\text{Treynor measure} = \frac{r_p - r_f}{\beta_p}$$

Gives:

$$\text{Fund A} = \frac{19\% - 8\%}{1.05} = 10.48$$

$$\text{Fund B} = \frac{22\% - 8\%}{1.20} = 11.66$$

Hence, we can say that on a risk-adjusted basis (systematic risk) fund manager B has outperformed fund manager A, the same conclusion as we drew above with the alpha value measure (the Jensen measure) based on systematic risk and the securities market line.

3.4.3 Information ratio

The information ratio considers, in comparison to the benchmark, the excess return of the portfolio against the excess risk. Again, this can be compared to the Sharpe measure for the benchmark in order to determine the impact of active performance.

The information ratio is calculated as:

$$\text{Information ratio} = \frac{r_p - r_b}{\sigma_p - \sigma_b}$$

where:

r_p	=	portfolio return
r_b	=	benchmark return
σ_p	=	portfolio risk
σ_b	=	benchmark risk
$\sigma_b - \sigma_b$	=	known as the standard deviation surplus

If the information ratio exceeds the benchmark Sharpe ratio, then the active performance has been good, as the extra return has more than compensated for the additional risk.

3.4.4 Excess return to relative duration

The excess return duration measure is suitable for **bond portfolios** where the measure of risk is the duration. The measure can be calculated as:

$$\text{Excess return to relative duration} = \frac{r_p - r_f}{d_p / d_m}$$

where:

r_p	=	portfolio return
r_f	=	risk-free over the same period
d_p/d_m	=	duration of portfolio (d_p) relative to that of the market (d_m)

Again, the higher the measure, the better the performance and the calculation of this measure is very similar to the above.

10: PERFORMANCE MEASUREMENT AND APPRAISAL

4 RISK-ADJUSTED PERFORMANCE ATTRIBUTION

4.1 Introduction

Having measured the performance of the fund and made suitable adjustments for the risk, the next task is to identify the sources of that performance. This involves breaking down the total return into various components. One way of doing this is known as Fama decomposition of total return.

The illustration below shows how we can decompose the total return in the case where the relevant measure of risk is systematic risk or β.

4.2 Fama decomposition

4.2.1 Analysing total return

Introduction

Suppose that fund P generates a return r_p, has a beta of β_p and has performed well over the period being considered. Then, it has a positive alpha value, equal to $r_p - r_2$, where r_2 is the CAPM expected return for this level of risk β_p.

This total return r_p can be broken down into four components.

Return on the portfolio = Riskless rate
+ Return from client's risk
+ Return from market timing
+ Return from security selection

Diagrammatically:

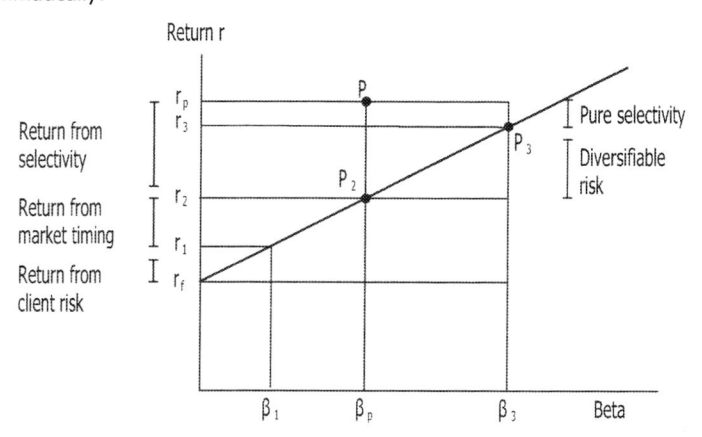

Riskless rate

The first component of the return on the portfolio is the riskless rate, r_f. All fund managers expect to earn the riskless rate.

Return from client's risk

The fund manager will have assessed the client's degree of risk tolerance to be measured by, for example, β_1. The client is therefore expecting a return on the portfolio of at least r_1. The return from the client's risk is therefore $r_1 - r_f$.

Return from market timing

The return from market timing is also known as the **return from the fund manager's risk**. This is because the manager has chosen a portfolio with a beta of β_p which differs from that expected by the client. The fund manager has implicitly taken a more bullish view of the market than the client. He has consequently decided to raise the beta of the portfolio above that expected by the client.

He has done this by selecting a portfolio with a larger proportion invested in the market portfolio and a smaller proportion invested in the riskless asset than the client would have selected. In other words, the fund manager has engaged in **market timing**. He has invested more heavily in the market in anticipation of favourable price movements. With a portfolio beta of β_p, the expected return is r_2, so that the return to market timing is $r_2 - r_1$.

Return to selectivity

The fourth component is the return from selectivity or the return from **security selection**. This is equal to $r_p - r_2$ and is known as the return to selectivity for the following reason. Consider portfolios P and P_2. Both have the same amount of market risk because they both have the same beta, β_p. However, they have different total risks. Portfolio P_2 contains no diversifiable risk, since it lies on the security market line.

Portfolio P, however, lies above the SML. It is, therefore, not a linear combination of the market portfolio and the riskless asset (only portfolios along the SML are). It must contain an active portfolio of risky assets that differs from the market portfolio. Thus, P differs from P_2 because P's manager has engaged in active security selection. This has resulted in portfolio P earning an additional return, but the fund manager has had to take on diversifiable risk to do so.

Subanalysing the return to selectivity

Is this extra return (the return to selectivity) worth the risk? To answer this question, we need to compare portfolio P with another portfolio, P_3, which lies on the SML and which has the same **total** risk, but how do we find this portfolio?

Suppose that the total risk of P and P_3 is $\sigma_p = 33\%$. Since P_3 lies on the SML, we know that all the risk of P_3 is undiversifiable and is equal to $\beta_3 \sigma_m$. If $\sigma_m = 30\%$, it follows that:

$$\beta_3 = \frac{\sigma_p}{\sigma_m} = \frac{33\%}{30\%} = 1.1$$

10: PERFORMANCE MEASUREMENT AND APPRAISAL

Pure selectivity

The return of P_3 is r_3 (given that the beta of P_3 is β_3), while the return of P is r_p. Since r_p is greater than r_3 in this example, it means that the risk in selecting the stocks in P was worthwhile.

Diversifiable risk

The extra return from taking on additional diversifiable risk is $r_3 - r_2$. But the fund P manager has done ever better than this, and earned an additional return $r_p - r_3$, due to pure selectivity.

4.2.2 Conclusion

Thus, the return can ultimately be decomposed as:

Return on the portfolio = Riskless rate
+ Return from client's risk
+ Return from market timing
+ Return from diversifiable risk
+ Return from pure selectivity

The Fama decomposition was done in terms of beta and is therefore important for share portfolios. It is possible to perform similar decompositions for bonds based on relative durations.

Example

Portfolio and market parameters have been as follows.

$r_p = 20\%$ $r_m = 16\%$

$\sigma_p = 15\%$ $\sigma_m = 12\%$

$\beta_p = 0.9$ $r_f = 10\%$

Solution

Decomposition

Return from client's risk

The client's desired beta is given as $\beta_1 = 0.8$. Using this, we can calculate the expected return on the client's desired portfolio as:

$r_1 = 10\% + 0.8(16\% - 10\%) = 14.8\%$

This means a return from client's risk of:

$r_1 - r_f = 14.8\% - 10.0\% = 4.8\%$

10: PERFORMANCE MEASUREMENT AND APPRAISAL

Return from market timing

The actual beta of the portfolio is 0.9. This implies an expected return on the actual portfolio of:

$$r_2 = 10\% + 0.9(16\% - 10\%) = 15.4\%$$

This gives a return from market timing of:

$$r_2 - r_1 = 15.4\% - 14.8\% = 0.6\%$$

Return to selectivity

The actual return of the portfolio was 20%. Hence, the return to selectivity is:

$$r_p - r_2 = 20.0\% - 15.4\% = 4.6\%$$

Subanalysing the return to selectivity

Return from diversifiable risk

The next step is to find the portfolio P_3 with the same total risk as our portfolio P. This portfolio has a beta of:

$$\beta_3 = \frac{\sigma_p}{\sigma_m} = \frac{15}{12} = 1.25$$

The expected return on this portfolio is:

$$r_3 = 10\% + 1.25(16\% - 10\%) = 17.5\%$$

Therefore, the return from diversifiable risk is:

$$r_3 - r_2 = 17.5\% - 15.4\% = 2.1\%$$

Pure selectivity

This leaves the return to pure selectivity as

$$r_p - r_3 = 20.0\% - 17.5\% = 2.5\%$$

10: PERFORMANCE MEASUREMENT AND APPRAISAL

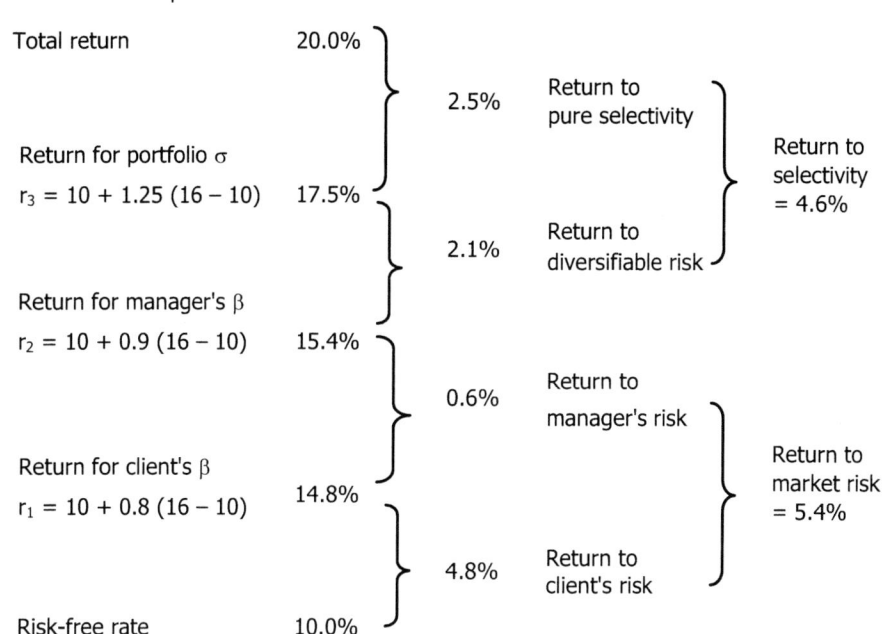

We have decomposed the total return as follows.

Total return	20.0%				
		2.5%	Return to pure selectivity		Return to selectivity = 4.6%
Return for portfolio σ $r_3 = 10 + 1.25(16 - 10)$	17.5%				
		2.1%	Return to diversifiable risk		
Return for manager's β $r_2 = 10 + 0.9(16 - 10)$	15.4%				
		0.6%	Return to manager's risk		Return to market risk = 5.4%
Return for client's β $r_1 = 10 + 0.8(16 - 10)$	14.8%				
		4.8%	Return to client's risk		
Risk-free rate	10.0%				

4.3 Conclusion

The decomposition of total return can be used to identify the different skills involved in active fund management. For example, one fund manager might be good at market timing, but poor at stock selection. The evidence for this would be that his $r_2 - r_1$ was positive, but his $r_p - r_2$ was negative. He should therefore be recommended to invest in an index fund, but be allowed to select his own combination of the index fund and the riskless asset.

Another manager might be good at stock selection, but poor at market timing. He should be allowed to choose his own securities, but someone else should choose the combination of the resulting portfolio of risky securities and the riskless asset.

10: PERFORMANCE MEASUREMENT AND APPRAISAL

Executive Summary

- The holding period return, money weighted return and time weighted return are methods of measuring a manager's performance.

- The time weighted return is typically the preferred method of calculation by fund managers since it is not biased by the size and timing of inflows and outflows.

- Performance attribution may be undertaken to establish a manager's skill in asset allocation and stock selection.

- The Sharpe measure, the Treynor measure and the Information ratio are all performance measures for identifying risk-adjusted return.

- Fama decomposition further breaks down the manager's return to establish additional sources of performance.

Index

Abnormal return, 100
Active investment management style, 22
Affordability, 19
American style options, 251
Annual compounding, 30
Annuity discount factor, 41
Arbitrage Pricing Theory, 115
    Assumptions of APT, 119
    Expected return, 116
    Limitations of APT, 119
    Portfolio under APT, 118
    Risk under APT, 117
    Sensitivity factors, 117
    Uses, 119
Arithmetic mean, 55
Asset allocation, 21
Asset-based valuation of shares, 202
Assumptions and limitations of CAPM, 109
Australian Government debt, 128
    Treasury bonds, 128
    Treasury notes, 128

Basis point value, 194
Benchmark indices, 305
Beta, 100
Bond risks, 194
Bond pricing, 160
Bonus issues, 201

Call options, 251
Callable bonds, 158
Canadian government bond market, 129
    Bank of Canada, 130
    Government of Canada marketable bonds, 130
    Government of Canada Treasury Bills, 130
Capital Asset Pricing Model (CAPM), 96, 109
    Beta, 100
    Carhart, 115
    Degree of diversification, 107
    Fama and French, 114
    International CAPM, 113
    Investment appraisal under CAPM, 99;
    Limitations of CAPM, 109
    Portfolio beta, 104
    Practical calculation, 103; R2, 107
    Securities market line (SML), 97
    Systematic risk, 97
Capital market line (CML), 93
Capital markets are in equilibrium, 110
Capital risk, 5
Carhart four factor model, 115
Charities, 16
Collective investment schemes, 14
Compound interest, 30
Convexity, 186
    Callable bonds 191
    Convexity formula, 188
    Use of convexity, 189
Corporate bonds: Secondary Market, 136
Correlation, 67, 78
    Correlation coefficient, 67
Coupons, 156
Covariance, 65
    Perfectly negatively correlated, 67;
    Perfectly positively correlated, 67;
    Uncorrelated, 67
Credit and default risk, 179
Credit risk, 154
Currency risk, 180
Currency swaps, 269

Day count conventions, 167
    30/360, 168
    Actual/365, 167
    Actual/Actual, 167
Day count conventions/30E/360, 168
Decision-making with risk, 68
Degree of diversification – R2, 107
Delta, 261
Difficult to estimate the β factor for an investment, 110
Discount factors, 41
Discounted cash flow valuation of straight bonds, 161
Diversification, 5, 73
Diversified investor, 95
Diversified portfolios, 109
Dividend cover, 208

INDEX

Dividend growth rate – 'g', 206
Dividend policy, 207
Dividend Valuation Model (DVM), 49, 203
Dividend yield, 207
Dividend-based valuation of shares, 203
Domestic corporate bonds, 154
Dual currency bonds, 157
Dutch government bond, 141
    Dutch Treasury Certificates (DIC), 142

Earnings-based valuation of shares, 208
Efficient frontier, 83
    Correlation coefficients, 83
    Indifference curves, 85
Emerging bond markets, 150
    Brady bonds, 151
Equity swaps, 270
Eurobond issuance, 159
Eurobonds, 158
European style options, 251
Excess return per unit risk, 312
Exchange traded funds (ETFs), 16

Fama and French three factor model, 114
Fama decomposition, 315
Financial information, 19
Fiscal risk, 180
Flat yield, 170
Floating Rate Notes (FRNs), 157
Foreign currency hedging, 285
    Borrowing and depositing, 287
    Currency option, 288
    Forward contract, 286
Foreign exchange rate: Cross rates, 282
    Factors affecting exchange rates, 282
    Fisher effect, 284
    International Fisher effect, 285
    Purchasing power parity, 284
    Spot rates, 279
Foreign exchange risk, 275
    Economic risk, 277
    Transaction risk, 275
    Translation risk, 276
Forward rates, 179, 279
Freely lend or borrow at the risk-free rate, 111
French government bonds, 143
    Bons du Trésor à Taux Fixe (BTFs), 143
    Bons du Trésor à Taux Fixe et Intéret Annuel (BTANs), 143
    Obligations Assimilables du Trésor (OATs), 143

Fund of funds, 17
Future: Cheapest to deliver, 246
    FTSE 100 Index future, 240
    Futures dealing profit, 239
    Hedge ratio, 242
    Hedgers, 235
    Long futures position, 233
    Long hedge, 238
    Risk in a hedged portfolio, 242
    Short futures position, 234
    Short hedge, 236
    Three-month sterling contract, 244
    Tick size, 239
    Tick value, 239
    UK Gilt futures contract, 246
    Users of futures, 233
Futures, 230

Gamma, 262
General insurance funds, 14
Geometric mean, 56
German bond market, 145
    Bobls (Bundesobligationen), 145
    BU-Bills, 145
    Bundesschatzanweisungen (Schatze) and Kassenobligationen, 145
    Bunds (Bundesanleihen), 146
Gilts: Competitive auctions, 135
    DMO, 134
Gordon's Growth Model, 205
Gross redemption yield (GRY), 172

Hard facts, 19
Hedge funds, 16
Holding period return, 296
Homogeneity of investor expectations, 111

Idiosyncratic risk, 95
Indifference curve, 69
    General characteristics of indifference curves, 71
Inflation risk, 5, 179
Inflation swaps, 271
Institutional investment management, 9
Interest rate parity formula, 281
Interest rate risk, 5, 179, 180
Interest rate swaps, 268
Interest rates, 29, 260
Internal rate of return (IRR), 46, 50
International CAPM, 113

INDEX

In-the-money option, 260
Investment management, 2
Investment management process, 21
Investment trusts, 14
Investors' required rate of return, 205
Issue specific risk, 180
Italian government bonds, 147
    Buoni del Tesoro Poliennari (BTPs), 147
    Buoni Ordinari del Tesoro (BOT), 147
    Certificati di Credito del Tesoro (CCTs), 147

Japanese government bond market, 131;
    Bank of Japan, 131
    Government bonds, 132
    Medium Term Notes, 132
    Treasury bills, 132
Japanese gross redemption yield (GRY), 171
Jensen measure, 310

Liability matching, 3
Life assurance, 13
Limitations of the standard deviation measure, 63
Liquidity and marketability risk, 180
Loan stock, 154

Macaulay's duration (economic life) of a bond, 182
Market portfolio, 94
Market risk, 95
Market timing, 22
Market value, 49
Minimum variance frontier, 83
Money-weighted returns, 299

Net present value, 40
Net redemption yield (NRY), 173
Nominal liability, 3
Non-annual compounding, 32
No-one can influence the market, 110

Offshore investment, 20
Option pricing, 258
Options, 249
Options trading strategies, 262
Ordinary (equity) shares, 198
Out-of-the-money option, 260

Overseas investment, 274
    Overseas diversification benefits, 274
    Returns on overseas investment, 288
    Risks of overseas investment, 274, 290

Passive management style, 22
Pension funds, 12
Performance appraisal: International investment appraisal, 309
Performance attribution, 315
Performance evaluation, 304
Performance measures, 296
Perpetuity discount factor, 42
Personal information, 19
Population standard deviation, 61
Portfolio selection, 83
Portfolio theory, 73
    Portfolio theory formulae, 79
    Return of portfolio, 79
    Risk of portfolio, 79
    Tabulation approach, 76
Pre-emption rights, 200
Preference shares, 199
Present value, 33, 37
Price to earnings ratio, 208
Pricing bonds: clean price, 163
    Ddirty price, 164
Property: Distinguishing features of property, 212
Property investment, 217
    Direct property investment, 217
    Freehold, 217
    Indirect investment, 218
    easehold, 217
    Real Estate Investment Trusts, 218
    Shares in property companies, 218
Property types, 216
Put options, 252
Putable bonds, 158

Real liability, 3
Return, 55
    Arithetic mean, 55
    Geometric mean, 56
Rho, 262
Rights issues, 200
Risk, 54, 94
    Factors contributing to risk, 54 Systematic risk, 95

INDEX

Risk measures, 58
    Limitations of standard deviation, 63
    Normal distribution, 63
    Standard deviation, 58, 61
    Variance, 58
Risk tolerance, 20
Risk/Reward profile, 8

S

Sample standard deviation, 61
Selecting a fund manager, 24
Semi-deviation, 64
Semi-variance, 64
Share buybacks, 202
Share valuation, 202
Shares – secondary market, 200
Sharpe measure, 312
Shortfall risk, 5
Simple interest, 29
Single-period (one year) model, 109
Size of efficient portfolios, 89
Soft facts, 20
Spanish government bonds, 148
    Bonos del Estado (Bonos), 149
    Letras del Tesoro (Treasury bills), 149
    Obligaciones del Estado, 149
Specific risk, 95
Spot rates, 178, 279
Standard deviation, 58
Stock selection, 22
Stock split, 201
Swaps, 268

T

Terminal (future) value, 33
Theta, 262
Time value of money, 29
Timescales, 6
Time-weighted returns, 300
Total risk, 95
Treynor measure, 313
Types of funds: Banks, 18

U

Undiversified investor, 95
Unlimited short selling, 113
Unsystematic risk, 95
US government bond market, 136
    Treasury bonds (T-bonds), 137
    Federal agencies, 139
    Federal reserve, 136
    Treasury bills (T-bills), 134, 137
    Treasury inflation protected securities, 137
    Treasury notes (T-notes), 134, 137
    US corporate sector, 139

V

Variance, 58
Vega, 262
Volatility, 184, 260

Y

Yield curve, 175
Yield measures, 170